ESTHER
The STAR and the SCEPTRE

ESTHER
The STAR and the SCEPTRE

A Novel by
GINI ANDREWS

ZONDERVAN PUBLISHING HOUSE
OF THE ZONDERVAN CORPORATION
1415 LAKE DRIVE, S.E. | GRAND RAPIDS, MI 49506

Scripture references are, when possible, from the Torah; otherwise, with one exception, the Revised Standard Version has been used, as the author believes this version is the most acceptable to the Jewish reader. For the same reason, the name "Adonai" has been used rather than the familiar "Yahweh."

ESTHER: THE STAR AND THE SCEPTRE
Copyright © 1980 by Gini Andrews

Fourth printing March 1982

Library of Congress Cataloging in Publication Data
Andrews, Gini.
    Esther the star and the sceptre.
    1. Xerxes, 519–465 or 4 B.C.—Fiction. 2. Esther, Queen of Persia—
Fiction. I. Title.
PS3551.N4178E8   813'.54   80-20388
ISBN 0-310-20181-0

Designed and edited by Judith E. Markham

Printed in the United States of America

To Jim and Helen Boyd
who know the true meaning of friendship

Characters in the Story

ESTHER (HADASSAH) a young Jewess, foster daughter of Mordecai
MORDECAI a prominent lawyer at Xerxes' court
XERXES absolute monarch of the Persian empire
VASHTI his first queen
HAMAN an ambitious man of Susa
ZERESH a concubine of one of Xerxes' guards

*BILSHAN an elderly Jewish scholar, friend of Mordecai
*DAVID BEN-BILSHAN his grandson, childhood friend of Hadassah
*RUTH and JAKOB friends of David and Hadassah
*RACHEL and RABOS their parents
THE SEVEN princes closest to the king
    Admatha, Carshena, Marsena, Memucan, Meres, Shethar, Tarshish
HAMAN'S SONS Parshandatha, Dalphon, Aspatha, Poratha, Adalia,
    Aridatha, Parmashta, Arisai, Aridai, Vajezatha
HARBONAH Xerxes' chamberlain
HEGAI eunuch in charge of women in the king's harem
HATAK king's chamberlain, in charge of the queen's household

EUNUCHS and CHAMBERLAINS Abagtha, Bigthan, Biztha, Carcas, Zethar
*SIROMUS Hegai's servant
*CHERSIS servant under Siromus
*HAREM GIRLS Armis, Arunah, Lura, attendants to the queen
*HULDAH nurse/servant to Hadassah
*MORDECAI'S SERVANTS Kusuru, Shirik

MARDONIOS a general in the Persian war with Greece, cousin to Xerxes
MASISTIOS a general in the war with Greece
ARTABAZANES Xerxes' brother, former rival for the throne, commander
    of the Persian fleet
ARTABANUS Xerxes' uncle
PATIRAMPHRES charioteer for Xerxes
ATOSSA Xerxes' mother
VAHUSH treasurer in Parsa
ARTATAKHAM master bronzeworker
*GIGIS worker in bronze
*MENOSANES worker in gold

*Imaginary characters (Others are historical, biblical, or both)

*MUL   master carpet-weaver
*DILOS   Mul's assistant
*SHISHIA   an immortal, Zeresh was his concubine
PYTHIAS   wealthy supporter of Xerxes' Greek campaign
*RHASA   a harem girl from Bactria
BHINDI   the man she loves
PARNAKKA   a doctor

Places

PASARGADAE   where Achaemenid kings were crowned
ECBATANA   (Hamadan) summer capital
SUSA   (Shushan or Shush) winter capital
PARSA   (Persepolis) ceremonial city for the New Year (March 21)

Weights

TALENT   about 66 pounds, according to Herodotus. Commonly cast as a
disc or oval in silver or gold. The talent was subdivided into the mina
(60 to a talent) and the kharsha (about 6 to one mina).

Measurements

PARASANG   an hour's walk (estimated to be about 3 1/2 miles). A day's
walk was about 5 parasangs.
FURLONG   about 220 yards
CUBIT   about 18 inches

Coins

DARIC   98% pure gold, about 3/4 inch in diameter, weighing about 1/3
oz.
SHEKEL or SIGLOT   90% pure silver, same size as daric, about 1/5 oz. (20
siglots to one daric).

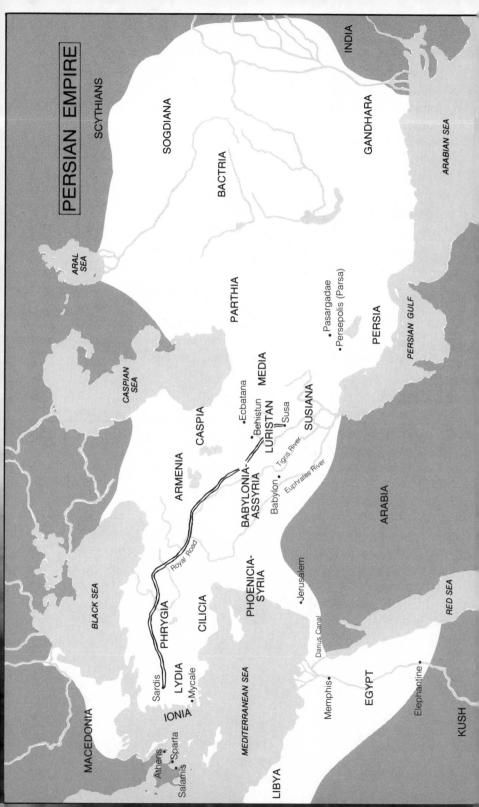

He saved them for his name's sake that he might make known his mighty power. —*Psalm 106:8*

I now know that evil is real and so is good. But there is a choice and we are not so much chosen as choosers. —*Rabbi Hugo Gryn*

PROLOGUE

Darius was dead.

DARIUS, THE GREAT KING, KING OF KINGS, KING OF PEOPLES OF EVERY TONGUE, SON OF VISHTASPA, AN ACHAEMENID, A PERSIAN, SON OF A PERSIAN . . . the titan whose shadow had reached across thousands of parasangs was dead.

Throughout the vast empire, from the Indus to the Nile, from the Caspian to the Red Sea, the word flashed out. Couriers, the fastest in the world, traveled on great Nisaean horses like winged things. They thundered over hills and swept over the plains of the Royal Road. They sent men racing up mountains to light the flares that would strike both terror and grief into those who saw. Gloom settled on the land like smoke.

Darius dead? Impossible.

Darius dead? But he was godlike! He had been the center of their lives, the one they obeyed and served with awe. Fear him they might, but life found its cornerstone in him, his will, his awful glory.

What now?

In Egypt and Sogdiana, in Bactria and Ionia, from Ethiopia to Greece the question blew: What now? Xerxes? What was he like? Would he be as good a ruler? Would he be worse? Only Babylon had any answer: "As crown prince he governed us for twelve years. He was not bad, as princes go, but (this was spoken in hushed tones only to those one trusted) *now that he is supreme?*"

The unknown struck a chill.

Almost at the heart of the empire, in a funeral train carrying the body of the dead king, Xerxes rode gloomily. At thirty-five he was now the reigning monarch of the greatest empire in the world.

From his birth, his mother, Atossa, had schooled her eldest for

11

kingship: "You shall rule, Xerxes. One day you will sit on the throne of the empire."

"But I am not the king's first-born! What of Artabazanes? He is the first-born."

"Leave it to me, my princeling. Your time will come; we'll find a way." Atossa had smiled; it was not a particularly nice smile.

As he prepared his campaign against Greece, Darius had given in to the pressure to name a successor to his throne. A royal row ensued; the harem intrigue, boiling below the surface for years, erupted. The first of his several wives pressed the claim of his first-born, Artabazanes. But she had reckoned without Xerxes' mother, the powerful Atossa.

This daughter of Cyrus had begun life with ideals and dreams; spoiled and willful as a child, she was not wicked. It took the years as wife to her cruel brother, Cambyses, and later to the false Smerdis, the Magus, to change all that. (Even in becoming Darius' wife, she married the man who had stabbed her second husband.) She had lived too long with brutality and treachery; ambition hardened into lust for power when other lusts were done. All her dreams settled on her son, Xerxes.

In her own way, she loved him, but it was a love controlled by ambition. Their relationship was unpredictable: one day she was over-attentive, the next she ignored him. Never affectionate, her attitude had a calculating element that left him emotionally starved.

In the succession struggle it was Atossa who gave Xerxes the tool that delivered the deathblow to the dream of the first-born, Artabazanes. She sent Xerxes into the royal presence.

"August sire—" his manner was reverent but the black eyes sparkled with that unpredictable brilliance Darius found irresistible. In Xerxes he saw a temperament he understood, though he was dimly aware of some core of weakness in his son which he himself never shared. "—Artabazanes is your first-born, but he was born *before* you became king. I am your first-born *after* your accession to the throne. Surely then, the throne is mine?"

And it was.

Xerxes was publicly proclaimed Darius' successor with shouts and cheers and celebrations.

Now, twelve years later, Darius was dead.

The procession moved along cuts in the hillsides, across valleys, by the water's edge. It was winter now, and they dared not use the mountain routes. Behind, the long line swung over the horizon; ahead, it stretched to infinity: horses, carts, palanquins, supply wagons, and people, people, people.

By law, every province must send a certain number of mourners, so hundreds of satraps and other high officials, wailing, beating their foreheads, tearing their clothes, proclaimed Darius the best king they had ever had. Behind, in Susa, were the bodies of Darius' chief eunuch and chief staff-bearer who had killed themselves when the great king died.

"Eighty-five parasangs . . . eighty-five parasangs. . . ." Xerxes' throbbing thoughts kept time to the monotony of the march. "Will it never end? Why now? Why did he have to die? Why?" He pounded his fist in grief and anger. The Achaemenids were not accustomed to events they could not control.

He shifted his cramped legs. Underneath the grind of the relentless questions and the grief were emotions he dared not look at: fear of the future, fear of the men who would jostle for position unless he was swift and sure, and fear he dared not admit even to himself—fear of failure. No matter what the future held, Darius would always be looking over his shoulder. Would he approve? His courtiers, would they? Would they think Darius could have done better?

He moved suddenly, and one of the horses reared.

"Fool!" Xerxes was glad to have an outlet for his emotions. "Curse you, driver! Control that beast or—or kill him. Or I will."

An eagle, that's what his father was, or—had been. He was not yet used to that tense. And like an eagle, Darius had swooped at the right moment and come up with a crown in his beak. A high-placed officer with King Cambyses in Egypt, he had moved to the throne without scruple or hesitation once Cambyses was dead. With towering genius, born to rule, Darius had consolidated the sprawling empire founded by the incomparable Cyrus and expanded by the forgettable Cambyses.

Darius had been religious, almost a monotheist. Usually inscribing his thanks to Ahura Mazda on monuments and buildings, he was not above putting in a precautionary, "and what other gods there be," just in case. His beliefs had been passed to this son who now rocked back and forth, partly from the road's unevenness, partly from sheer misery.

"Parsa! It's Parsa!" The word hummed up and down the line, and the wailing, hushed by fatigue, was taken up again.

Xerxes, who had been dozing fitfully, poked his head out. Even on this sad journey he thrilled to the sight of the ceremonial center that was his father's dream and his.

Silhouetted against the Mount of Mercy, the unfinished buildings glowed red-gold in the afterglow. Unfinished blocks like giants' playthings and huge, standing columns caught the light. Torches burned in welcome, though fewer and dimmer than at ordinary times.

Tonight, all the dignitaries would sleep in buildings on the high platform where Darius had placed his palace; the servants would camp below in the plain. In the morning the satraps and other luminaries would join the large family and proceed to the tomb which Darius had ordered cut from the rock, over which his artisans had carved his self-evaluation: I COULD DO EVERYTHING . . . UNDERLING, VIGOROUSLY MAKE KNOWN HOW GREAT I AM AND HOW GREAT MY SKILL AND HOW GREAT MY SUPERIORITY. . . . His wax-covered form, in the stone sarcophagus, would be placed with reverent ceremony in the tomb.

Nearby, in the square stone fire-tower, the flame, which always burned except when monarchs died, went out.

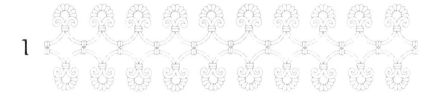

1

In Susa, Xerxes, King of All Peoples, was giving a feast.

Harbonah, overseeing preparations, moved about muttering to himself. The towel over his arm, badge of his eunuch status, was snowy, his flowing robes were faultless, the band around his curled dark hair immaculate. But he was nervous, and his hands shook.

My first major assignment since my promotion, he was thinking. Everything must go well. It had *better* go well; Xerxes was not one to suffer fools gladly. "If I fail—I pray Mithra my death will be quick."

He'd done well at the one hundred eighty days' feasting for the satraps. But that was months ago, and this was different. Never before had Xerxes opened his lavish gardens to the horde that would pour through them today and for the next seven days.

Harbonah twitched his fastidious nose, small like his eyes and mouth. Aristocracy he was willing to serve, but this feast included even the lowborn. *Slaves! Scum!* He flicked a fly from a golden plate piled high with fruit. *The garden will never be the same; they'll ruin it.*

He walked to one of the doorways piercing the enamel brick walls, where archers with spears were depicted on the blue tiles. Tonight their living counterparts, the Immortals, would stand against these same walls, one behind every guest.

Harbonah snapped waspishly at the stream of servants hurrying through the walled gardens. The beardless chamberlain could not endure one thing out of place, demanded absolute punctuality from his subordinates, and his emphasis on cleanliness was almost irrational. But underneath the fussiness lived a frightened little man.

On a vividly colored pavement thrust out into the foaming foliage were gold couches for the most honored guests, silver couches for the less important. Rings of silver in marble pillars supported exquisite hangings and a great translucent curtain that would screen the king.

15

"Nearer the king, nearer to trouble," mumbled Harbonah as he cuffed a slave who was mauling a priceless carpet.

He looked around sharply but found no more to criticize. The great hall was illuminated with the copper intensity of the setting sun, barred with the columns' straight shadows.

Harbonah went to rest his tired feet.

It was evening. For hours the throngs had been pouring into the palace gardens. High in trees, in flowering shrubs, gold lamps winked. Perfume from gold scent-burners mingled with the heady fragrance of jasmines, lilies, lilacs, and roses. Water cascaded into ponds, shimmered in lakes, doubled the beauty in reflections. Lutes thrummed underneath the hum of voices; a nightingale sang. It was a Persian "paradaiso."

The bibulous guests were already giddy, while the more abstemious were relieved to find no one was being compelled to drink. At most parties the host set the drinking pace and guests were made to follow him even if it meant being held down and forced.

Inside, the hall was a vast jewel, faceted with color and light. Great bull capitals surmounted a forest of columns. Everywhere the gold was overpowering: the lights made it blaze, sparkle, gleam.

"The king! The king! The King of All Peoples arrives!"

There was an instant hush, and every guest was prostrate on the ground.

Carried by bearers, the throned king was set down, and he moved to his dining couch. Right and left of him were his seven nobles, descendants of some of the original Seven Conspirators. Advisors and confidants of the king, they alone had access to the royal presence without appointment.

The king signaled the beginning of the festivities by raising his gold rhyton, a large horn-shaped drinking vessel flaring out from a crouching ram.

"Drink!" he shouted, and the seven-day feast was officially under way.

Memucan, keenest of the Seven, smiled to himself and thought his king looked unusually handsome, black eyes sparkling, sensual mouth curving with pleasure. Gold flickered in his long, squared beard, and on his hair he wore a fluted gold coronet over a blue and white cloth diadem.

The robes of the nobles fell in the classic crescent folds of the Achaemenids. The king's was purple, heavy with gold embroidery and intricately worked gold ornaments, his linked belt clasped with Darius' gold, turquoise-studded buckle. Bracelets, rings, and heavy earrings threw back the torchlight.

No one was more keenly aware than Memucan of his king's failures and weaknesses, yet he never underestimated Xerxes' power. When it came to placating the notorious Xerxesian temper, Memucan was the most skilled man in the kingdom.

"And how is your lovely queen, sire?"

Xerxes' glance met his with amused understanding. It was Memucan who had arranged the meeting between Vashti and the king and had managed to maneuver Xerxes into a marriage he thought his own idea.

The queen had an impressive lineage, an unremitting sense of her own importance, a cool awareness of her influence over Xerxes. She was the second strong woman he had loved, the second who knew all too well just how to manage the dependency that was part of his nature. The first, of course, had been his mother. The hundreds of virgins and concubines from his well-filled harem he selected according to his mood, as he did his wardrobe, and just as carelessly discarded.

Vashti was different. He found in her something that held him, challenged him. She knew just how long to act the disinterested royal lady, all the time rousing him to distraction. At just the right moment she would capitulate, making him feel the conqueror. Xerxes mistook her sensuality for love.

Now, at the banquet table, Xerxes sat toying with his food, smiling over his memory of last night. She had been at her best: exotic, imaginative. While she had stroked his head, he found himself pouring out his deepest feelings. It was good he had not seen the contemptuous curve of her lips.

"Vashti?" He came back to the present. "She is having a feast of her own, Memucan, as you know." He lifted the refilled rhyton. "Your wife is there, surely?"

"Of course." Memucan drank too. He was keeping pace with the king, rule or no rule. "We've heard of nothing else in my house for the past two months."

Xerxes looked through the gauzy curtain into the garden humming with laughter. One pair of guests caught his attention: a voluptuous woman seated by a man of extremely proud bearing.

"Who are those people?"

Memucan lifted his shoulders in a gesture that effectively dismissed the pair.

"The man's name is Haman; the woman's just one of many. He's a widowed social climber with a large family scrambling behind him."

"Sons?"

"He has ten sons, sire."

"Well done! Have we rewarded him?"

"Generously. Some of them are old enough to serve Your Majesty in the army; they will be of service in the Greek campaign."

Xerxes nodded absently. He had already lost interest.

"I've sent for Egyptian dancers tonight, Memucan, and Hasnari will dance."

"The one who is so—ah—?"

Xerxes laughed. "You don't think I want *only* talent in my court, surely?"

The meal went on. Pheasants and cocks, dozens of whole roasted animals, were brought in and went out as picked bones. The hour grew very late, the company very drunk. At last the king, more than a little drunk himself, signaled his throne-bearers, and the night's party was over.

And so for six days and nights the crowds flowed in and out in braids of color; pleasure became sensuality, sensuality became debauchery. The intensity of the excesses was most noticeable in the king.

Memucan looked at the other six nobles. What were they thinking of the king just now? Admatha on his right. Carshena next, and then Meres. On the king's left sat Tarshish and Shethar. Although the others had the swarthy skin, the black eyes and hair of the Persians, Shethar, fleshier than the rest, had lighter hair and beard, lighter skin, and long, narrow eyes that were almost gold. A good man, Shethar; Memucan enjoyed him. Last was Marsena. There was something disturbing about Marsena. A whiff of treachery? A certain deviousness? He could not pin it down.

Xerxes' voice cut across his thoughts. "What do you think, Memucan? A good plan?"

Memucan dared not admit he had no idea what the king had been saying, but since he did not imagine it was anything earthshaking he bowed and said, "Of course, sire." He raised his cup. "To Your Majesty's plan."

Xerxes preened and gestured to the impassive row of eunuchs behind him.

"Biztha!"

The man stepped forward, prepared for anything. With Xerxes one never knew.

"Carcas! Harbonah!"

18

Why didn't he call me first? Harbonah fumed. I am in charge here. He should have called me first.

One by one the chamberlains came from their place behind the king. By now the king had so relaxed protocol that these men, too, were half-drunk. "Go." Xerxes made a sweeping gesture. "Go now and bring me— the queen!"

It came too suddenly. There was a sound of indrawn breaths like wind rattling the leaves of oleander trees.

Xerxes raised a strongly angled black eyebrow. "At once! I want Queen Vashti here! And tell her she is to wear the royal crown, the new one."

Weaving a bit unsteadily, they went.

Queen Vashti here? It was not done; it broke all precedent. The Persian women sometimes joined the men in feasting, but left when the serious drinking began. This was the seventh day of hilarity, exotic dancers, and erotic scenes. The beautifully decorated tables were a shambles; the elite were having trouble staying awake.

Memucan's mind raced. Would she come? The royal lady was nothing if not independent.

Lately he had worried as he saw the queen's influence growing. Those highly coveted satrapies she had awarded relatives—the Seven had their own favorites for these; how dared she? Too many servants, carriages, horses, pets—and her wardrobe! It took up one entire wing of the new palace the king had built her. As for the crown—it was a sore point with all the Seven.

It had all begun with Babylon. Suddenly that satrapy had revolted. Jettisoning any attempts at conciliation, Xerxes had acted swiftly and savagely. Walls were leveled, buildings ransacked, and, as the ultimate in sacrilege, the twelve-cubit statue of their god Marduk was destroyed. Fifty-two thousand talents of purest gold melted into a bubbling pool. He could have done nothing more shocking to the Babylonians.

Some of the gold that had once been Marduk had become Vashti's new crown. "Surely," the Seven had muttered among themselves, "nothing good will come of this; this crown is ill-omened." Vashti only complained that its weight hurt her dainty head.

Memucan shifted his eyes to Tarshish who elevated his well-draped shoulders. Meres? Meres rolled his eyes toward the impassive bulls, then looked quickly to see if the king had observed. He had not. Smiling rather drunkenly, Xerxes was playing with his beard.

19

"Vashti is a beauty, my Seven," he was saying, "a great beauty—the most beautiful woman in this country—in any country—of any time." His speech was thick. "And in bed, my lords! Ah, if I could describe to you—"

Memucan was shocked. They were all lusty men with wives and concubines, but this was not something to discuss at a formal occasion—and certainly not of Her Majesty.

"Sire—" he began, not knowing what he would say, but feeling he had better say something.

"It's true, Memucan; she is a treasure and—and—"

He seemed to lose the thread of his thought and was silent a moment, still toying with his beard.

"Ah, yes, the crown. You have not seen it yet?"

"Not yet, my lord."

"A masterpiece. My own design. Thermistes, that—that Greek—he made it. All lapis lazuli and pearls—you cannot imagine." His head lolled a little; he jerked it up. "Vashti—she—she is inc—incredible."

The Seven were absorbed with the possibilities: Would the queen come? Would she sacrifice her dignity for this unprecedented request? But a refusal hardly bore thinking about. Tension hummed in the room like a taut bowstring.

2

"But I assure you, it is quite true."

Bright laughter, brittle as glass, broke round the room.

Vashti, her beauty heightened by wine, was telling the ladies some court gossip.

Her dining room, smaller than the king's, was lavishly appointed in colors chosen to enhance her beauty. There were those who found that beauty cold. There were those, too, who said she felt contempt for the king, that she loved no one but herself.

Reclining on draped couches the wives, sisters, and mothers of the important men in Susa had also been wining and dining for seven days. Here the perfumed air was still sweet, though there were wine stains on fragile robes and the coiffures were not what they had been.

"And then—" Vashti lifted her head at a stirring of the curtains at the doorway. "What is it? I do not wish to be disturbed."

With an imperious gesture she waved her head eunuch away and turned to her guests.

"Your Majesty, I—I—"

"I said," the voice was icy, "I do not wish to be disturbed."

Then, seeing the eunuch was seriously upset, a slightly mocking smile curved her lips. "What's this? Are we at war again? Has the king ridden off with a slave girl?"

A wave of laughter applauded her.

"Messengers, my lady."

"Messengers? From whom? I am not holding court. Tell them to come tomorrow."

"My l-lady, they—they are from—"

Vashti was curious. Curious and a little puzzled, but with no hint that the answer to her query would change her life.

"Speak out. Who sent them?"

"The king, Your Majesty."

"The king?" Vashti was listening now. "Send them in then. Don't keep the king's messengers waiting, you fool."

The curtains were swept aside and in weaved the seven eunuchs on their unwelcome errand. They prostrated themselves before her, not without difficulty.

Vashti wrinkled her nose.

"Tell me your message and then leave. Quickly."

No one spoke.

"Harbonah! You at least have some sense. What does the king want?"

Harbonah raised his head. "The king wishes—the king—wishes—"

Vashti's voice was metallic, "What does the king wish?"

Harbonah told her.

Stillness settled on the bright room. After a quick lift of her head, Vashti sat like a statue.

Slowly, unbelievingly, she spoke. "The king—King Xerxes—wants me—to come to him—? There? Now?"

"Yes, Your Majesty. And, with the crown."

What madness was this? Drunk. Of course he was drunk. She looked at the eunuchs on the floor. If the king were not in his cups, he would never have tolerated their reaching such a state. But he had been drunk before. Often. This was different.

Every person in the room waited in an agony of suspense for her reply. She will have to go, they were thinking. She has no choice. Yet if she dares refuse? What will happen to us? Banishment? Prison? Death?

He won't dare kill me, thought Vashti. If they were together, she could charm him out of this nonsense. Perhaps she'd better go.

The seconds went by.

Suddenly, with a snakelike movement, she was on her feet.

"Am I a concubine that he sends eunuchs for me? To come before his drunken lords?"

She adjusted her jeweled collar.

"I am his reigning queen, with blood in my veins as rich as his own. *How dare he?*"

Moving from the table she accidentally pushed over an alabaster jar. The shards skittered along the polished floor.

"Am I a cheap slave picked up on one of his campaigns? A trinket to show the tradesmen of the town? If they need to be amused, let him parade his horses, his concubines, his—his Egyptian dancing girl!"

She looked round the room, from the cringing eunuchs to her frightened guests.

"Go tell your master that Vashti, the queen, sends her answer in one word. No!"

Shaking, the eunuchs rose and hurried from the hall. Outside, they looked at each other in silent dismay. What would Xerxes do? His blazing irrationality was notorious. And this was a public insult from his wife! Who was to tell him?

"You, Harbonah," the other six turned to him. "You are in charge of this feast, and this is part of it. You must tell him."

"Me?" Harbonah raised his curving eyebrows. "Did you notice that when he sent us here, I was not called first, or even second. Shall we go over the order? First, Biztha, it was you. And then you, Carcas; you were next. I decline the honor." And he moved down the hall.

"Harbonah! Come back! We have to return together; you know that."

They were right. Seven chamberlains had been sent on this errand of madness; seven must return.

Harbonah came back, his shadow thrown ahead of him, twice his size.

"It really doesn't matter who tells him," he said. "If he kills one, he'll kill us all."

"But *how* it is presented is important, Harbonah. You know how to be diplomatic. You will be the speaker?"

"No. We will cast lots. Agreed?"

Agreed. What choice was there?

From under his loose robe Carcas drew die stones. They cast lots. First one was eliminated, then another. Finally, the choice was between Biztha and Harbonah.

They cast the lot once more and—

Harbonah!

Biztha sighed. At least he would not have to say the fateful words.

"Cursed, cursed, *cursed!* By all the black powers of Angru Manyu! May she never give birth except to monsters! May she roam forever in the world of dark spirits! Curse Vashti who dares defy Xerxes!"

The Seven, veterans of a hundred court scenes, had never seen the king like this. Angry, yes. But this was a madman.

He was standing, all color drained from his face, his body vibrating with rage.

"Am I, Xerxes, the Great King, the King of Kings, King of Nations—" he choked, "King of This Great Earth—to be crossed by a—by a—a woman?" He spat out the word.

Sleeves swinging, he swept the table in front of him. Rhytons rolled in all directions, spilling their contents, painting the floor with vintage wines. Glass from Egypt splintered against pillars; alabaster and marble bowls cracked like broken skulls.

A final crash—a few tinkling sounds—the last goblet rocked to stillness.

No one spoke.

Black beards stood out sharply against hundreds of fear-bleached faces. With the king in this mood, whose life was safe?

One heavy rhyton remained standing on the table. Xerxes snatched it up and flung it against a tiled wall picturing a pacing lion. The enameled beast lost its nose. Unnerved by the ugly scene, Shethar's son giggled shrilly. The giggle ended in a squeak.

It was flame to a tinderpile.

"Dare you! Dare you laugh at me, Xerxes, King of All Peoples? I—will—kill—"

Memucan decided it was now or not at all. If the king was not cooled down, there would be a massacre.

"My gracious lord! You are a just ruler. This is the son of one of your greatest nobles, a beardless child; he meant no harm. No one here challenges your mighty presence, Lord of the Whole Earth."

Xerxes seemed to come back from a far country. The familiar red mist of his rages began to clear; the pounding in his head stopped. He recalled where he was, who he was. His eyes met Memucan's: grave, respectful, expecting the best of him. One by one he looked at the Seven, then at the wise men, the scribes and lawyers, the Magi at his table.

He signaled Harbonah. "Dismiss the guests. You Seven, remain." Only too glad to escape, the hundreds of guests went silently.

"Well, my lords," the lightning change of mood again, "what shall we do with this—this vixen, this she-wolf?"

A slave brought a freshly filled rhyton to the wine-taster who sipped and passed it to the king's cupbearer who then presented it to Xerxes.

"She has disobeyed me. You are my councilors; advise me. What does the law say?"

The Seven breathed again. Who knew? This crisis might deal once and for all with the threat of Vashti.

"My royal lord," Memucan touched his mouth respectfully, "Vashti, the queen, has not wronged Your Majesty only"—he stressed the last word to show Xerxes he did not minimize the personal insult—"but she has done violence to all your princes."

Xerxes turned quickly.

"All?"

"All," repeated Memucan. "To all the people in all the satrapies of the Great King."

"Explain yourself, Lord Memucan. I'm a bit tired."

"This despicable thing the queen has done will be known to every woman in Susa by tomorrow morning. I'm sure even now our wives are buzzing with it. When the women of the empire hear, they will spit in their husbands' faces and say, 'King Xerxes ordered his queen to come to him and she refused.' And they will follow the queen's lead."

"And your suggestion?"

"If it please the king, let a royal edict go out, written into the laws of the Persians and the Medes that may not be revoked. The edict will say that Vashti comes no more to the Great King and—" Memucan was gauging his effect with care, inching toward his goal, "that her place as queen—" he took a deep breath, "be given to someone better." He finished in a rush.

Xerxes looked at Carshena and Shethar, who nodded; at Admatha and Tarshish, Meres and Marsena. Their faces said, *Yes, this is good counsel.* These were his trusted men. So be it.

His throne-bearers, trembling with fatigue and fear, responded to his signal. As they came, he said, "Call the scribes. The letters must be drawn up at once and sent into every satrapy of my empire. The message will read: 'Every man is to be ruler in his own house.' It is my command."

His malicious satisfaction could be heard as he was carried down the corridor.

"Vashti is queen no more!"

3

The morning after Vashti's disgrace, Memucan, summoned to Xerxes' private apartments, found an irate and disheveled king striding about with a whip in his hands. Dark crescents under his eyes showed he had not slept well.

Thoughts of Vashti had plagued him all night. How dare she treat him in such a way? He had been certain she loved him, certain of his power over her. He had made her his queen!

With her he had tried to share his loneliness, his longing for understanding, his unnamed fears, exposing himself in a way extraordinary for him. Misinterpreting her silence, he felt she was the one person in the world who understood him.

What was she thinking of him now?

His stomach knotted as he imagined her cool disdain, the laughter among her intimates. And what were his own intimates thinking? What would Darius have done? None of *his* wives had ever rebelled against him. He realized Darius would not have violated precedent in sending for his queen.

He had cursed and sent for more wine.

Now, "In the name of Angru Manyu, Memucan, where am I to put her? I cannot turn her out into the street. She *has* been consort to the Great King."

Petulantly, he slashed at an unfortunate lizard sunning itself in the window sill. "I don't ever want to see her anywhere."

"A suggestion, sire."

"And what is that, O great Lord Memucan? You have such superlative ideas—so original, so unique. You were the one who brought Vashti to me." Another swat at the lizard. "In fact, if it had not been for you—"

He squinted at Memucan whose back was toward a narrow window.

"Come over here. I can't see your face, and I don't trust you when I can't see your face."

Memucan moved.

"Surely Your Majesty has no reason to distrust me?"

"Of course not. Don't be ridiculous. Don't ruffle my temper at this hour of the day. Now, what brilliant, inspired scheme have you concocted?"

"I should send her to Ecbatana, sire."

"But, you fool, *I* go there in the summer. Do you think I am going to stay in this pesthole in the hot weather?"

"Exactly, sire. When you go to Ecbatana, she and her entourage will come back here. Wherever your royal person is, there she will *not* be."

Xerxes laughed. "You are an evil daeva, Memucan. Sometimes I think you really are possessed by one of those wicked spirits. All right. Take care of it. And soon. I do not like things hanging over my head."

Xerxes pulled at his beard, then met Memucan's look a little shamefacedly.

"I shall miss her, you know, Memucan. There's no one like her in bed."

"But my lord Xerxes has many beauties in his harem."

"Yes, I know. But I don't suppose there is much there that's very interesting; it takes a lot to interest me these days. After Vashti, they will seem pallid."

He sat down dejectedly.

"And what do I do about a consort? I have no queen. What solution do you have for that?"

Memucan, who had no solution whatever, decided it was time for the king to attend to more important matters.

"It is a decision which will take time. Any highborn lady in the land would give everything she owns to be your consort. You will need to select with care. Meanwhile, beautiful women are easily come by; my lord has only to reach out and choose. And—this is not the most pressing problem, sire."

"Not the most pressing?" snapped Xerxes. "Tell me then, my gifted one, by all means tell me, what is?"

"I think what is uppermost in your mind now is surely—Greece."

The urbane nobleman knew he was taking a chance.

Greece. The word went into Xerxes' brain like an incendiary arrow.

"Curse them! May they know the darkness of Angru Manyu! They mocked my father; I will destroy them!"

27

Memucan was relieved. Military strategy appealed to him much more than harem intrigue.

Even before the Babylonian uprising, plans had been set in motion for a monumental attack on Greece. Months ago, Xerxes had held a convocation for all his satraps; they had come with their retinues from all over the dominion.

For one hundred eighty days he had wined them and dined them, arranged great hunts in the royal parks, horse races, chariot races, and mock battles. The highlight of the entertainment had been a display of thousands of carefully selected objects from the treasuries at Parsa. Alabaster and marble dishes. Silver in cool, shining abundance. And the gold! Besides all the dishes, one whole wall was given over to personal jewelry: hair ornaments; bracelets inlaid with garnet, amethyst, turquoise, and lapis; necklaces like thick, gold lace; rings and brooches ornamented with tiny granules of gold; exquisite earrings. Loose in gold dishes were pearls and emeralds by the handful, turquoise, and the deeper blue, gold-shot lapis lazuli.

The nobles had emerged from the treasure room blinking like owls, shaking their heads: "We are fortunate to be part of such an empire; fortunate to be ruled by such a king." Any who disagreed kept their opinions to themselves.

The king's purpose for the gathering had been to discuss with his satraps, his generals and commanders how he would carry out his campaign against Greece. Already he had ordered a canal cut through the probing finger of the Mount Athos peninsula.

True to his nature, he blew hot and cold. What would Darius have done? Would the Seven approve? Was it wise? Greece? Yes, he wanted Greece, but was now the time?

The great General Mardonios, the king's cousin, knew all about the king's ambivalence where Greece was concerned; at this war council he had set about to change it.

"You will recall, sire, that when your father sent messengers to the Athenians for the tokens of vassalage, earth and water, they put his envoys in a well and told them to get their tokens there."

Xerxes hit the table, and the wine goblets rattled.

"Abomination!"

"And those who were sent to Sparta—"

"They killed!" roared Xerxes, now thoroughly worked up. "My father's memory must be avenged."

He addressed the council: "My noble lords, I come from a line of the most illustrious conquerors and rulers the world has ever seen. My father, Darius, conquered and ruled with such brilliance that he will be honored forever."

The men had heard this many times before, but dared not show signs of boredom.

"I have no intention of doing less for my empire. I have the blood of both Darius and the inimitable Cyrus. We are chosen to be conquerors, we Achaemenids. Since my father died before he could revenge his wrongs, I will finish what he began."

One would think, mused Mardonios, that he had originated this idea himself instead of having to be pushed into it.

A slave moved a golden whisk as a fly circled the king's head.

"On my father's behalf, and for my many subject peoples, with no regard for personal comfort—" Xerxes liked the sound of that; he tried it again: "—with no regard for personal comfort, I will not rest until Greece is mine. Your work, my lords, is to prepare. I want men, equipment, animals—your best. Mardonios, you wish to say something?"

The king's cousin touched his lips.

"The Greeks, sire, need a lesson—a sharp one. You have a vastly superior army, wealth beyond reckoning. The Ionians, the Aeolians, the Asian Doraians, and the Thracians are already on your side. With millions in your army—" Mardonios was getting swept away, "and a great fleet, your victory is assured. Why, with your consummate skill, with the best army and navy in the world, you will wipe them from the map."

Xerxes was pleased with Mardonios and showed it.

Day after day they planned; night after night the palace lights burned. Maps were brought and discussed; new ones were made and pored over. Soldiers came and went, the clank of arms as familiar now as the clatter of banquet dishes had once been. Clutching rolls of leather and parchment, scribes hurried along the hallways. Messengers galloped into the courtyard, threw the reins to a groom, and strode into the council rooms from which loud voices could be heard discussing and arguing.

Finally, the satraps had left to arm for war and compete for Xerxes' rich prizes. They took with them glittering tales of Susa and its glories that were only half-believed at home.

Now, after the emotional upheaval that had ended last night's banquet, Memucan sensed it was time to rekindle Xerxes' enthusiasm for the campaign.

"Yes, I must have Greece, Memucan. They humiliated the Great Darius, Emperor of the World, Lawgiver—"

He began to sound like Darius' own self-commendatory inscription on the high cliff at Bisitun. Memucan sometimes felt amused tolerance for the king; occasionally he felt contempt. There were other times when his admiration bordered on affection. But he never was indifferent.

He's no Darius, but he's not a fool. And what influence he has! He has a conqueror's mind—

"Why are you smiling?" The question had an edge.

"Forgive me, sire. I did not realize I was smiling. I—"

"Go on."

"I appreciate standing in the presence of greatness."

Xerxes smiled. He liked Memucan.

"You were always astute, Lord Memucan. You are my closest friend."

Memucan placed his hand to his mouth in the time-honored gesture of reverence and was dismissed.

As the curtain swung behind the nobleman, Xerxes' euphoria drained away, and he thought of Vashti again. His anger was appeased; his just sentence would be carried out. But the pain of his loss was real. Who would listen to his intimate thoughts now? Who else could understand him?

He crossed to his sleeping apartment and sent the slaves away. Looking down at the empty bed, he felt very alone. Atossa had never allowed him into her heart, but he had been so sure of Vashti.

Tears of pain and anger surprised him. Furiously he wiped them away.

"I hate her! Despise her! I tear her from my life! From now on, I think of Greece."

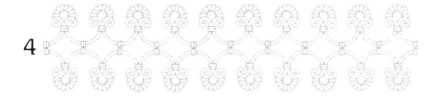

4

Mordecai was late this evening. He wrapped his warm wool cloak closer about him against the rough wind and rain blowing into Susa from the plain.

Born in Babylon, grandson of one of Nebuchadnezzar's captives from Israel, Mordecai was a prominent lawyer at Xerxes' court. During Darius' reign, while Xerxes governed Babylon as crown prince, Mordecai was building a formidable reputation in Susa. He was a distinguished looking man. His hair and beard, worn in the tight-curled Persian fashion, were strikingly streaked with gray. Burly eyebrows grew close to keen dark eyes and met in a thick tuft over his nose which was large, high-bridged, yet somehow delicate in structure. To an ingenious mind too secure in its own skill to curry favors, he linked steely ambition. Grounded in Hammurapi's Code, on which Darius had based the Persian laws, he seldom failed to win a case; his fortunes and ambitions vaulted together.

Already well-known in Susa when Xerxes had succeeded Darius to the throne, Mordecai studied the new king carefully. What were his weaknesses? Where did he and his father differ?

The grandeur of Susa did not impress Mordecai. He had come from mighty Babylon. That city had fallen; so could this one. As for religion, his faith in Adonai and his loyalty to the Great King seemed to him two separate things; he made no attempt to reconcile them. Most of his colleagues were not even aware that he was a Jew.

From the citadel he could hear the shouts of the changing guard whose torches were reflected on the wet walls. The rain-soaked streets were nearly empty. Carriages with foreign representatives went by; a doctor hurried to a patient. He saw a mounted soldier patrolling the street and a few other men late, like himself, for dinner.

He was on the Street of Oleanders now, his own street, lined with head-high walls varying in color and design. In places these walls were broken by gates. His own was of heavy wood with bandings of beaten copper; above it burned two torches. He was proud of his gate.

He rapped three times, and the gate swung open; his gatekeeper bowed, and Mordecai wondered again where Kusuru had learned to move so gracefully. Had he been a dancer in his youth? What matter? Kusuru was too old for that now.

Mordecai crossed the paved courtyard. Ahead, Kusuru opened the wooden door of the house itself. Oil-burning alabaster lamps lit the entrance hall; the sound of singing was muted by thick curtains at the end of the hall.

"Hadassah?" Mordecai asked his servant.

"Yes, lord. She has been playing and singing all afternoon."

Mordecai nodded and moved quietly down the hallway. Kusuru drew back the heavy curtain.

"By the waters of Babylon there we sat down and wept, when we remembered Zion. . . ." A remarkably pure voice was singing a Hebrew melody to the accompaniment of a hand harp. The girl's figure was turned away from the doorway, her throat and shoulders outlined in lamplight.

Mordecai's foster child, daughter of his dead uncle Abihail, was his earthly source of peace. No matter what the confusions at court, no matter what storms shook the pagan city, Mordecai felt he lived in the eye of the storm where there was quiet, where there was Hadassah.

She felt his presence and turned.

Mordecai caught his breath. Sometimes he forgot how extraordinarily beautiful she was. Tonight she seemed lovelier than usual—and there was something else. He realized she was not a little girl any more; she was a young woman of fourteen.

"Father!" Hadassah put down her harp and ran across the room, flinging her arms around him, hugging him, running round and round, holding his hands. Her laughter was irresistible.

A woman? Perhaps not quite yet.

"You are wet through," she said, shaking her head disapprovingly. "And your hands are cold. *And* you are late, sir. Where have you been? Kusuru, send for Shirik, please. Take the master's wet things and bring dry house shoes."

"Come." She pulled him toward a copper brazier which added light and heat to the lovely room. "Sit down."

He did so obediently, his eyes twinkling with his delight in her as she poured wine from a ewer of Egyptian blue paste.

"Peace, my father," she said, handing him his cup.

32

"Peace." He lifted the cup and drank.

"Now," she settled at his feet, "tell me about today. Did Dakia the Mede win his case? What did you learn about the runaway slave? And that man who wanted—what was it?—a judgment on the man who rode into his dog and injured it?"

"Yes, yes, my daughter," Mordecai's stern mouth was smiling. "One thing at a time. Dakia won his case and—"

"Because he had you for a lawyer. He would win, of course."

"Possibly. But we had a very fair judge."

"And what about the slave?"

Mordecai shook his head. "There has been no word. It will go hard with him when they catch him."

"Don't you mean *if* they catch him?"

"No, my dear, when. He has no chance." And then he was sorry he had said it, for Hadassah's big eyes seemed to get even bigger.

"What will they do to him, father?"

Annoyed with himself, Mordecai concentrated on putting on his embroidered house shoes. He certainly did not want Hadassah to know about the atrocities that were sometimes done in the name of just punishment. He might deplore them, but as one of the king's lawyers he accepted them as a fact of life.

"They will act according to their ideas of what is right, my dear." He was relieved to see Shirik gesturing for them to come. He held out his hand. "Dinner is ready. Tell me what good things you have planned for me."

Hadassah's eyes danced. "No. A surprise. I have planned something special for tonight."

Mordecai breathed a sigh of relief; she seemed to have forgotten the slave.

After the meal they returned to the big room where Mordecai took some papyrus scrolls from a chest. He laid these on the table with some leather documents inscribed with colored ink. "It is time for your lessons, Hadassah."

"Which shall we do first tonight, father? Our Scriptures or the history of Persia?"

"Which would you prefer, my dear?"

She wrinkled her nose. "You always make me choose."

"But you must get used to making decisions, daughter, even small ones. You are growing to be a woman."

"But, father, I make decisions all day long: what is to be done in the garden, what shopping Huldah is to do, what we are to have for meals, what is to be cleaned and polished in the house each day, which of your robes needs washing and airing, how to discipline that lazy son of Kusuru's—"

"Stop! Stop!" he laughed. "I agree. You make all these decisions, and you make them well. But there are other kinds of choices."

"Choices." She moved restlessly. "You are always talking about being free to choose. Sometimes I don't like this idea. It makes me feel so—so—"

"Responsible?"

"Yes, I suppose so. It's easier just to blame everything on Adonai."

Leaving the subject, Mordecai said, "We shall have a review!"

"What happened to the dog, father?"

"Dog? What dog? Oh—" He shook his head at her. "Hadassah, we are studying. I want you to take this seriously."

"Yes, father, I do. But we did not get that question answered before dinner, and you don't let me ask questions about your work at meals, so please tell me and then I promise I'll settle down to work. Did the dog live? And did the man get a judgment against the stupid man on the horse who ran into the dog?"

Mordecai sat up straight. "First, Hadassah, you will not speak of your elder, *any* elder, as a stupid man."

Hadassah put her hand over her mouth, but her eyes were not very penitent.

He looked at her quizzically. "Sometimes I think you feel more tenderly toward animals than you do toward people."

"But they are nicer than people sometimes."

"Still," Mordecai had a little trouble keeping back a smile and wished for the hundredth time that there were a mother in this home, "you are not to call your elders stupid. That dog lived; the man was fined. Now, who was the founder of the Persian Empire?" He spoke to her now in Persian. Normally they spoke in Aramaic, but since he had no son, he was determined Hadassah would have the best education he could give her. Besides Persian, he was teaching her Hebrew.

"Cyrus was the empire's founder. Why was he called the Shepherd?"

"You remember that, do you? It seems as if we shall combine Persian history and Scripture study tonight." He took up one of the scrolls. "Listen to what the prophet Isaiah said—"

"About *Cyrus?* What did Isaiah know about a Persian king?"

"Listen! 'Thus saith the Lord, your Redeemer, who formed you from the womb: I am the Lord who made all things; who stretched out the heavens alone, who spread out the earth. . . . who says of Cyrus: he is my shepherd—"

"Adonai's shepherd!"

" 'And he shall fulfill all my purpose, saying of Jerusalem, "She shall be built" and of the temple, "Your foundation shall be laid." ' "

Hadassah's eyes were shining, and she hugged her knees. "Go on, father. Go on!"

"There is not much more. 'For the sake of my servant Jakob and Israel my chosen, I call you by your name, and I surname you, though you do not know me. I am the Lord and there is no other; beside me there is no God.' "

The room was quiet. The glorious phrases sang in the air. Outside, water dripped from the trees.

"And did he?" asked Hadassah.

"Did he what?"

"Did he do Adonai's pleasure, this founder of the empire?"

"And what city did he defeat?" Mordecai used the familiar Jewish technique of answering one question with another.

"He defeated Babylon, for one."

"And do you recall how he did it?"

"Oh, yes, I remember." She recited the story of how Cyrus had dammed the water of the Euphrates so that the river running through the vast city's center had dried up and Cyrus took Babylon with almost no resistance.

"Do our Scriptures say anything about Babylon?"

He read: " 'Sit in silence and go into darkness, O daughter of Babylon. . . . I was angry with my people, I profaned my heritage; I gave them into your land. You showed them no mercy. . . . Evil shall come upon you . . . . disaster shall fall upon you, which you will not be able to expiate and ruin shall come on you suddenly. . . . let them stand forth and save you, those who divide the heavens, who gaze at the stars, who at the new moons predict what shall befall you.' "

"I don't understand that last part about the moon and gazing at stars."

"The art of astrology began in Babylon and is very old. From the stars and their positions priests and star-readers say they can predict the future."

"Why don't we have astrologers? I think I'd like to be one. Do they have some in Susa?"

35

"Probably they do, but it is expressly forbidden for a child of Israel to have anything to do with such things," Mordecai said firmly, reading on, "'Let no one be found among you who . . . is . . . a soothsayer, a diviner, a sorcerer, one who casts spells, or one who consults ghosts or familiar spirits, or one who inquires of the dead. For anyone who does such things is abhorrent to Adonai and it is because of these abhorrent things that Adonai your God is dispossessing them before you.'"

Hadassah was thoughtful. "But how did Cyrus do Adonai's pleasure?"

"It was Cyrus who decreed that the Jews in Babylon could go back to Jerusalem at the empire's expense. He even allowed them to take the gold and silver dishes that had been stolen from our temple—" Even now, so many years later, the desecration shocked him. "The sacred things that had been taken to that pagan city."

"Did many of our people go back?"

"No, too many were comfortable, as we are comfortable, I suppose, in a foreign land. They felt at home; they had houses and vineyards and businesses."

"Does that mean Cyrus believed in Adonai?"

"Not necessarily, Hadassah. Cyrus was a great ruler, very wise. He was tolerant; those he conquered were allowed to continue their customs and religious practices."

"But what were our people doing in Babylon in the first place, father? I know they lost a war, or a battle, or something to—whoever the king was."

"Nebuchadnezzar. You have much too fine a memory to forget important names. You mustn't be lazy."

"Nebuchadnezzar. But you always say Adonai is behind all history. Couldn't he have done something for his people? Why did he let it happen?"

"Choices again, Hadassah. Adonai does not force his ways on man, not even on his chosen ones. Do you remember the covenant Adonai made with Abraham?"

"Yes."

"He said that certain things would happen if we did not obey him. He said that if we failed him, we would go down before our enemies, that those who hate us would reign over us." He picked up another scroll. "Here in the Fifth Book of Moses it is written, 'Take care then not to forget the covenant that the Lord your God concluded with you and not to make for yourselves a sculptured image. . . . The Lord will scatter you among the peoples and only a scant few of you shall be left among the nations to which the Lord will drive you.' So you see, the Jews went into exile because they disobeyed Adonai. But he *is* faithful, even when we are not; his eye is still on us. He says, 'I will maintain my covenant between me and you and your offspring to come as an ever-lasting covenant throughout the ages, to be God to you and to your offspring to come.'"

"What made Adonai choose the Jews in the first place, father?"

"I have no answer for that, Hadassah."

"We must have been a bigger and better nation."

"I think not." Mordecai read again from the same scroll. "'Of all the peoples on earth the Lord your God chose you to be his treasured people. . . . It is not because you are the most numerous of peoples that the Lord set his heart on you and chose you. . . . but it was because the Lord loved you and kept the oath he made to your fathers.' Do you understand that, Hadassah? He loves us because—he loves us."

"Oh, yes, I understand that. I love you because you are so good to me and you are my father and I respect you. I have good reason to love you. But I love my bird and the flowers just because—well, I just love them, that's all."

Mordecai nodded. "Do you remember the passage you learned last week, the one you liked so much?"

"'He that keeps Israel shall neither slumber nor sleep.' Only Israel? Doesn't Adonai care for other nations? What about the Persians?"

"Adonai is Lord of the whole earth, Hadassah. He always longs for men to turn to him. All men—never forget this—*all* men have been made in his image."

"In his image? What does that mean?"

Mordecai smiled and stroked her hair. "What are the qualities of our God?"

Hadassah closed her eyes and recited from the ancient Book of the Law: "'The Lord! The Lord! A God compassionate and gracious, slow to anger, abounding in kindness and faithfulness.' Oh, I see! It's inside we are made in his image. We can love because he does; we can be kind because he is kind. Is that it?"

"Yes, that is at least part of what it means."

"But then—but then—" Her cheeks were flushed and her eyes large with excitement.

Mordecai stood up and pulled the girl to her feet. "Enough for tonight, little one. To bed with you."

Hadassah threw her arms around him, kissed him, saying, "I'm so glad I'm Jewish!" and obediently went upstairs where Huldah, her nurse from babyhood, waited for her.

For a long time Mordecai sat staring into space. He found himself praying for wisdom in training this ward of his. He knew she had a good mind and that her beauty could prove a heavy load. *Adonai, protect her!*

She was already of marriageable age. He sighed, realizing it was time to think seriously about it. But who? David ben-Bilshan? Friends since childhood, they seemed fond of each other. He himself liked his oldest friend's handsome grandson, but was David ambitious enough? How high would he set his sights? Mordecai wanted a brilliant marriage for his daughter, but Hadassah—in this she would want to make her own choice. Well, time would tell. Telling Shirik to snuff out the lamps, he went to bed.

5

Never had such an army marched before. Color spilled over the plains like a moving patchwork, highlighted for parasangs by the sun's rays glancing off spears, arrowheads, and helmets.

Half of the army moved ahead of the king, parasang after parasang, sweat-streaked and footsore but excited by the change brought into their ordinary lives. A long train of mule-drawn wagons carried countless silver containers of boiled water for the king, water from Susa's river Choaspes, the only water he would drink. The first section of the great army ended many parasangs from its beginning, and a two-furlong gap was scrupulously maintained; no common soldier must come near the Great King.

In this section the whole mood changed. Here was taut discipline, order, wealth. Under their decorated tunics, the Persian soldiers wore coats of Egyptian mail; on their heads were soft felt hats. One thousand cavalry, their horses' coats silk in the sun, preceded a thousand spearmen. After them came ten of the sacred horses from Nisaea.

A space of stillness seemed to settle round the vehicle that followed. Eight white horses, sparkling with gold trappings, drew a golden chariot. In it was nothing visible, nor would there ever be. The charioteer walked behind, holding the reins. No mortal man, not even the Great King himself, dared sit in the chariot of Ahura Mazda, the supreme god.

Next came the royal chariot carrying only Xerxes and his charioteer, Patiramphes. When the jolting became too much for the king, he stopped the procession and was carried to his covered carriage.

One thousand more highborn spearmen were behind him, another thousand cavalry, and then the Immortals, all ten thousand of them. They moved in a great square formation, carrying gold- and silver-topped spears. After ten thousand more Persian horsemen there was a second empty space. The remainder of the vast horde followed.

At a place called Celanae, Xerxes had a surprise.

Pythius, one of his wealthiest and most loyal subjects, not only entertained him in regal style but offered him his entire fortune for the war. The king sent for his handsome general, Masistios.

"Can this Lydian afford such gifts?" he asked.

The reply nettled the king.

"He is second only to you in wealth, sire. He is the man who gave your father the plane tree and the vine made of solid gold."

The king stayed on with Pythius, and his host again offered to give him all the gold darics he had—3,993,000 of them—insisting he could live comfortably on his estates with his servants; he did not need the gold.

"Pythius," the king extended his golden sceptre, "I make you my friend." He gave Pythius time to absorb this honor. "As a reward for your loyalty, you may keep your darics, and *I* will give *you* a gift. I will round out your fortune with enough gold darics to make it a full 4,000,000. Enjoy your wealth; you deserve it."

And Xerxes went on his way, leaving behind a man convinced he served the most gracious monarch who had ever lived.

The army rumbled westward over the Royal Road and eventually reached the city of Sardis where Xerxes would winter. Demanding the usual surrender-tokens of earth and water, he sent out messengers to the Greek states. He sent no messengers to Athens and Sparta; he had other plans for them.

It was a bright spring day. Xerxes was in fine fettle. After being cooped up in Sardis for the winter the men were like prisoners suddenly freed from cages. The captains had all they could do to maintain the order and discipline of the march.

Above them arched the cloudless sky, brilliant as lapis. Suddenly, inexplicably, the light began to fade. The sun seemed dimmer, but there were no clouds. The light faded more and more.

A handsome, richly dressed man of middle age picked up a piece of dark Egyptian glass and looked through it at the sun, his eyes streaming. A superstitious man, he gasped at what he saw. When he told his captain what it was, he was brought to Mardonios.

"It is an omen, my general," said the captain. "Surely it means disaster of some kind."

Disturbed, Mardonios went to the king who was wondering what gods pursued him.

"Sire," said the general, "this man has seen something I think you should know about."

"It is time someone had *something* to tell me," the king said impatiently and waved permission.

The man was shaking as he said, "Please do not be angry, great lord, but—but—"

"Speak up. What is it?" The darkness was growing, giving the landscape an eerie look. "Have you some explanation for this?"

"I looked at the sun through this, sire." The man held up his treasured bit of Egyptian glass. "And I could see the sun and—it—it is dreadful. It is partly burned out."

"The *sun?*"

"The sun, Great King."

"Here. Give that to me." Xerxes waved to his nearest eunuch.

The glass was handed to him, and he, too, peered into the sky. By now the eclipse was nearly total, and even the animals were growing restive. A strange hum, a vibration of fear, came from the crowd. Men made signs against the evil eye. Some swore. Others prayed.

"Send for the Magi," Xerxes ordered.

The Magi came, looked, and conferred.

"This is good news, great Lord Xerxes," said the head Magus. "The sun is that which warns the Greeks. This is a good omen. Look! Now it grows brighter!"

It was true. The light was returning. Looking through the glass again, the king saw that the sun's burned-out area was on fire once more.

"This means," said the Magus, "that the Greeks will be obliterated by the vast armies of the Ruler of All Peoples."

"Victory!" shouted Xerxes. "Forward! The gods are on our side, even the Greek ones!"

Later, he called Mardonios to his tent.

"Who was that man with the piece of glass? Could he be a messenger from Mithra? We must reward him."

"His name is Haman, sire."

"Haman?" The name tugged at his memory. "The man with the ten sons?"

"The same, Majesty."

"What extraordinary eyes he had—almost hypnotic."

A dust cloud in the distance put an end to the conversation. A caravan came up, no ordinary caravan, and Xerxes gave the order to halt. Accompanied by only one servant, a man approached.

"Sire," announced Masistios, "it is your friend Pythius."

"Pythius! My wealthy host from Celanae? Bring him here at once." Xerxes extended his sceptre to the man he had honored with his friendship. "Welcome, Pythius. What brings you here?"

"Great King!" Pythius prostrated himself. "Your generosity and your pledge of friendship, of which I am most unworthy, have given me courage to come and make a request. To you it will be small, but to me—"

"But my dear friend! And my father's friend! Of course. We have not forgotten your loyalty and hospitality."

Xerxes, pleased at the day's omens and having had a good lunch, chose to be charming. Encouraged, Pythius lifted his head; the breeze blew his white beard. "The king is most generous. You know that every one of my five sons is serving you in this campaign."

The king inclined his head very slightly.

"It is a great privilege for me to have them serve my lord, the king—a proud privilege. But I am old, and I entreat Your Royal Majesty to allow me one son only—my eldest, Oromedon—to stay and care for me and my estates. Keep the other four with my blessing."

With no warning, Xerxes' face contorted with fury as he lashed out at the old man. "Insolence!" he roared. "Ungrateful Lydian! Here am I—I, the ruler and master of your fate and the master of every one of your sons, sweating and burning in this filthy heat. For what? To defend your home—*yours!* Yes, and with me are my royal brothers, cousins, uncles, men from the greatest families in Persia. Who do you think you are?"

"Sire—"

But Xerxes was in the country of the evil daevas. If Darius was looking over his shoulder now, he was ignored. "How *dare* you ask for the release of a son of yours? Masistios! Send word to the executioners—"

Pythius paled.

"—and have them hack in half this Oromedon, son of this dog."

"My son! O Gracious King! Take me! Kill me! I was your father's friend—"

"Cut his son in two pieces!" Xerxes spat the words out one by one. "And impale each piece—one on either side of the road over which my army will march." The king's face was now the cruel mask his enemies knew: nostrils flaring, eyes blazing with near-insanity.

Masistios turned aside to hide the revulsion he felt. Accustomed as he was to violence, he was shaken by this wanton bestiality.

42

The ugly thing was done.

Deaf to his sworn friend's terrible cries, Xerxes gave the order to move on. And the squadrons of the king's army marched through the grisly gateway, warned that no one offended majesty with impunity.

Ahead was the most imposing natural barrier of the campaign: the straits of the Hellespont, separating them from Europe. Violent discussions had gone on in Susa over this crossing. One strategy after another had been considered, shouted over, and discarded. It was the king himself who had devised the final plan.

As they went on toward Abydos, the town from which the crossing would be made, dust blew and blinded, gritting into everything—food, baggage, into every crevice of their bodies. Sometimes gales came, lightning cracked, and men died.

Losses and discomfort only settled the stubborn king deeper in his resolve to go on. Zoroastrian he might be, but in Troy he ordered a sacrifice to the Trojan goddess of warfare and wisdom, Athene. Nothing must be left to chance.

"What would Darius say, I wonder?" murmured Masistios to Mardonios, watching the Magi preparing a thousand oxen for the ceremony.

"Darius?" Mardonios laughed. "Surely you have not forgotten how Darius treated these things? His reverence for the sacred bull in Egypt? His temple to the god Amon at the Kharsa oasis? Darius was a pragmatist, my lord. Whatever his personal feelings for Ahura Mazda, and I don't doubt they were sincere, he was not a man to let them interfere with policy. He would have understood this perfectly."

So Xerxes believed also. Knives flashed, oxen bellowed, blood settled in lakes. The smoke of sacrifice stung the eyes. Chanting as they walked around the bloody scene, the Magi poured libations of wine to the departed spirits of the great.

"Mithra we worship whose words are correct, who is challenging, has one thousand ears, is well built, has ten thousand eyes, is tall, has a wide outlook, is strong, sleepless, ever-waking. Well may he bring them terror and fear; off he throws the evil heads of the men who are false to the treaty; off fly the evil heads of the men who are false to the treaty."

Xerxes was nodding approval. "This spells doom for Athens and Sparta," he said to Mardonios.

The chant went on.

"Four coursers pull at his chariot, all of the same whiteness; they are

43

immortal, they have been reared on supernatural food, their front hooves are shod with gold, their hind hooves with silver."

The whole procedure unsettled the men. Those farthest away could see nothing but fire and smoke, and the wildest rumors flew up and down the line. During the night superstition and wine melded into panic, and even the whistling whips had hard work to restore order.

At dawn they were again on the march, grinding over the interminable parasangs. And then, at last, Abydos.

Xerxes looked over the plains stretching to the horizon. "See there, Mardonios, the men of Abydos have prepared a throne for me, there on the cliff. I'll review my army from there."

Fascinated, he watched them pass before him. They came from every country in Asia, from Egypt, from Ethiopia; there were even many Jews. Each nation wore its own costume, brought its own weapons: spears tipped with iron, flint, or antelope horn, swords, javelins, daggers, battle-axes, and immense bows which shot cane arrows. The Assyrians carried clubs which were knotted or iron-studded. Shields were of crane-skin, ox-hide, and wicker.

Xerxes asked questions and ordered his secretaries to take notes. Looking at the whole of the Hellespont covered with ships, the great plains and roads and beaches black with people, he preened like Nebuchadnezzar at Babylon years before. "They are *my* men, *my* power, *my* wealth. My name will last forever. Yet my greatness has only begun."

"To be sure, sire. We will take this polyglot mass of people—"

"*I* will take, Mardonios. Do not forget whose army this is."

"That is understood, sire. *You* will make of this mixed group the greatest fighting force on earth."

It took days to complete the review of the troops. In the distance, rain hung a curtain. To his left, the waters narrowed and the opposite shore showed gray and mauve. The wind whipped his robes, and a servant draped him with fur.

Without warning, tears ran down his face, cutting furrows through the dust. His uncle, Artabanus, asked him the reason.

"Life is so short, uncle. Look at all these men: brave, strong, the best in the world."

"Yes, sire?" The old man was puzzled.

"In a hundred years not a single valiant man will be alive."

Artabanus was reminded of the boy Xerxes who had wept when his slaves were whipped. Somewhere under the seasoned soldier and the cruel monarch there was still a vestige of compassion.

44

From the headland at the Hellespont the king's engineers planned to run two bridges across nearly seven furlongs of water. His Phoenicians spent days making great flax cables for one bridge, racing the Egyptians who made papyrus cables for the other. No sooner were the bridges completed than a violent storm whipped them away and carried them down the strait in splinters and foam. Again the great Xerxesian rage erupted.

"How dare mere water interfere with my plans! I am King of the Earth! Mardonios! Masistios! Send men with whips. They must lash the waters!" He glared at the Hellespont, churning under gray clouds. "Filthy stream!" he bellowed. "I need no man's permission and no river's. I will cross you!"

The men flailed the waters with long whips, working off some of their own anger and frustration—glad, too, that the kingly rage was directed against something inanimate for a change. But worse was to come.

"And now—" Xerxes swung round to his officers who stood immobile, but pale and shaken. "Now, the bridge builders." He ground his teeth, and spit dribbled on his beard. "Every single man of them!"

There was a long pause. Gulls screeched overhead, oblivious to offended majesty below; the waves broke on the beach; horses whinnied. The suspense was dreadful.

"Behead the bridge builders! All of them!"

Xerxes stumbled into his tent and sent all but Harbonah away. His rage and frustration had drained him. Watching him, Harbonah knew from past experience what would come next: self-doubt, remorse, uncertainty. He would be ill for hours; after the execution of Pythius' son it had been days. At times like these, the eunuch, who had wasted little love on Vashti, almost wished for the clever queen. For reasons of her own she had been expert at soothing and reassuring the king during these terrible aftermaths.

Not that she gave a silver siglot about the man himself, Harbonah thought. She had simply known how to look after her own interests. Perhaps he might learn. He looked at the figure on the couch: eyes closed, mouth slack, body still shivering even under fur robes.

Harbonah's small eyes looked around the tent where the dimly burning lamps cast wavering shadows. "Strange," he murmured, "all his wealth, his power—what good are they now? He will kill himself with one of these attacks. King of All Peoples, but ruled by his moods." In his own way he loved the king.

Xerxes opened his eyes at that moment and reached out his hand. "Come here."

Harbonah clasped the king's hand; it was cold.

"I was right, wasn't I, Harbonah? Discipline is necessary in wartime; that's what my father always said. He would have had those men killed, wouldn't he?"

"I am sure he would, sire."

"You are a faithful servant, Harbonah. You must never tell anyone about—me—being like this." He waved feebly.

"Never, my lord king."

"And, Harbonah, when we get back to Susa after this war is over, I must find a new queen. I need someone to comfort me."

Harbonah held his hand till he slept and remained by him all night, concern mingling with a terrible jealousy.

Like many eunuchs, Harbonah was a complex man. He had served Xerxes for years. Intelligent, ambitious, hard-working, he was fiercely possessive of anything he considered his own. In a position of real power, he had achieved nearly everything he wanted from life, but the threat of a new queen unsettled him. He did not mind how many girls Xerxes called from the harem or the house of the concubines. But a queen, someone who would be closer to the king than he was, someone who would become an object of confidence and love? That idea was nearly intolerable. How far would he himself go, he wondered, in attempting to defeat a new queen? He looked into the depths of his own confused heart and realized he did not know.

Now there was a new problem: the king had short-sightedly killed off all his experienced bridge builders. However, the newly chosen men, goaded by a healthy fear for their lives, found a solution. They lashed galleys and triremes together into two bridges—three hundred and sixty boats for one bridge and three hundred and fourteen for the other. From wooden winches on the shore they twisted cables of flax and papyrus and sank heavy anchors on both upstream and downstream sides. Three lanes were left open for water traffic.

For days and parasangs men chopped down trees, making planks the length of the boats. They placed these over the cables, tying them together. Hundreds scoured the countryside to bring back mountains of brushwood which they layered thickly on the planks. Tons of earth were shoveled onto this, and then men jumped and walked on it, tramping it into hardness. A protective railing on each side, acting as a blinder for the skittish mules and horses, brought the work to completion.

Xerxes had his bridges.

6

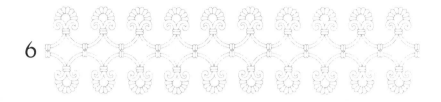

The sun drove down in straight, hot fury. It was the noon rest time, and the camp was relatively quiet. In the distance, heat shimmered over the rocky terrain like a gauze curtain. The overripe smell of a dozen varieties of fruit mingled with the stench of sweat and human excrement. Flies made a druzzing sound. Children sired on this campaign cried or whined or laughed. Donkeys brayed, camels grumbled, horses neighed. Most of the men and women rested in what shade they could find, amusing themselves after their fashion.

One such pair, carefully screened by a large rock, was Haman and Zeresh. Auburn-haired with topaz eyes, she was the newest concubine of an Immortal named Shishia and played a dangerous game in even speaking to another man, but she enjoyed danger. Haman found her challenging. She knew just how far to go in titillating his appetites before she withdrew with a light laugh. "My impulsive Haman! You are an exciting man. But remember—we must both remember—I belong to Shishia."

Haman sometimes strode off in a fury of frustration; at other times he would let her go and look at her speculatively. "I am going a long way in this world, Zeresh. My aim is high."

Amused, Zeresh rearranged her hair. "Tell me about it, Haman. I know you are ambitious, but tell me more. I want to know all about you."

"I am rich."

"Very rich?"

"Very. I contributed heavily to this war."

"And where did you get all this money?"

"I got it through my own efforts. My father was very poor, a skilled carpet weaver in a tiny village, but no businessman. When he died, his one little shop was all I had to begin with. From that I developed a good business. Now I have some of the greatest carpet ateliers in the kingdom. I have—other interests as well."

"I can imagine," murmured Zeresh. "Do go on. You have a wife, of course?"

"No, she is dead. But I have ten sons—magnificent, all of them. Several are here with me in the campaign. In fact—" he pointed to a couple embracing under a tree, "there is the eldest, Parshandatha."

"Ten sons! You *are* a man, aren't you! And Susa is your home?"

"I was not born there, but it has become my home. I have a house there, and I shall return to it after this war is ended. As I told you, my aim is very high."

"You want to be Captain of the Immortals? Come now," she laughed, "I admire ambition. My own has put me where I am. But as soon aspire to be one of those falcons flying up there as to be the Immortals' captain. You're not even a Persian!"

"The Immortals' captain, commanding only ten thousand? Do you think that would satisfy me? I aim far, far higher than that."

"Higher? Would you dare—" her voice dropped. "Surely you are not considering— What *are* you considering, Haman?"

Haman put his hands in his full sleeves. The sun shone on the oiled hair and beard, the aquiline nose, the thick, smooth lips. He made her a mocking bow.

"You shall see, Zeresh. Think what it might be like to be second lady of the land some day."

As he swung away from her, his mind was busy with schemes for the future. The war—he shrugged at the war. That must be gotten through somehow, and he would continue ingratiating himself with the king whenever he could, but military exploits required too much bravery. When he returned to Susa he would strengthen his many contacts there and set up his sons in key positions. Parshandatha, for instance, had a keen mind for finance. Already he had made sharp profits from land, but banking was his main interest. He wanted to buy his eldest the best, but the best banking business in Susa was owned by a Jew as were so many other banking firms in the empire. Haman spat.

He could hardly remember when he had not loathed Jews. His mother, who adored him, fostered his sense of uniqueness by telling him he was descended from royalty, from Agag king of the Amorites, a great king whose fiercest enemies were the Jews. Long before the day King Saul defeated their ancestors and the wretched prophet Samuel killed Agag, she told him, there was bad blood between Jews and Agagites. They had not changed. His mother assured him he was never to forget this.

So the boy Haman would set his dog on Jewish playmates or contrive cruel practical jokes. Instead of punishing him, his mother rewarded him with praise and cakes. By contrast his father, while having no love for Jews, doled out punishments streaked with sadism. This contradiction in his parents' attitudes had twisted his character to some degree, but he himself nurtured the deep-rooted narcissism that had turned him into the amoral man he was.

As the years went on, Jews always seemed to get in his way. Did he want to buy a rug shop? It was owned by a Jew too shrewd to be cheated. Did he plan to expand his estates? Who but a Jew owned the land around his? And now as he thought of Parshandatha's future, a Jew stood in his way again.

Watching him go, Zeresh was thoughtful. Second lady? Whose office was he after? She thought about Susa and its glories. Someone had once said, "If you take Susa, you need not hesitate to compare with Zeus himself for riches." The lavish court, the luxurious life, position, power! Haman lusted for power, and she—who else would he find so helpful, so serpent-wise?

At times she was nearly wild with desire for him, but knowing the risk and wise in her dealings with men, she had never allowed him to take her. Some day . . . .

For Zeresh there was no right or wrong; she had no beliefs against which to measure conduct except what suited her. Nothing was right that gave her the slightest inconvenience, nothing wrong that gave her a moment's pleasure.

Shishia had noticed that she was becoming less interested in him; her attention wandered during love-making. Jealous, he questioned her.

"Unfaithful to you, my lord? What nonsense! I have been yours for— who remembers how long?"

"You have been mine for exactly two months."

"Has it been so short a time?" She pulled him down to her. "I feel as if I had belonged to you all my life."

Shishia's look remained cold. "You know quite well what the penalty will be if I ever find you with another man. I will kill him, but you I will mutilate."

Zeresh shivered. She knew he meant it.

Preparation for the crossing accelerated. Shouts, animal noises, and shrill cries of women filled the air. Men dropped from exhaustion. Quarrels broke out. The eunuchs jostled for preference; the female cooks fought the camp followers; the Indian dogs snarled and bit the pack animals.

But the day came at last.

In the gray chill before sunrise, spices of all kinds were burning on the bridges and myrtle boughs were laid along the route. The pungent flames cheered the shivering crowd, sleepy and fearful in the dawn.

As the sun rose, Xerxes, in his shining clothes, poured wine into the sea from a golden goblet. At times like this Xerxes seemed superhuman; his men were captivated. The scarlet stream was blown into rubies by the wind, then dissolved into the salt water. Still facing the sun, he prayed to Mithra: "Forcefully Mithra comes forth, strong in power he flies, with his beautiful far-shining glance he looks round with his eyes. On account of his splendor and fortune I will audibly worship Mithra with libations. Listen, O Mithra, to our prayer; satisfy, O Mithra, our prayer; condescend to our prayer. Approach our libations, approach them as they are sacrificed, collect them for consumption; deposit them in Paradise."

He flung the cup into the Hellespont, following it with a bowl and a short gold sword.

The crossing began.

Pack animals and underlings swarmed over one bridge, the men shouting, swearing, sweating. First to cross the other were the ten thousand Immortals, wreaths on their heads, sun glinting on the gold that covered them like fire.

The bridges proven, the king, standing in his chariot, followed the empty chariot of Ahura Mazda.

Men marched, walked, staggered—for seven days and seven nights the mighty progress continued. At last, all were across; the Abydosians were left behind to guard the cables, and the army continued on its way.

The arrival of the king and his hordes brought disaster to even the friendliest Greeks. In preparation, every available smith who worked in gold, silver, and copper made dishes for the state visit. Calves, sheep, and fowl were gathered for the final slaughter. The land was ransacked—the best of everything collected. Afterward, taking with them everything not consumed, the departing troops left behind impoverished peoples.

Xerxes and his forces eventually reached the vital pass at Thermopylae. Here the Greeks had decided to defend their land; a better place could hardly have been found. Only thirty-odd cubits wide, it sometimes narrowed to a single wagon track.

For days the Spartans drove Xerxes' men back in hand-to-hand struggle. He poured in men: first the Medes; then, realizing how formidable his enemy was, his Immortals. For every Spartan killed, two new ones seemed to appear. Was he to lose his whole army in this humiliating pass?

Malis, a Greek opportunist, came to the Persians, slyly seeking a fortune in exchange for information. "There is a small track that leads *over* the hills to Thermopylae; you can avoid this deadly pass."

Covered by the oak wood, Xerxes' forces crossed the narrow defile at night. As daylight came, the king poured his libation to the rising sun and attacked.

Hopelessly outnumbered, the Spartans were doomed, but the Persians paid heavily. Blood greased the rocks, and many fell screaming into the sea and drowned. Others slipped and were trampled to death by their friends. Driven relentlessly by whips, men died of shock and exhaustion. Two of the king's brothers were killed.

It was carnage.

During long, hot marches, during short, star-hung nights, Haman continued his personal campaign, plotting his rise to power. His was a nature so intensely self-oriented that things not directly associated with himself seemed hardly real; conversely, anything that was his or even associated with him took on grandiose importance. Unintentional slights became insults; indifference was an affront. But he also knew how to be charming; his eyes, large, black, almond-shaped, could mesmerize.

How best ingratiate himself with the king; how achieve his goal? His subtle mind wove and rewove. Threaded through this pattern of ambition was the strand of his desire for Zeresh. The fact that she belonged to one of the king's own guards only added zest to his aim to have her. He would outflank, outwit, outmanage everyone, and she would be not just his concubine, but his wife. Exotic, ambitious, unscrupulous, she was perfect for him. He would reach the palace itself, and Zeresh with him.

Inordinately proud of his sons, he had given them the finest education possible. They were a handsome lot which he saw as extensions of himself, his own assurance of immortality.

One day during the campaign in Greece, he sent for the five who were with him in the campaign. Parshandatha, the eldest, arrived first, then Dalphon and the twins, Poratha and Aspatha.

"Where is Adalia?" asked Haman.

"With a woman, of course," said Poratha.

Haman laughed. "He's my youngest son here, but he makes the rest of you look like boys without beards. Oh, there you are, Adalia." Haman studied him sardonically. "You are my son all right. But be sure that pleasure never interferes with business. Do you understand?"

"Of course, father."

"And it's business we'll discuss today," Haman said. "By the time we return to Susa, we must have a complete plan for building up my position in the capital. You are my most valuable weapons. Together, we'll infiltrate all the avenues of power: banking, trade, the military. You, Parshandatha—you'll continue to make profits from land, but we must establish you in banking also."

"Banking, yes. But not any little bank. You know the one I want," his son said boldly.

"The one owned by that tight-fisted Jew?"

"That one. He had the gall to tell me I wouldn't live long enough to learn what he already knows about banking."

"Was he threatening you?" Haman asked.

"He wouldn't dare! They're a cowardly lot, these Jews."

"Well, they're becoming altogether too powerful for my taste. But forget the leeches for now. Think about Susa. We'll be socially successful—we'll give the best banquets."

"You'll need a wife for that," laughed Parshandatha.

"I've chosen someone," his father said.

"Are you serious?"

"Who?"

"Tell us!" Outwardly amused, the brothers were inwardly disturbed. They were used to their father's women. But someone in their home with status, closer to their father than they were? This was something else.

"No one you know." Haman waved aside their questions and abruptly changed the subject. "Trade. That's the vital link with the satrapies, and the best way to keep tight control on faraway places. Dalphon, you've shown a good head for such things. What sort of trade would interest you?"

"Jewels for me, father."

"A good trade for someone with such an interest in women, Dalphon."

Adalia laughed. "In that case, we'd better all be jewelers."

"Is that what you want, Adalia?"

"Women, yes. But jewels—no, thank you. I want to study law. I'll become the best lawyer in Susa."

"You haven't the brains," snapped Dalphon. "Anyway, the smartest lawyers in the capital are mostly Jews. It's a tightly controlled group."

"Jews again! You forget—I'm clever."

"You're conceited. Do you think you stand a chance against the Jew, David ben-Bilshan?"

"Who says ben-Bilshan's going to be a lawyer? He's nothing but a schoolboy."

Dalphon shrugged. "Schoolboys grow up. When we left for the war, he was already speaking three languages and his teachers were calling him brilliant. He's a lad to watch."

"Well," said Haman shortly, "we'll watch him. Aspatha, Poratha, what do you want to do?"

"Poratha already knows a lot about rugs, but as for me—" Aspatha tipped an imaginary goblet. "Wine, lovely wine."

Haman nodded. "Parshandatha, you're making notes of all this?"

"Yes, and it occurs to me that both the rug and wine trades are in the hands of Jews! Do you know what one Jew said to me when I wanted to buy his shop? 'If King Saul of the Israelites had done a better bit of work on your ancestors, you wouldn't be here to bother me.'"

Haman swore. "There are just too many of them! And they multiply like hares. Business, banking, estates—they'll soon have us by the throat."

"Well, we'll show our loyalty to the king by cleaning up the empire," said Dalphon. "You've always told us they're our ancient enemies."

"And so they are. And remember, you're all of royal blood. Now, pay attention, all of you. The younger boys at home will be ready to play an important part by the time we return. We must be prepared to move into every area of influence in the capital the day we return."

And through the night they discussed the steps by which Haman could reach his objective.

Parshandatha, most like Haman in both subtlety and sharpness of mind, had the best ideas; but all the others, trained by their father, made contributions. Together they were formidable.

Before the discussion ended, Haman sent for a man who was a secret priest of Angru Manyu to offer sacrifices. The gods must be on their side.

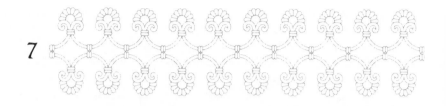

7

In a room warmed with light, flowers, and quiet laughter, Mordecai and Hadassah were dining with their old friend Bilshan, a Jewish scholar who had taken his son's large family under his protection when that son had been killed in the war with Greece. He lived in an even finer neighborhood than Mordecai's, one that bordered the river Choaspes.

During the meal the talk had been of the war. Mordecai, in a position to hear more than most, told them the latest reports. "Our troops found Attica deserted, and in Athens the only people left were zealots who barricaded themselves behind wood ramparts on the Acropolis."

"But they would be trapped like animals!" David, Bilshan's eldest grandson, broke in.

"They were. Our Persians shot blazing arrows over the wooden walls and then swarmed up the great rock below the buildings. The poor Greeks died pleading with Athene."

"Who is Athene?" Hadassah wanted to know.

"She is the Greek goddess of wisdom." David flashed her a quick smile; he enjoyed showing off before Hadassah.

"How do they send the messages about the way the battles are going?" asked a younger grandchild.

"They use fire signals. They light a series of fires, and these are seen by men faraway who then light similar fires."

"And all goes well with the Persian troops?" asked Bilshan.

"Not entirely," Mordecai replied. "A three-day storm has wrecked hundreds of our ships."

Bilshan nodded his white head. "The Great King of All Peoples is finding there are forces that even he cannot control."

"How many men are in the army, Uncle Mordecai?" the youngest wanted to know. "Hundreds?"

"Thousands, silly," said David, gently pulling at his brother's ear. "Thousands and thousands."

"How can he count them all?"

Mordecai laughed. "That was a stroke of genius on the king's part. You see, except for the Persians, the army is a rabble of many nations, hampered by lack of training. Each contingent fights according to its own native customs. So our king decided that at least he would number them and separate them by nations. Ten thousand men were jammed together and a circle was scored round them in the dirt."

"Like fish in a net!" exclaimed David.

Mordecai nodded. "They were dismissed, and a fence was built along the circular line."

"So that's how they did it," marveled David. "Ten thousand in the enclosure at a time."

"You say that the Persians are the best-trained?" asked Jakob, David's closest friend.

"Oh, by far, Jakob. They have the strongest motivation for fighting, you see. In a particular way, the Great King is their own."

"How do they look, Uncle Mordecai?"

Mordecai turned to the youngest and smiled. "They are wonderful to see—colorful robes, gold bracteoles—"

"Gold what?"

"Bracteoles—tiny gold ornaments sewn on their clothes." It was Hadassah's turn to show off.

"What are they for?" the youngest wanted to know.

"To show what a rich king we have," laughed David. "And they have gold anklets and chains and gold-hilted scimitars."

"Huldah said their women lie on gold and silver couches and eat and drink from gold and silver dishes," Hadassah put in. "That's just a silly tale, isn't it, father?"

"I'm afraid it's true, my dear."

"But all that luxury—doesn't it make the men weak?"

"Weak!" scoffed David. "The Persian soldiers are the fiercest in the world!"

The youngest was thinking hard. "All those men and animals— what do they drink? What do they find to eat?"

"One whole lake, more than a parasang wide, was drained dry by just the pack animals. River after river simply disappeared. As for food—"

"The countryside must look as Egypt did after the locusts had swept through," said Bilshan. "What a waste!"

The little one was jumping up and down in his seat. "Do you think they will still be fighting when I'm old enough to be in the army? Do you? Oh, I hope so!"

David tousled his hair, but his voice was hard. "I shall go first, little brother. I'm not old enough yet, but I soon will be."

"When you go, I'll be right beside you," said Jakob.

"May it please Adonai that the war be ended before any of you go," murmured Bilshan.

Mordecai pursed his lips. A successful campaign was important to the empire and to his plans.

After the meal, the young people and children went into the garden.

"Hadassah!" David took her hand, drawing her toward the pear tree. They were the same age; they had known each other since babyhood. David thought her the most beautiful girl in all Susa. He realized, too, that she had something besides beauty: she had strength—more, perhaps, than he. He remembered the way she had comforted him when the news came that his father had been killed. Until that event, nothing had touched the young Jew. He had looks, wealth, love. The war had seemed exciting but faraway until the day he was told of his father's death; then reality was ragged-edged and ugly.

Jakob and his sister Ruth joined them by the tree.

"It's been months since we've been together. Have you seen the new lute David's grandfather gave him, Hadassah?" asked Ruth.

"It's lovely, David. Play for us. Please?"

"All right, but I don't play nearly as well as you do."

"You're fishing for compliments, sir! Very well, I shall give you one. You're the best lute player in—in—"

"In this garden!" laughed Jakob. "Come now, David—play something lively."

They began dancing to David's vigorous twanging. Hadassah, flushed and laughing, was dazzling. David and Jakob were entranced; Ruth watched wistfully. Hadassah's nature was too generous to incite jealousy, but Ruth wished Hadassah would find her own brother Jakob more attractive and leave David for her.

The moon silvered the pear tree. The younger children went off to bed; Jakob and Ruth tactfully wandered indoors. David looked at Hadassah and grew serious.

"Do you think they will betroth us, Hadassah?"

She was startled for a moment, then laughed softly. "I have no idea, David. Come, let's go in. It's hardly the time for us to talk of that yet."

She took his hand. He tried to pull her back, but she slipped away.

"Last one in's a donkey," she called over her shoulder and ran into the house.

The Persian juggernaut rolled on. Naïvely trusting in a deliberately deceitful report from Athens' general, Themistocles, Xerxes decided to trap the Greeks in the narrowest part of the Saronic Gulf between Salamis and the mainland. After that, he would push on to Sparta.

Seated in splendor, he called a council of war and ordered the leaders placed according to his chosen protocol. Mardonios went to each for his opinion and then took it to the king. All were in favor of engaging the Greek fleet except the strong-willed woman commander, Artemisia, from Halikarnassos, who had contributed five ships and felt entitled to speak her mind.

Artemisia was a widow with a grown son. Stocky, with powerful arms and hands, her skin was leathered by sun and salt wind. She had icy green eyes that could skewer a lazy seaman. And she was wise.

She warned the king: "Do not fight at sea; the Greeks are too experienced. You have Athens and the rest of Greece. Just keep your fleet at anchor; they cannot hold out, and they will not dare resist you."

Her friends were terrified that her independent thinking would bring down the wrath of the king; her enemies hoped it would.

Xerxes listened carefully, then laughed. Unused to women speaking their minds, he found her intriguing. He eyed her speculatively. He was her sovereign, but he saw she found him attractive as a man. What a pity she was so ugly.

"Our lady commander is wrong this time, Mardonios. What failures we have had occurred because *I* was not there. We will fight the Greeks at Salamis, and this time I *shall* be there, watching from the shore. We will win."

On a little island between Salamis and the coast he placed a large contingent of men who were to deal with escaping Greek seamen and care for wounded or shipwrecked Persians in the coming battle. A triple line of Persian ships blocked the east exit at Salamis; on the west were two hundred more ships. The Greeks were trapped. They lacked supplies; they squabbled interminably. Left alone, they would have devoured each other. But the ambitious Xerxes had his heart set on a spectacular victory. He had not come all those long parasangs just to play a waiting game. Before scything his way on to Sparta, he would humiliate the Greeks.

At the base of Mount Aegaleos, across the strait from Salamis, Xerxes sat on a silver-footed throne to watch the battle. The Athenians took the initiative; Xerxes' Ionians trounced the Spartans. The battle was a boiling cauldron in the king's well-guarded trap. Any act of valor that caught the king's eye was recorded by one of his secretaries. "Who was that?" he would ask. "Write that down for the royal annals."

At one point when the battle was very hot, he saw a Greek ship swooping down on one of his own that was straining to get out of range. Squarely in the path of his trireme was a third ship. The king's craft rammed solidly into it, sinking it with all on board.

"Well done!" roared Xerxes. "Who commands that ship?"

"Artemisia, sire."

"Artemisia! Are you sure?"

"I know her ensign well, my lord king."

Xerxes shouted with laughter. "Well! It seems my men have become women and my woman has become a man."

He would have been less enthusiastic had he seen what really happened. Artemisia, pursued by the Athenian ship, saw that the vessel in her path was her own ally. It was her ship or theirs; she did not hesitate. "Forward!" she shouted, and with a rending shock her ally's boat went down.

Now the caged Greeks were fighting for their lives. With annihilating force, they butted into the tightly bunched Persian ships, splintering the sides, snapping the oars, upsetting, turning, ramming with the fury of trapped tigers. Some ships stampeded; the strait became a snarled mass of bodies, boats, and weapons. Greek hoplites and archers poured over the Persian ships. Orders were shouted and ignored.

Finally, Athens broke through the strangling Persian blockade. Javelins glinted in the clear light, bows twanged, arrows sang. Screaming with pain and fear, the Persians, many of whom could not swim, fell from blood-slimed decks. Two hundred of their ships went down. Even the king's brother, Artabazanes, Commander of the Great Fleet, was killed. Artemisia's advice about the Greek's experience on water had been well-founded; the Greek allies lost only forty ships.

The Athenian Aristides and his foot soldiers now converged on the little island, Psyttaleia, that was to have been a Persian shelter and a trap for stranded Greeks. He slaughtered every man there, including three of the king's nephews.

The victorious Greeks shouted their triumph, while on shore Xerxes was white with horror and shame. Darius and Atossa had schooled him in the mentality of kingship. The word *defeat* was not part of the Achaeminean vocabulary. In his mind had been no flicker of doubt: things would go on forever as they had been, only more so. He would finish everything his father had died too soon to complete; he would put down all resistance, expanding more, building more. He envisioned a greater empire, more wealth, finer buildings. The great name of the Achaemenids would lose no luster during his reign; its light would reach all civilization. Perhaps southern India and beyond, perhaps Italy . . . there were no limits to his dreams. He had swept across Thrace and Macedonia, hardly slowing down. He had outwitted the tough Spartans at Thermopylae; he, Xerxes, had burned the Acropolis.

Now, in one day, his hopes were smashed as his fleet was smashed down there on the bloody waters. He thought of his brothers, Artabazanes and Ariabignes, whom he would never see again, of his three nephews on the island peopled with the dead.

From the strait below, the cries of the dying came to him like voices of the damned; the great triremes and penteconters cracking and splintering were a scene from the underworld. Unaware of those near him, he lost all sense of time and space. A curtain seemed to hang between him and reality as he watched the mayhem beyond his throne.

Now the light was fading after a sunset filled with color and light. To the Greeks, who found their omens in the sun, it was a joyous endorsement of their victory; to the Persians it was an insult. A cool breeze rippled the water and moved the pieces of wreckage and floating bodies.

"Great King—" Harbonah finally attempted to recall him.

A shuddering sigh from deep inside, a gesture that was utter defeat. "Take me away," Xerxes said, and Harbonah hardly recognized the voice.

What had gone wrong? How could they have been defeated? Scene after bloody scene filled Xerxes' mind. For once, the tragedy and horror of human suffering and death seemed to become a reality almost too painful to bear. In an agony of confusion and humiliation, he turned to Harbonah. "Where was the god Mithra? Has he deserted me? Where was the righteousness of Ahura Mazda? Who failed me, that such a thing could happen?"

All night he lay awake reliving the battle, not daring to admit he had made a mistake. That way one teetered on the crumbling cliff-edge; below was a chasm of failure and fear he could not contemplate.

Suddenly, he sat up in bed. His bridges! The Greeks would rush to the Hellespont; they would burn the cables he had left behind when the ships moved westward. One-third of the Imperial Army stranded in Europe? Unthinkable!

Forgetting he had a fleet still, that he had men, and that the Greek Allies were depleted, he failed to see Salamis simply as a check to his progress. He forgot Artemisia's advice; he lost his sense of balance.

Only Harbonah saw him agonize over the decision. For once, Darius' name was not even mentioned. Finally he decided to deceive both the Greeks and his own troops into thinking he would stay and continue to fight. Everyone was taken in. Except Mardonios. He knew the king as no one else knew him, and he was not fooled.

Sending for his general, Xerxes unfolded his plan. What did he advise? Mardonios' brilliance in handling Xerxes and his unblemished record for bravery had kept him in the king's good graces. He had no trouble now. Another war council was called.

The king smiled ingratiatingly. "What do you think? Where am I needed most? Shall I personally attack the Peloponnese, or shall I leave Mardonios here with three hundred thousand men and go home? He claims, and of course I believe him, that he can deliver all Greece to me. He wants to show his mettle. Give me your opinions."

Once again, Mardonios went the rounds of the leaders seated a respectful distance from the king; once again it was Artemisia who was most decisive: "Do not endanger your royal person. Of course, leave Mardonios behind. If he succeeds, it will be *your* victory, for your minions will have done it. If he does not, at least you will be safe. As long as you and your house survive, the Greeks will have their hands full." She shrugged as she gave the general her message for the king. "Mardonios does not matter."

Mardonios looked through her. A woman commander! He wished he dared spit.

Xerxes decided this was good advice. "Send my compliments to Artemisia."

So Xerxes, escorted by sixty thousand of Mardonios' select troops, left for the Hellespont and Sardis, his head high. Only Mardonios and Harbonah understood the torment underneath the majesty. Although Salamis had been a defeat for the Persian military and naval forces, for Xerxes the man it was a searing personal calamity.

The return was bitter. Advancing, the king's troop had gorged on the riches of the land; now they ate grass and stripped the bark off trees. Plague and dysentery decimated their ranks. More tragedy waited in

Abydos where many of the men, frantic for food, stuffed themselves and died.

All the next year Xerxes stayed in Sardis, ostensibly keeping an eye on the Ionians. He was morose, withdrawn, but with occasional flashes of white-hot rage.

In the ranks withdrawing with the king, Haman learned that the guard Shishia had been killed. He was overjoyed, then frightened. Zeresh! As the concubine of a deceased Immortal, she would be killed—unless she had somehow managed to escape, and that was most unlikely.

He went up and down the lines, in and out of camps, making discreet inquiries that hid his inner fears. Yes, people remembered Zeresh. No, they did not know what had happened to her. These women always were put to death. But no one had seen; no one was sure.

He sought his god, Angru Manyu, with sacrifices and incense. A deeply ingrained strand of superstition in his nature made of Zeresh's disappearance a dark omen. Zeresh was an important part of his plan for the future; what forces were interfering at this crucial point? He followed every lead and never stopped trying to find out what had become of her.

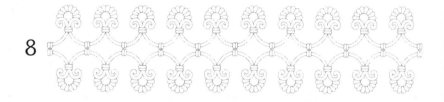

8

Susa was in mourning.

When the capture of Athens had been reported, the city had celebrated. Roads were strewn with fragrant myrtle boughs; incense burned in every home. And then Salamis! It was like going from a lighted banquet hall into a tomb. They had no warning. Xerxes, their king, with that numberless army? They were invincible!

Salamis!

And after the shock came fear. What if the king himself were dead? If that great army could be defeated in faraway lands, where was Mithra? Had he withdrawn his protection? And if he had, then what of Xerxes? The king! The king! Men tore their clothing and wailed in the streets. Homes were draped with mourning, and the great palace on the acropolis showed few lights at night.

"Mardonios! It is Mardonios' fault. He talked the king into this venture. Wait until he comes home. . . ." They did not know he would not be coming home—that he and his great horse would die near Demeter's temple in Platea.

The winter passed at last; spring colored the land. Suddenly the word hummed through the capital: *The king comes!*

Susa erupted into a volcano of color. From the acropolis, where the color glowed richest, it poured down onto the housetops and walls and ran like paint into the streets. Waves of sound washed up and down the highways and alleys. There would be a recession of noise, and then cheers would break out again.

The housetops were dark with people; so were the tops of the city walls. Rugs and banners draped the houses, hung out of every window. The streets were a mass of humanity, held sternly back by a solid row of armed men. Guards patrolled on horseback. Here and there groups of musicians were playing; people sang. All shops and businesses were closed for the day, but hawkers with fruit drinks and wine, delicate pastries and bits of roasted meat were everywhere.

"He comes!"

For parasangs in every direction bushes, trees, and crops waved in the breeze, and the scent of flowers was blown about in waves. Far to the east were the snow-etched mountains. The people were drunk with relief and exhilaration. Later in the day they would be drunk for other reasons.

At last the vanguard arrived and was admitted by the welcoming guard at the north gate of the city. For a long time men poured into Susa, some heading for the citadel, others packing the streets.

Then came the king's own advance guard.

If the populace was shocked by the condition of the army, it made no difference in the vociferousness of its welcome.

As the royal chariot swept into the King's Gate, the people were prostrate. Xerxes stood in his chariot, looking straight ahead. By not so much as a muscle in his face did he betray any emotion. As Ahura Mazda's representative, it was beneath his dignity to bow and acknowledge their devotion. The roars of the early morning now receded into a sound like a giant sigh. "Great is Xerxes, King of All Peoples! Great King of All the Earth! King of Kings, King of the Whole Earth! Great is Xerxes, the Achaemenid!"

When they dared, the people stole a look, shocked at the changes they saw. Gray streaks in the black beard and glossy curled hair. Deep lines along the mouth. The king's posture was still regal, but he could not hide the marks defeat had left on his face.

The chariot moved on to the foot of the double staircase that led up to the acropolis. Slaves were waiting, holding the throne with its fringed canopy of gold and purple. Xerxes was carried to the top of the staircase. There he signaled the bearers to stop and slowly raised his golden sceptre toward the thousands below him. It was a gesture of compelling majesty. Then, at his signal, the bearers took him into his palace.

In the streets the merriment began again.

In Mordecai's house, too, they celebrated. Influential men with whom he associated at the palace came with their wives. Piles of steaming food were brought in on copper trays; wine flowed freely. Hadassah, who had planned the feast, was nowhere in sight. When their Jewish friends visited, she was allowed to take part in the meal and often played her harp and sang. But Mordecai had no intention of allowing pagan eyes to look at his daughter.

This morning he had allowed her to go, heavily veiled, to the roof with the women of their household. She had come down breathless with excitement. The pageant, the noise, the color of the royal progress had exhilarated her even though she was too far away to see much. Watching her, eyes sparkling, color in her cheeks, Mordecai renewed his vow to keep her away from the profligate court. The less she knew of that life, the better.

Hadassah found his restrictions aggravating, but he had told her his reasons: She belonged to the people of Israel. Where women were concerned, their way of life was different from that of the Persians. Hadassah argued vigorously for more freedom; Mordecai remained adamant. And since he was the hub of her life, she obeyed. Even chafing at his restrictions, she understood that he loved her.

Tonight, shut upstairs in her own suite of rooms, she was feeling more pensive than annoyed. She picked up a silver mirror. *Fourteen, and I don't even know anyone I want to marry. Of course, there is always David. Dear David. But he's more like a brother. Still, I don't know anyone else as nice. And I do want children.*

She went out on the balcony that overlooked the garden. *Perhaps Adonai will be kind and allow me to be the mother of the Messiah!* Then she looked up at the stars and laughed. *Hadassah, you are an idiot! Every Jewish girl in Susa, in Persia, in the world is hoping the same thing tonight and every other night. How can Adonai say yes to all our prayers? To most of us, to all but one, the answer must be no.*

In the palace, Xerxes was padding about his sleeping room and talking with Memucan.

"Tell me what has been happening, Memucan."

Memucan began his reports on palace intrigues, on taxes and tribute, on the satrapies, on progress of the buildings at Parsa. At mention of his favorite project, Xerxes' eyes lit up for the first time since he had come home. "Parsa goes well, then?"

"Yes, sire, very well. Your father's palace is nearly finished, and the workmen are beginning on your own."

"Excellent. And the reliefs? The figures on the stairs?"

"They are magnificent. I will bring you some sketches. Now, if Your Majesty wishes."

"No, no. Tomorrow will do. Parsa is going to be one of the wonders of the world. You know that, don't you, Memucan?"

"It will be a monument to your greatness, my lord king."

"And to my father's greatness."

"Of course, Majesty."

But as the days wore on, the Seven began to worry about Xerxes. He was not as he had been before the Greek campaign. The humiliation of Salamis, the later defeats of the army, the deaths of Mardonios and Masistios, the loss of the fleet had sapped something vital. Moody, irritable, and bored, he prowled his rooms and growled at people for no reason. He began brooding about Vashti again. The more he thought about his queen, the more deprived he felt.

"It's your fault, Memucan—all your fault. Without you, I would not have done anything so drastic. Why did she have to be deposed? I could have punished her, refused to sleep with her for a while. Then everything would have been all right."

Memucan dared not mention that it had been only the law that had kept the king from killing Vashti on that memorable night so long ago.

"I miss her! I'm lonely!" He swung savagely on Memucan. "Curses on you and your progeny!"

To be cursed by the Great King was not something to be taken lightly. As Ahura Mazda's earthly representative, his power was second only to the god's. Memucan's lean hawk-face was sober. "Your Majesty, please believe I am your loyal servant. With your excellent memory—you will recall how seriously Your Majesty was offended by the queen's behavior. My lord behaved most unselfishly. All the wise men and the Seven—"

Xerxes' eyes narrowed. Was this man going to remind him that he had asked their advice?

"—we all realized the great sacrifice you were making for the cause of your kingdom."

That was better. Xerxes waved him on.

"It was because of the effect on the homes throughout the kingdom that you took this difficult step. You put royal duty above pleasure, the kingdom's good above your own desires."

"You are right, Memucan." Xerxes plumed himself. "I am moody today—not like myself. But where can I find a replacement for Vashti? Now that I think of it, I seem to recall that when we began planning the Greek campaign you were going to tell me some brilliant idea you had on this subject."

At the time of which Xerxes spoke, Memucan had had no ideas about selecting a new queen. Since then, however, he and the other princes had discussed this at length; he was ready. "The idea, my lord king, is that we seek virgins throughout your whole empire. Appoint officers in all the provinces to bring together the most beautiful young women. The virgins will be brought to Susa to the House of the Women and put under Hegai's expert care."

"But, Memucan, I have concubines galore and virgins right here in my harem now."

"These would be new faces from many lands. As they entered your august presence—"

Xerxes interrupted with a sound between amusement and a snort. "I am not exactly august at such times, Lord Memucan."

"I understand, Majesty. But for these young women, coming to the Great King is an awesome experience."

"At the start, perhaps." Xerxes smoothed his mustache. "They love me before the night is over, I assure you."

"I am certain of that, sire."

"But go on. You were saying—"

"They will each come to you once; then, from all these lovely girls, this vast selection, you will choose your queen."

Xerxes looked at him for a moment that seemed very long indeed. Memucan became uneasy. Suppose this ploy did not work? What then?

"Ah, yes," the royal voice was purring. "I try all these virgins, and finally, one night, *she* will come and she will be very, very beautiful and very, very bed-worthy. Yes, Memucan, I see." He was smiling now, moving around the room in quick strides. "The cream of my kingdom! All mine! Magnificent! Quick, Memucan, get this edict out at once! What a treasure you are! And send someone to the harem right now. Tell Hegai I want the most exciting girl he has."

Next morning, Susa hummed. Extra scribes had worked through the night transcribing the king's edict into many languages. The courtyard was filled with the jangle and stomp of horses and riders as they prepared to carry the proclamation to every corner of the empire.

"Good morning." A young courier dropped a friendly hand on the shoulder of an older man. "We're off again. Which way do you go?"

"To the south, worse luck, where it's hot."

"What do you make of this edict?"

"Quiet! One does not question the Great King."

"This king is not the man his father was. Why, when Darius reigned, he—ouch!" A sharp elbow in his ribs caught the young man off balance. "Fool! What are you doing? I—Oh—"

Not fifteen paces away was one of the Immortals. Fortunately he had not heard the careless remark and continued on his way, but the scare had finished the reminiscences.

"Hurry!" the older courier snapped to a sweating groom. "We have to leave by sunrise." He looked out over the plain; in the distance the mountains were turning pink. The younger man was Ahmet, the Egyptian, the fastest postal courier in the king's service.

"Since you are going toward India," said another young courier, "do you think you could find someone to send back some perfume for me? I have a little friend—"

"Another little friend?" asked Ahmet.

"Well, yes, but this one is the loveliest yet. Such charm, such grace—"

"And such expensive tastes, eh?"

"Money is no object." The younger man reached into the folds of his short tunic and pulled out some silver shekels. "This should take care of it."

Ahmet stared. "Angru Manyu! Don't tell me you got those on a courier's pay?"

"Not exactly." He shrugged. "Some of us are lucky with dice."

"I see. You want to spend all of this? You do like the lady, don't you?"

"You have no idea how much I like her."

"Very well, then. I'll try." Then, to the groom, "A coin for you. See that I'm first away."

The courtyard bustled with noise and activity. Couriers strapped swords tighter, grooms checked horse trappings, flasks of wine were filled. Oaths and shouts everywhere, some good-natured, some not.

"Is this all the fruit you could find, you wandering Israelite? How far do you think this will take me? Get me some great blue grapes, pears, and at least a few oranges. Quickly!"

"Slave! Tighten this girth. Do you want my bones rotting in the Arabian sun? I suppose you might, but it won't be this time, my sexless young friend."

"By Ahura! If you do not move quickly, I'll cut your ear from your Greek head. Foreigners! *Move!*"

Grooms worked hard, often sullenly, but all knew enough to keep silent. Punishment came swiftly and without mercy.

As the first shafts of sunlight leveled across the courtyard, a messenger from the king came down the steps. "Thus says Xerxes, the Great King, King of Kings, King of Nations with Their Many Peoples, King of the Great Earth even to afar. . . ." He read through the proclamation calling in the virgins. Slaves handed out copies of the edict written in the appropriate language for each courier.

"I'm off to Arabia, land of perfume and horses!"

"And women, no doubt?"

"That's your statement, my friend. I said nothing about women."

Laughing, they swung their horses' heads in line with others, clattered down the shallow steps, and headed out on the hard-packed road. The sun was in full glory, the sky clear. Clouds of dust swirled as they dispersed north and south. Later they would fan out in many directions.

The king's word was on the march; in a fortnight the whole empire would be covered. No word of death or war this time. This time they carried the great net which would bring in the beauty of the monarchy for one man's pleasure.

Back in Susa with his sons, Haman began implementing their plans for power. While Adalia studied law with a Babylonian, Parshandatha insinuated himself into the banking firm he'd sworn to control one day. Dalphon was supplying the richest ladies in Susa with imported jewelry and personal attentions. Haman's finest rug atelier was now controlled by Poratha, while Aspatha was fast becoming an expert in wines. As for the younger five, they were all training under skilled masters paid to make them accomplished courtiers, as expert in arms as their brothers.

Haman's impressive house on the Choaspes riverbank overflowed with servants, his sons, their women, and his own. Until they married, his daughters lived there as well. All the years of struggle, the accumulation of wealth by good means and bad, stood him in good stead now. Widely traveled, skilled in languages and dialects, astute in administration, knowledgeable in industry and the culture and customs of the widespread kingdom, he bought estates in a dozen satrapies and saw to it that powerful men were cleverly put in his debt.

Determined to make himself invaluable, he studied the king's tastes in everything from horses to women. In this he was helped by Marsena, of the Seven, who shared his greed, lust, and intense ambition, as well as his contempt for Jews. An inveterate gambler, Marsena always needed money. In exchange for a wide variety of information, Marsena received a steady flow of treasure.

The Jewish community continued to be a burr under Haman's saddle. Not only their business and professional expertise chafed him, but their houses of wealth and taste, their culture, their women and children.

"No wonder our ancestors fought these scum!" he said to his sons. "Hoarding up wealth! Sending it to Jerusalem, that pesthole in the provinces. I tell you, the king should know the Jews will never adapt and become part of this empire!"

9

From every satrapy they came: sloe-eyed Egyptians, exotic Babylonians, regal Assyrians. There were Arabian girls, lissome and seductive; there were Medes, Armenians, Parthians; there were girls from Cappadocia and Chorasmainia and Gandara, lovely Sarangians, Bactrians, and girls from Sogdiana. The Savaens and the Sattyadades had said good-by to their loveliest women; others had been snatched from Aracholia and Maka. Never, even in Hammurapi's reign, had there been a greater collection of beautiful women in one place.

Some were thrilled. Some were ambitious. Others were terrified, torn apart, wrenched from home, family, country. Many had left behind men they loved.

Day after day they poured into the capital: tall, short, blonde, dark, red-haired. None of the girls could have been over eighteen; most were thirteen or fourteen.

They came riding on camels, on richly caparisoned horses, in hand-carried litters with slaves in attendance. Some from India were on elephants. Great palm fronds waved incessantly, and fly swatters swished. Each satrapal contingent was preceded by an accompanying official. Subtly jockeying for position, some of the women leaned out and shrilly called each other names in their own languages. Rivalry, anticipation, excitement, and fear vibrated as palace officials moved in and out with accommodation lists. Hegai, the eunuch-in-charge, came as close to losing his composure as he ever had and was heard saying distinctly uncomplimentary things about women in general and these in particular.

Not all the girls were wealthy. A few, looking rather shamefaced, came on foot, accompanied by only one female servant and the soldier. These were always particularly beautiful, but their poverty put them beneath contempt for the wealthy. Young and very frightened, they shrank from the brassy stares and lewd comments.

"We are like cattle up for sale," said Rhasa, a Bactrian. "Only we already know who the highest bidder is. It's degrading."

"How strange you should feel that way," said a regal blonde. "Why can't you see it as I do—a privilege to be in the harem of the greatest of all kings? What exactly do you want from life?"

Rhasa held her head up so the tears wouldn't fall. "All I want is my Bhindi."

"Ah," the other girl's voice softened, "someone you love?"

"We were to have been married next month."

"I understand now. You will never see him again, of course."

"Never. There is nothing to live for now."

"Don't be absurd!"

"How can I be the plaything of a man who has had so many women, used for a night and then discarded like—like a worn-out sandal."

"Sshh." The blonde pressed her hand. Guards were closing in, sent to bring order out of the international chaos.

A fat eunuch was in charge of the grooms who stood by the animals. "Now then, you men. Line these beasts up! Get out of each others' way! Mind where you step there, you fool! *Must* that elephant take this time for—Wah!"

The immaculately dressed eunuch moved too late. Shrill female laughter subsided as he cracked his whip. He strode to the platform above the courtyard and continued his shouting from this vantage point.

More and more people arrived. No sooner had a lady dismounted and gone through the elaborate doorway to the House of the Women than the next pushed or was pushed forward and all shifted position.

Getting each girl settled in and arranging lodging for the attendants took time. Many of the girls were from noble families; some were satraps' daughters. And every courtesy must be extended to the highborn men and women who accompanied them.

The long line twisted through the streets all the way to the North Gate, out beyond the city walls, up the different roads converging on the capital. There it was even worse than in the city. The unseasonable heat of the sun hit the bronze-hard ground with an almost audible impact. Tempers, taut with waiting, began to ravel. Drivers cursed the weather, the officials, the dumb beasts, and each other; horses snorted and reared. The camels grumbled and snapped nastily at anything within reach. Only the donkeys, by nature unmovable, seemed to find delay pleasing.

The vivid colors became dust-grimed, sweat-darkened. The virgins, who had arrived meticulously groomed, expertly coiffed, showed signs of wear. Tendrils of damp hair straightened; kohl-darkened eyes became smudged. Some of the girls were still giggling, chattering like sparrows, flirting with the nearest males. Some complained loudly. Others were sunk in dullness—their bodies in a sedan chair, on a camel, or sidesaddle, on a horse, but their minds and spirits drawn deeply into some inner place of memory and longing.

As time wore on and there were still many in the slow-moving lines, laughter and talk simmered away like water in a hot pan. Apathy settled heavily, and only a few took any interest in the regal sunset which strung out banners of gold, purple, and scarlet, only a few saw the one lantern star burning in a sky like green crystal.

Up on the acropolis, enjoying their vantage point, were Marsena of the Seven and Haman.

"What a sight!" said Marsena, rubbing his hands. "Look at that little redheaded girl."

His companion shook his head. "I like the Bactrian. She looks all fire."

"Well now, Haman, you are getting closer to the king every day; he is certainly not going to want all those girls."

"True, he has always been very generous to me, as you know. But from this group comes the queen."

"I know. Frankly, I do not see one who can come close to," he dropped his voice, "the lovely—former queen, do you?"

"Perhaps not, but my daughter—"

"Look, here comes Mordecai."

"Mordecai?" Haman could see by the man's dress that he was wealthy. It didn't occur to him that he was a Jew.

"He is an excellent lawyer. Greetings, Mordecai! This is Haman, the man who is rising so fast in the king's favor."

"Marsena exaggerates, I assure you." Haman was memorizing the newcomer's features. Instinctive antagonism crackled between the two men. Mordecai barely inclined his head, and since Marsena was not his favorite member of the Seven, he started to move on.

"Don't go. It has been too long since we have seen you, Mordecai."

"I have been away."

"Where?"

"In Bactria."

"On business?"

"Yes."

Marsena ignored the curtness of Mordecai's replies. "You went in connection with this selection of virgins, I'd guess. Fortunate man."

Mordecai's expression gave nothing away. As the king's representative he had done what he was ordered to do, but the whole procedure was distasteful to him.

"What do you think? Is the new queen in that group?"

"One learns not to have opinions about some things, Marsena."

Disappointed, Marsena went on. "I suppose we shall have a new queen soon enough; if not from these foreigners, then from our own Susians."

Mordecai looked at the turbulence below. He found the scene depressing, even frightening. There were rumors that when this group was settled in, the girls from Susa would be taken. That could mean. . . . The fear in his throat had a taste.

Haman joined in. "Personally, I cannot imagine why the Great King went to all this trouble."

"Lower your voice, you fool," hissed Marsena. "Do you want us impaled?"

"Surely Susa itself has the most beautiful women in the world," Haman said softly. "Why should he look further? Mordecai?"

Not wanting his despondency noticed, Mordecai smiled. "Faraway jewels have a bright glitter."

"Besides," Marsena added, "the king's appetite is jaded; he may find something exotic from, say, Sogdiana."

"My eldest daughter outshines every young woman down there," boasted Haman. "Lomar would please the king. All my other daughters are beautiful too."

"Perhaps you have forgotten," said Mordecai, with quiet malice, "that the first requirement is not beauty; it is virginity."

Haman's eyes were dangerous. It was evident from his face that the shot had gone home. He turned and clumped down the stairs.

It was true that he was rising fast in the king's esteem. One could almost see his progress. Six of the Seven were not pleased.

"He's no Persian; he's an Agagite."

"Upstart!"

"It's unprecedented."

Marsena, dependent on Haman's fees for information, refrained as much as he dared when the others tried to undermine his influence, but the king found Haman interesting and clever. His phenomenal memory, ready to be tapped for anything from dates and battle casualties to maps and history, impressed the king who was also impressed by his wealth and his ten sons.

"It is a pity you don't have a daughter, Mordecai," Marsena was saying, not unkindly, as he, too, went toward the palace stairs; it was not wise for any group to stand talking for very long.

Shadows slid over the pavement as clouds filmed the sun. Shivering, Mordecai moved swiftly away. The whole scene had made him uneasy. He wanted to get home quickly, to see Hadassah, to be reassured.

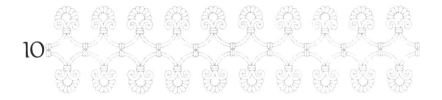

10

Hadassah was embroidering. Unobserved, Mordecai watched the lamplight painting shadows on her face.

She's like her mother. Pictures flickered in his mind: his uncle, nearly his own age—his aunt's kindness—Hadassah playing in the garden. And the desolate little girl he had brought home with him after her parents' death.

"Father!" She put down her work and ran to him. "You were so quiet! Oh, it's good to see you! I've missed you! There's so much to tell you. Did you have a good trip? Was your business successful?

He held her close and did not answer. She stepped back.

"Is something wrong?"

"Noth—" he began and stopped. He had never lied to Hadassah. Since they might soon be facing the greatest crisis of their lives, this was no time to begin. He had not told her the reasons for his journey, but it was pointless to avoid the issue now. "Let's have our meal, dear, and I want to show you what I've brought you. Later we'll talk."

After dinner, he began in what he hoped was a casual manner. "You've heard of the king's edict?"

"The one about the beautiful girls?" She broke into spontaneous laughter. "That's all the servants have been chattering about for weeks! I can hardly get any work from them; they want to watch the processions. Yesterday I went up on the roof—"

"Hadassah! I forbade it!"

Her lips set rebelliously, then relaxed. She patted his hand.

"I was veiled, father, and I only peeked over the top of the ladder. Some of them were splendid, and such clothes! Some were funny, though, like swans or peacocks." She minced around the room, mimicking.

"This is a serious matter, Hadassah. It could change our lives."

"*Our* lives? Why, how could it affect us? We are Jews."

He put his hand under her chin and tilted her head. Was it possible she did not know how beautiful she was? "Hadassah, the edict is for the entire empire. You know the purpose, of course?"

"Of course. The king wants a new queen. Now that the proud Vash—"

"Hush!" instinctively Mordecai looked over his shoulder. "That name is not to be mentioned."

Hadassah saw that Mordecai was genuinely troubled. She became serious. "I'm listening, father."

"The king wants a new queen. These young women from all over the empire are being taken into his harem. Do you know what a harem is, Hadassah?"

She shrugged. "It's a place where the girls live before the king chooses one to be queen. The servants say they have a marvelous time: rich food, beautiful clothes, jewels, games, pets—"

This was going to be harder than he had thought. "Do you have any idea how the girls are chosen?"

"Why, for their looks, I always thought. The king comes and looks at all of them," she was miming again, "then he points to one and says, 'You! You are the most beautiful woman in my kingdom. I crown you my queen.'" She swept a mock bow as the imaginary queen accepted the honor.

"And then?"

"Then she becomes his wife in a big ceremony and is queen forever after. Unless she is disobedient like—well, like you know who."

"Do you understand what it means to be married?"

"Oh, that!" Hadassah chortled. "Don't worry, father. Huldah told me all about that ages ago. About babies, and—yes, of course, I know what it means."

"I see. You understand, Hadassah, that the virgins are first placed in the harem, where there are many small rooms. In charge of them is a friend of mine, Hegai, a eunuch. Do you know what a eunuch is?"

"A castrated man," she said matter-of-factly. Perhaps the fledgling was a little more grown-up than he had thought.

"So the girls are oiled and bathed and anointed, fattened up a little if they are too thin, trimmed down if they are a bit fat—"

Hadassah giggled. "Do they all have to be the same size? How dull!"

"The king is very fastidious in his tastes."

"And then what happens?"

"Then—" Mordecai hesitated, "each girl in turn goes to the king for one night."

"So he can see her better?"

"No, Hadassah, so he can sleep with her."

"Sleep with her! Before he marries her?" Raised in the Jewish tradition of the Law and the family as the basis for all of life, Hadassah found this shocking.

"He probably will marry only the one he chooses as his queen, though he may have more than one wife. That is the Persian way."

"But, but—all those other girls—" She strained to comprehend. "What happens to them after that one night?"

"They go to the House of the Concubines."

"And then?"

"Then, if the king wants them, they are sent for again."

"Anytime, whether they have liked him or not, whether they want to or not?"

"Yes, Hadassah."

She sat very still. Mordecai was quiet. He knew she could not be an innocent forever, but it hurt him.

"Suppose," she looked at the glowing coals of the copper brazier, and her voice was almost inaudible, "suppose he never sends for them again?"

He shut his eyes. "Then, Hadassah, they go on living in that house."

"With no husband? No children? Forever?"

"With no husband and no children. Unless, of course, they are fortunate and conceive that first night."

Hadassah was silent a long time. Suddenly she sat up very straight. "Are you trying to tell me, father, that *I* may be taken for this contest and that *I* could end up in that House of the Concubines?"

Mordecai walked round the table and put his hands on her shoulders. "My child, my Hadassah, I pray that Adonai— but you must understand that it could happen."

There was a swirl of brilliant color. Racing across the room, she stood in the doorway, her face colorless, her eyes big and dark. "Never!" she shouted. "Never! I will never allow myself to be touched by those soldiers. I will never go with them. I will never be shut up in a pen like a—a sheep. I'll run away!" And she raced upstairs.

Mordecai was agile and was there almost before her. "Hadassah!"

She struggled under his hands, weeping with fury and fear. "Let me go! Let me go! What are you thinking of, father? How can you imagine I would agree? I am a daughter of Israel! I am *your* daughter."

"I command you! Listen to me!" And for the first time in his life he shook her.

She was gulping and choking, and she had never looked at him like that before.

"Do you suppose that there is any way, or scheme, or place that I have not considered to keep you safe?"

"I'll run away."

"Do you realize what would happen if you ran away?"

She turned her head from side to side.

"This edict covers thousands of parasangs. There are soldiers on every road. You would either be killed or maimed."

"I'd rather that than—"

"Your ears cut off? Your tongue cut out? Your eyes—?"

Mordecai was gray, and the droop of his figure made him look old. He had wrestled with this for weeks. He must make her understand. "There would be reprisals against the household. They might kill all the servants. And in the end, you would be caught and dragged, a disgrace to your name and mine. Then the end would be much worse."

She was listening, but she looked as if she had seen Gehenna.

He drew her tense figure into her room. Huldah was there and would have left, but Mordecai motioned her to stay. "You heard?"

Huldah could just manage a nod. Hadassah was her world. This edict they had laughed about, could it invade this sanctuary, touch her beloved?

Mordecai led Hadassah to her couch and sat down beside her, his arms around her shoulders. No tears now. Just the great watchful eyes. "Listen carefully, daughter of Israel." He was deadly serious. "This thing may never happen to you. It may be in the mercy of Adonai that you will be spared." Neither of them really believed it. "But in the event that you are chosen, then you must behave as a princess. If, I say *if*, you are taken to the king's house—" he could not make himself say harem, "I want you to go, trusting in Adonai, who will go with you as He went into the fiery furnace in Babylon with the three Israelites. Do you remember?"

Hadassah nodded just a little.

"What did the pagan king see when he pushed those three young men into the fire?"

Hadassah pulled her thoughts back from some faraway place, "He saw a fourth figure," she whispered.

"And what did he say about that fourth figure?" Mordecai was relieved that he could get her attention even for a moment.

"He said he saw—one—like—a son of God."

"That same fourth figure, my Hadassah, will go with you into the palace, if such is to be Adonai's will. You will not go alone."

Hadassah looked at him from swollen eyes and could not speak.

"Think on what I have said, little love. Huldah, prepare your mistress for bed. I will come back, Hadassah, and—and—tuck you in as I did when you were a little girl."

Downstairs, his reserve went completely and he sobbed. Was there really no way out? Suppose he took her tonight and fled? But it would be no use: Hadassah mutilated? It was unthinkable.

Why had Adonai given her such beauty? Why hadn't he let her die when her parents died? Was it for this she was kept alive? It was as if it had already happened.

Could he hide her with friends? But every house would be searched when the day came. He had no right to endanger other lives, other daughters.

He went upstairs to say good-night and held her gently before he pulled the covers about her. It was like touching cold stone.

Outside the door, he spoke to Huldah. "Stay close to her and call me at any time. And, Huldah, can you do something, anything, to make your mistress look plainer, less attractive?"

"I will try, my lord Mordecai. I can pull her hair back, dress her in plain clothing, take her jewelry, but her beauty—it is not something that comes from adornment, master. It comes from inside."

"I know, Huldah. Just do what you can. Remember, nothing at all may happen."

Uneventful weeks went by. Life was fairly normal but always shadowed.

One night they were again at Bilshan's for supper. The young people were in the garden, and Bilshan himself ushered Hadassah there.

David embraced her gently. "How funny you look!" said the youngest. "What have you done to your hair?"

"Hush," said David. "It's rude to make such remarks to a guest. Go play with your brother."

The youngster went, but mumbled, "She *does* look funny."

When Bilshan was back inside, he looked keenly at his friend, Mordecai. "The little Hadassah is very pale. The edict—?"

"What else?"

"Ah, yes. The rumors reach even me, you know. You are more vulnerable than I. To me, my granddaughters are queens already, but they are not beautiful enough, I trust, for the royal— forgive me."

"What can I do?"

"There is nothing you can do, Mordecai. Absolutely nothing. Live quietly and trust in Adonai. Do not borrow trouble."

Mordecai wasn't listening. He thought that death might be bearable, but not disfigurement, blindness. . . . "Bilshan! I shall kill her—I'll kill her myself!"

The older man grasped his arm and shook him. "What are you saying? Adonai would never countenance such cowardly behavior. It is written, 'Thou shalt not kill.'"

"It is also written," Mordecai countered bitterly, "'Thou shalt not commit adultery.'"

"Certainly. But if she is taken—*if*, remember—she will in no way be an adulteress."

Mordecai shivered. "A point of law."

"*Not* just a point of law. It makes a difference to you, to us in the Jewish community who love you both, and certainly to Adonai. She is not consenting to this, nor are you. And remember, it may not happen."

"Do you really think that?"

"The important thing is that they do not get a look at her. Continue to keep close watch. I notice she's plainly dressed; that is good."

"I need to *do* something, Bilshan. My money, my position ought to be worth something. Instead, I find myself impotent."

"Mordecai, this earth is the haunt of violence," his friend said sadly. "If only the promised Messiah would come!"

Neither of them had noticed the shadow that moved in from the garden where the sound of play and music still tinkled. Hadassah sat down near the pillared entryway.

Bilshan rocked back and forth, eyes closed, chanting from memory: "'What I see for them is not yet; what I behold will not be soon. A Star rises from Jakob and a meteor comes forth from Israel.'"

A small voice said, "Please?"

"Well, my young eavesdropper!" said Bilshan. "Do you want to ask something? A stroll with my David perhaps? The young scamp! Why doesn't he make his own request?"

"Thank you, Uncle Bilshan. David is my good friend, but—no—what I want to ask is about the Coming One."

Bilshan looked sharply from under craggy white brows. "My friend here has not taught you of the Messiah Adonai will send us? My friend is remiss."

"Oh, he has, often. But I don't think I ever thought of *this* question before."

"And what is this question?"

"When the Anointed One comes, *where* will he come?"

"Ah! That is it? A good question, daughter. With Jews scattered all over the world, where will he come? Yes? Where would you think he would come, Hadassah?"

"To Jerusalem."

"Yes, of course. You think Jerusalem. Mordecai?"

"I am not of your scholarship, learned friend." Mordecai's eyes held the suggestion of a twinkle. "Suppose you tell us what you are evidently bursting to tell us. Do the Scriptures mention the place?"

Bilshan rustled through some scrolls. "I think I may have a surprise for you."

It was exciting for Hadassah to be allowed to even hear such a discussion. Girls, even women, were seldom present when men talked seriously.

"Listen," said Bilshan, "this is from a prophet of not so many years ago—Micah—"

"You are so old," said Mordecai, "that three hundred years is a mere trifle?"

"Hear me, even if you do not respect my white hairs. 'But you, O Bethlehem Ephrathah, who are little to be among the clans of Judah, from you shall come forth for me one who is to be ruler in Israel, whose origin is from of old, from ancient days.'"

"Bethlehem!" The two voices said it together.

"So it says. And why not? Is it not the city of the great David? And does not the Anointed One come of David's house? Why not?"

And the three Jews sat for awhile, wrapped in the glory of the messianic dream.

A crescent moon and one great star swung in the clear sky as Mordecai and Hadassah walked from Bilshan's through the quiet streets to their home. Hadassah seemed in better spirits, and Mordecai felt quieter than he had in weeks. They went along comfortably, his arm about her shoulder, and turned in at their gate.

How tall she is for her age, he was thinking. Like a young—

"*Halt!*"

He had not heard them come, but suddenly he and Hadassah and the servants were surrounded. The street seemed full of soldiers. One walked to Hadassah and wrenched loose her veil.

Mordecai rushed forward, but two of the soldiers grabbed him and held his hands behind his back. It was dark under the trees, and neither he nor the soldiers could see each other's faces. The soldier with Hadassah held up a torch.

"Well—Look here! What do you think of this one?"

"Take care, you fool," warned the other. "You're not picking up a harlot for an evening's fun. We're on the king's business. Here comes the captain. Put down that torch." They stood at attention as a well-dressed official came up. Hadassah wrapped her veil closer.

"In the king's name greetings!" He looked keenly at the girl.

"Would you please drop your veil? I regret having to ask you, but I have here—" He brought from under his robe a copy of the edict.

"In Susa?" Mordecai was unbelieving.

"I have authority from the great Xerxes, King of All Peoples."

"In Susa, too?" repeated Mordecai.

"In Susa, sir. You do know of the conscript of the virgins? Your veil, my lady."

There was a humming in Hadassah's head. *It's not true. It's too soon. I'm not ready. Where is Adonai? Can't he see?* The reality of Mordecai's voice cut into her confusion.

Anguished, he saw acceptance as the only way to help her; he must keep his own fears in abeyance. "Remember, you are my daughter."

She stood tall then and with a regal gesture let her veil fall.

The plain dress, the severe hair-style, the absence of jewels only seemed to enhance her beauty.

The captain stared. "By—by Angru Manyu—" Then, recalling his position, "Yes. You will come with me." He turned to where slaves held a litter. "Please get in."

Hadassah did not move.

"Wait!" Mordecai had to make one final attempt. "I am an employee of the king."

"So am I, sir. I am sorry; I have my orders."

"But her clothes— Preparations need to be made."

"Preparations *have* been made," said the captain crisply. "Her possessions will be sent for. Come, my lady."

Hadassah's courage nearly failed then.

For many nights she had lain awake, thinking of the possibilities. She had knelt by her bed and pled with Adonai, reminding him that she was one of his chosen; the heavens seemed hard and faraway. She was confused by the things Mordecai had told her of harem life; she realized how little she knew of physical love. Taught that this was a beautiful part of the way God created man and woman, she had always looked forward to it. But with a pagan king—! She had tried to relinquish her hopes of a Jewish marriage and children; to say good-by to the dream of being the Messiah's mother. Since Mordecai had told her that if taken she was to behave like a princess, she had made up her mind how a princess should act.

But here, now—her heart was pounding; there was a rushing in her ears, and she thought she would faint or be ill.

As she was being pushed, not rudely, into the litter, Mordecai whispered in Hebrew, "'Even though I walk through the valley of the shadow of death, I will fear no evil—for Thou art with me.'"

She turned and looked at him with an expression he was never to forget. Then the curtains of the litter swung shut, the order to march was given, and the party headed for the palace.

Kusuru had to help Mordecai through the gate. By the time he reached the big room, rage and grief cut into the shock and he began shouting: "Adonai! Where is he? *Why?* Why doesn't he help us?" Words from the psalms of David poured out. "'Our fathers trusted in you . . . you rescued them. . . . Now there is no one to help.'" His cries echoed through the house.

He went up on the rooftop and stared out across the city. Facing the lighted palace on the citadel, he shouted, "Thief!" The servants came and tried to quiet him. If people heard! "He has the world to command! Hundreds of women. Yet he takes my one treasure, my trusting innocent—"

Unseeing, he was moved by the servants down the staircase.

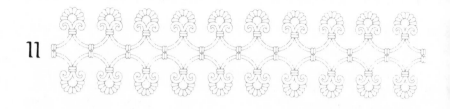

11

The curtained litter swung along the street to the palace. Inside, Hadassah sat very still, observing the scene as though it were happening to someone else. A story was being unfolded, and she, always a lover of stories, was watching. Only she felt no response, no excitement, no fear, no grief.

The whispers of the soldiers came in wisps of sound.

"This one is a goddess."

"Fortunate man!"

"Quiet, you fool!"

"She'll make even the Great King take notice."

"Silence!" The command cracked and conversation stopped.

From time to time there was a crisp military greeting, the sounds of other horses, other men—a sharp cry—sobbing—laughter. None of these had any meaning to the girl in the palanquin.

She felt motion, was aware of light through the opaque curtains. Looking down at the dull woolen dress she wore, she saw hands clutching a plain black veil. Who was this in the litter, this someone she watched? The hands seemed familiar, but they were not her hands. *Her* hands always wore many rings; these hands—one moved—were bare, or almost. There was one simple gold ring. She studied it carefully. What was this stranger in the litter doing with her mother's ring? It *was* her mother's ring? Yes, torchlight pushed the shadows from the litter momentarily: it was mamma's ring.

Jostlings, shoutings, horses' hooves ringing on stone. She felt hot. The flickering lights on the curtains looked like flames. Returning reality made her hands, her arms, even her head shake violently, and her sandaled feet made an involuntary tattoo on the floor of the litter.

The curtains were wrenched aside.

Like an explosion of light and sound, the mammoth buildings stunned her. They were giant crags against the night sky. She fell back as if from physical impact, then, regaining her icy poise, held her head high.

On every side of the court stood men dressed exactly alike—robes, felt hats, spears—man after man until they hardly seemed like human figures. Hundreds of them. They reminded her of something. Something to do with leather, when she was very little. Mamma cutting something from leather—yes, folding and refolding and cutting with the small, sharp silver dagger. The little girl watching, fascinated; mamma unfolding the whole strip into a row of little men, each one just like the other, holding hands. Only these men were not little; they were not made of leather; they were not holding hands. They were living and they were holding spears.

She felt walled-in, alive, in a gigantic tomb; the stone-winged guardians of the doorways menaced her. She could not make a sound, could not move. Then the soldiers moved her forward.

Through the vast courtyard, through the furlongs of corridors, on and on. She must fix the route in her mind, remember the turnings. After awhile she gave up; it was a labyrinth.

In a room with couches and a table, they filled a goblet. She drank thirstily, thoughtlessly. A little later they carried the unconscious girl the long way to one of the harem cubicles.

Muted sounds, feet marching, clattering noises, shouts.

Hadassah lay still, listening, struggling to orient herself. Why were the servants so noisy this morning? Had Kusuru left the front gate open? Careless—not like him at all. She would have to reprimand him severely. The soldiers—

Soldiers! She tensed, unwilling to open her eyes. Where was she? With the king? Was he sleeping? Here?

What day was this? What time? Slowly she peered through thick lashes.

She saw a heavy curtain, closing off a doorway. Light—sunlight—painted its edge. She opened her eyes a little wider. She lay on a narrow bed, alone, in a very small room. Painted mud-brick walls, a chair, a chest, a small table. Opposite the curtained doorway were two slots, high up, letting in light and air. Her eye measured the distance up to them, but, no, they were too narrow to get through.

She looked at the clothing on the chest. Nothing familiar—not one thing. She moved her hand, and the light caught the gold ring, mamma's ring, her link with reality. She looked down at the thin nightdress, soft and sweet-smelling but not hers. Who had undressed her?

Even when mamma and papa had died she had not felt so alone.

Stop it! she thought. Stop it! You are a daughter of Israel, daughter of Abihail, foster daughter of Mordecai. You are not a coward; you will act like a princess.

She slipped out of bed. Perhaps if she went very quietly. . . .

With a sleek sound of silver rings sliding on a silver rod, the curtains were swept aside.

"Ah. The lady is awake." A tall, beardless man in an orange robe stood looking at her. A silver belt was around his waist, a fillet of silver around his dark, curled hair.

She slid back in bed, wary, her heart banging in her throat.

"He will take me to the king. I'll not go. I'll scream. I'll—"

"Good morning, Esther."

A mistake. A reprieve. *He does not want* me.

"Hadassah. My name is Hadassah." She corrected him in a small voice.

The man shook his head. "Not any more, my dear. You have a new name, a special court name. I have named you Esther."

"You have named me!" She sat clutching the woolen coverings. *"Hadassah* is my name," she was getting angry. "Who are you to dare take that away from me?"

"I am Chersis. You are in my charge." The small chair creaked as he sat on it. "You are in the House of Women of the King of All Peoples; a wonderful honor has been conferred on you: you have been chosen."

"I am already one of the chosen," said Hadassah and then bit her lip as she remembered Mordecai's solemn and repeated warnings: *Never, under any circumstances, reveal to anyone that you are a Jewess. I know you are proud of your Jewishness, but if the day comes—may Adonai forbid it—that you are taken to the palace, you must never let anyone know who you are. Call it a special secret, Hadassah, but take it very seriously. It could mean your life and mine.*

"Yes, you are one of the chosen," the eunuch was saying, missing her special meaning, "and your new name is Esther. Everyone gets a new name here."

"My name," she said distinctly, "is Hadassah. Who are you anyway?" This man must be some sort of servant. She was used to handling servants.

"I told you; my name is Chersis. I am one of the keepers of the king's women."

"The king's women! I am not one of his women. I am—"

He disregarded her. "I am under Hegai, chief of the House of the Women."

Hegai. Father had said something about Hegai.

"Hegai can make you or destroy you. He has power of life and death in this house." He waved a hand heavy with rings. "Now get dressed and come to me in the courtyard. Do you understand, Esther?"

"Hadassah."

"You will be there by the time the sun has moved here." He marked a place on the floor tiles. "See that you are on time—Esther." He swung the curtain aside and left.

Too many new sounds, new sights, new smells. Heavy, pervading, rich scents; she did not like them.

She wondered if he would take her to the king. Surely not in the morning? Still, one never knew with pagans.

She sat huddled on the bed until the sun had moved halfway to the appointed square tile. Then she began to dress. Gossamer undergarments, a soft robe, a corded belt, embroidered sandals—beautiful but alien. She had no choice but to put them on, but she did so angrily.

They had taken her home, her father, even her clothes. Now they were trying to take her name. Well, let them try; she wouldn't answer. Her name was who she was; she would not give that up. She was encouraged by the thought that her father knew this Hegai; he would tell them.

She brushed her hair and, without looking into the silver mirror, left the room.

Somewhere down the long corridor she heard voices and followed the sounds. The corridor was close, lighted only by slots that let in the sun a few hours each day. A turn in the corridor, and she was in a rectangular courtyard with many doorways opening onto it. Water splashed into a green pool from rock terraces, skillfully placed. Eunuchs were escorting girls; slaves passed carrying food.

Some of the girls were older and plainer and wore robes alike: simple yellow cloth falling freely to the ankle and over that a white shawl. Brown fillets held their hair. Who were they? Young girls holding tame birds or musical instruments sat in the company of these yellow-robed ones.

Hadassah stopped by a painted pillar, and Chersis appeared. His habit of suddenly materializing from nowhere annoyed her.

"You are in good time, Esther. Come over here; I wish to talk to you."

She walked beside him, feeling oddly detached.

Chersis sat down and motioned her to do the same. Ignoring him, she stood very straight.

"Now, Esther—" Chersis yawned and crossed his legs. These new girls were often difficult, and more often than not a bore. How many hundreds of times had he made this speech? "Let us understand each other. You have been chosen for a very high honor. My lord Xerxes is the greatest sovereign alive, and you are one of the girls chosen to give him pleasure."

"When?" The word was a whisper.

"When?" Chersis laughed. "Oh, my dear Esther! Not for at least a year."

A year?

The irises of Chersis' eyes had the blurred look of the unsexed. He looked her over, taking in the simple hair-style, the browned hands of the girl who loved the sun. "At least a year. *After* we start the course of purification."

A year! She nearly laughed. In a year she would know the procedures, she could send a messenger to her father, he could bribe a guard. . . . A year! For the first time she smiled at Chersis.

"You will be very busy in that year, Esther, and—" he knew these girls, "forget any plans you have of leaving us. We have ways," he stared at her with the smudgy eyes, "very unpleasant ways."

"And what will I be doing during that year, Chersis?"

"For one thing," he snapped, "you will be getting used to your new name. And right now you will come with me to meet Hegai, chief of the House of the Women."

Hadassah looked down demurely, a strategy forming in her mind. She would win this man over. Hegai too. And one day . . . But a new name? No. "My name is Hadassah."

Chersis sighed. He had been having a wearing time with this vast beauty contest, and he had not much patience left. "Listen carefully. *Everyone* who comes here gets a new name, a court name. It is a break with your old life; an acknowledgment that you now belong to the king. You are no longer your own person. Your name is Esther!"

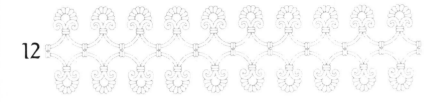

12

Hegai yawned and waved languidly at the remnants of his lunch. "Take it, Siromus. All this fiddle-faddle with the new virgins has taken my appetite. Are there many more?"

"There were a few brought in last evening from Susa itself."

"Angru Manyu! Local talent! All right."

A messenger presented himself at the door of the head eunuch's apartments.

"And what do you want?" snapped Siromus, who was getting infected by the master's ennui.

"A message for Hegai."

"From whom?" Siromus was a privileged servant.

"From a man called Mordecai."

"Mordecai?" Hegai came out of the dining area at the mention of his friend's name. He adjusted a silver belt around his full waist and fussed with his sleeves. He rather fancied himself in this new gray robe with the silver bracteoles.

The messenger handed him a small bit of leather sealed with Mordecai's seal: a bow and quiver with one arrow.

"Wait. There may be a reply." Hegai broke the seal and read.

"You will tell Mordecai that I send him greetings and that his request will be carried out to—ah—the best of my ability. Repeat that."

The slave did so.

Hegai nodded. "Go quickly."

He turned to Siromus. "This is interesting. Mordecai is concerned for one of the local virgins brought here last night. Her name is," he consulted the message, "Hadassah. He says she is someone he has known a long time, she's of excellent character, and will I please be good to her." He laughed shortly. "That, I think, will depend on the lady herself. Go fetch her, Siromus. Let us have a look at the girl the estimable Mordecai interests himself in."

Siromus met Chersis coming toward Hegai's apartments with Hadassah. "What is your name?" Siromus asked her.

"Hadassah."

"Esther."

The two sounds canceled each other.

Siromus looked coldly at Chersis; there was old enmity between them. "I asked the young lady."

"My name is Hadassah."

"Come with me at once."

Chersis was furious, but Siromus outranked him.

Hadassah was ushered into Hegai's luxurious apartments in a new frame of mind. Young and resilient, the possibility of a plan of action cheered her. Furthermore, wasn't this her father's friend, Hegai? She must not admit who she was, but this, at least, was a tie with home and things known. She was prepared to be charming.

Hegai, after a whispered conference with Siromus, was prepared to be critical. Bowing, Hadassah smiled her warm smile. Hegai's defenses shook a little.

Well, he thought, this one has beauty. She's in a class by herself. Steady, Hegai, steady. You've played this game too long to be influenced by either a pretty face or a friend's request. You've not kept your head on your shoulders by being impressionable. With no change of expression, he waved Hadassah to a chair. "Welcome to the King's House of Women."

She thanked him and sat down. Hegai expected an immediate barrage of complaints, requests, even tears. The girl looked at him calmly without speaking.

"I understand you do not approve of the name Chersis selected for you."

"There is nothing wrong with the name, sir. It is just that it is not *my* name. We—" She was about to say, We Hebrews give great importance to names. "My parents gave me this name, and it means a great deal to me. It is who I am, sir."

"Of course. What does it mean?"

"Myrtle."

"A very nice name, I'm sure. Your parents, do they live in Susa?"

"My parents are dead, sir."

"What a pity." Hegai felt relieved. At least she would not be wailing for them. "Let me explain about the name change, Esther, my dear. It is

90

the king's pleasure that all girls brought here be given everything new: clothes, living quarters, attendants, a new life. You have been promoted to the greatest honor possible for a young woman in the Persian empire."

Did he himself believe that, he wondered? He had some idea of what it might mean to a sensitive girl like the one in front of him. He was wise in the ways of the court and its evil, but not totally hardened.

"This is a complete break with your old life, to which you will not return." He said that casually. The girl kept her composure, but Hegai noticed her knuckles were white. "Let me repeat. It is the Great King's express order that a new name be given every girl who comes here—a Persian name. I cannot, even if I were so inclined, allow you to be an exception. You can imagine the chaos that would occur. And I value not only my position, but my head. I am afraid you will have to get used to a new name. What name did Chersis assign you?"

"Esther." She brought it out with hesitation.

"A beautiful name. Do you know what it means in Persian?"

"Yes, of course. It means star."

"I think it's lovely. Would you prefer another?"

Hadassah felt resistance building up inside her again. This seemed the last tie to her old life. She shook her head. "I am sorry, sir; I cannot do this."

Hegai narrowed his eyes. "Esther," he said distinctly, "get used to the idea that from now on," he repeated the words louder and more slowly, "from-now-on-you-will-not-use-the-word-'cannot'-about-*anything*. You have no choice any more. Is that clear?"

Hadassah sat stubbornly.

Hegai liked her spirit, but he knew he must curb it. He tried another approach.

"I have here, " he waved the slight piece of leather, "a message from a friend of yours."

Hadassah's heart missed a beat; she had seen the seal.

"A man named Mordecai. Do you know him?"

The flood of color in her face was its own answer.

"Very well. In this note he says that he is concerned for your well-being, sends you his greetings, and says that you are to do whatever I tell you." Hegai shared the age-old Persian horror of The Lie, but he could be flexible in his handling of truth. What Mordecai had said was that he was sure Hegai would find Hadassah a gracious and sincere girl.

A struggle was going on in Hadassah's mind. Father—he has heard from father! If I make a friend of this man, perhaps I may get messages. I am alone; the walls are high as heaven. He seems kind.

She said quietly, "Very well, sir. I choose to accept the name of Esther."

"You *choose* to—" Hegai's astonishment was genuine. She had said that like a queen. Who did this little girl think she was? She was smiling, a delightful smile that quirked at the corners. Hegai's defenses shook a bit more. At least this girl was not boring.

"Do you understand about the purification rites?" he changed the subject.

"No, I do not."

"Every girl chosen to the honor of being in the king's harem has to spend one year in the purification process."

"What does she have to do?"

"For her purification, she does very little. She is done *to*. For six months she is anointed with oil of myrrh; this bleaches the skin and purifies. The Great King must never be contaminated by one of his women in any way. The second six months is spent with sweet odors and other things that we Persians know about. Some of the processes are secret and go back as far as the Egyptian kings."

"I should think," Esther's eyes held a little of their normal sparkle, "that by this time the girl would be well-preserved."

Hegai was not amused. "During this period the virgins are not allowed in direct sunlight, and they are taught many useful things."

"What things, sir?"

"Embroidering, lute playing, weaving, dancing—"

"I do all those things."

"Languages—"

"I speak two." She must forget the Hebrew for the present.

"You will prove these skills to me soon." There was a touch of pity mixed with irony in his manner as he said, "There are other things even more important that I suspect you do *not* know." He looked at her sharply. "You *are* a virgin, Esther?"

More angry than embarrassed, she snapped, "I am. I don't suppose you will ask me to prove *that?*"

"Calm down, little one. I accept your statement. Looking at you, I could not really think otherwise."

Hegai thought, If she were a cat, her fur would be on end. "Do you have questions, Esther?"

She was fighting down her anger. "This period of purification—I don't understand why it's so long."

"It is tradition, in part. Also, it takes that long to make the skin like silk, to so penetrate the skin and hair with perfume that it is not something added for a moment; it becomes part of the woman. There must not be one rough place on any part of the body; it must be an exquisite work of art." He sat with eyes half-closed, describing curving motions with his white hands.

"And all this takes a year?"

"A year. *After* the process is begun, Esther."

"Oh. And when does it begin?"

His smile was enigmatic. "When I decide it is time to begin."

"Do you mean that a girl might be here for months before the purifying process is even started?"

He stood up. "She might. Now, you said you play the harp? Do you have one?"

"A very fine one."

"Good. Go and see if your things have been brought to your room."

"My own things? Here?"

"Surely. We allow you a few treasures from your former life."

Looking at her, slender and courageous, Hegai began to feel a genuine warmth toward her. She was obviously frightened, but doing her best to hide that fear. "If there is anything else you want from your former home, tell me and we will send for it. Now go and wait till you are sent for. Siromus will accompany you, Esther."

"Thank you." She did not even realize that she had automatically responded to her new name.

Back in the tiny cubicle, however, all her poise, her good resolutions left her, and she was just a very lonely girl who cried herself to sleep.

After Esther had gone, Hegai sat tapping his teeth with a golden toothpick, a present from Queen Vashti.

This little Esther had a quality he found strangely appealing; it drew out the protective side of his nature. No one had done that for years. His position made him the most cynical of men where women were concerned; not only was he not attracted to them, but he usually found them boring, if not exasperating. But this girl. . . .

"Angru Manyu! She is beautiful," he murmured, tapping away. "But she has more than beauty; she has brains, if I am not mistaken. And she is the Great King's type. Of course, perhaps I'm thinking of last year's type. I think he might take to her though. Hmm. The new queen? It might be worth a wager with Siromus. If I train her, win her trust, and she does become queen. . . . Siromus! Go and prepare the large western apartments."

"The big suite, sir? It has been closed for—"

"Go!"

"All ten rooms?"

Hegai's hand moved toward a heavy object on the table. Siromus moved.

"When it's ready, place the girl who was just here in that suite; we'll start the purification process at once. I'll give her her things and tell her how to use them."

Siromus grinned and thought he'd never seen the old cynic so solicitous.

"What are you smirking for?" growled Hegai. "Move!"

Two days later, Siromus came to take Esther to the new quarters. He found her dazedly looking at things from home: her harp, her small loom, her embroidery. But there were none of her clothes. Each morning she was given fresh, new clothes; finer things than her own, but she longed for old favorites.

She dream-walked through the move to the new quarters, only vaguely aware of light, open rooms, fine furnishings, colored hangings, a sunken bath. She had been assigned not one maid, but seven, wearing the yellow robes and white shawls she had noticed on her first morning in the harem.

Siromus mumbled to himself: One would think Hegai was grooming her to be the new qu— He stopped. Only this morning he—why, the marauding son of Ahriman! He wagered me a new robe that he could pick the next queen! What does he know that I don't?

Esther still felt she moved in a painted world. Every eunuch, every guard coming on duty raised the hope of some word from Mordecai, but silent day followed silent day.

Yet, not many cubits away, on the other side of the thick wall, Mordecai paced up and down. Every day he came to the portico outside the House of the Women where he bribed slaves to bring him news. He dared not send Hadassah a direct message; it could mean the life of the messenger, perhaps even his daughter's. When he had first asked for Hadassah, he was told there was no one by that name. Terrified, he had sent another message to Hegai and had received notice of her new name along with a crisp command not to make a nuisance of himself.

Star, he thought. Yes, she is a star. To me she will always be Myrtle, but Star suits her very well.

Since he paid well, the slaves who saw her coming and going to her various classes and treatments brought him news eagerly. And once he had received the day's news, he could throw himself into his work.

His reputation continued to grow, and so did his fortune. But anxiety for Hadassah made the success he had dreamed of taste like sand. He hated going home: the servants were desolate, Huldah cried endlessly; Hadassah's room was a wound.

Almost overnight he felt older, slower; he did not sleep well.

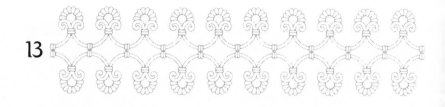

13

In the harem Esther was polite, cooperative, gentle, submitting listlessly to the massages, anointings, the smooth touches on her body—a puppet going through the lessons in court etiquette and dance.

But when there were no further requirements of her, she went to her garden, in the shade as ordered, or to her bedroom. The small, columned sleeping apartment and the walled garden became the only places where she felt secure. She would sit for long periods without moving or speaking.

Her serving maids tried every way they knew to interest her, to give her pleasure. Armis and Arunah were in charge of the rich unguents, ointments, salves, and perfumes. Another pair supervised the food that was sent in from the main kitchens which supplied the harem. There was one who specialized in lute and harp playing, another in embroidery and weaving. Lura, with coppery hair and skin, almond eyes, and a broad smile, helped Esther in dancing and deportment.

During the day's routine, Esther spoke when spoken to, thanked those who brought food and flowers, but at the end of the day she withdrew completely into herself.

The nights were the worst. She would lie sleepless, staring at the walls, listening, listening. Where was her father? Why didn't he send for her? The silence pressed against her eardrums. Couldn't he throw something over the wall? Send a messenger? Often she would creep to the door. The eunuch on guard would growl like a menacing dog, and she would turn back into the room and lean against one of the pillars, her head pressed against the painted wood.

Why? Why did she hear nothing? Perhaps he was dead! Her vivid imagination pictured Mordecai lying in some prison, saw him ill, wounded. *Adonai! Let people be kind to him.* Lura would wake. "My lady, you are cold. Why are you standing there? Come back to bed. Come."

And Esther, who did not know she was cold, would allow herself to be led like a dazed child back to bed.

Hegai found her a yellow bird and a little dog she named Siko. Soon she and Siko were inseparable; he even slept on the foot of her bed. Into his silky ears she poured secrets she shared with no human being.

Eventually she coaxed one of the guards to allow her into the little garden at night. He had to be awake anyhow, she pointed out, and he could keep his eye on her. He agreed, knowing the wall was high and that beyond it were many more guards. So she sat on the grass with Siko, her back against a small tree. Above her hung the great stars. The God who had made those stars had made her, she had been taught; could he hear her prayers? Did he care?

Adonai! she prayed, please listen. I don't pray for myself any more; I can face what I have to face. But please take care of my father.

So far, all the love and fierce loyalty of her passionate nature had focused on Mordecai. Her parents had died so long ago that their memory, while sweet, was vague. It was Mordecai whose love had made her most secure, whose thinking shaped her own. Without him, life had dissolved into shapelessness. She mourned.

The stars burned beautiful and cold. Why? *Why?* Over and over the blind silences wrung this cry from her. Surely he would never willingly abandon her; something terrible had happened. She beat the ground with her fist in frustration and pain.

The routine days ground on. The rains stopped; the spring came. There was some healing in the spring, a little comfort in the flowers. But she dreaded the twilight, harbinger of nothingness, when the silence became a weight and the questions closed in again.

One night the inner tension, the sense of betrayal, would not stay caged, and she woke the house with screams, sounds that made the hair on the watch dogs bristle. Siko, at the foot of her bed, threw back his head and howled.

Lights were lit, the eunuchs and maids rushed in, Siromus arrived. Seeing the figure on the bed, the intimidated servants, he clapped his hand firmly over Esther's mouth. She struggled briefly, then collapsed like a doll. Cowering, Siko crept toward her hand, and they shivered together.

Siromus reported to Hegai.

"This must stop. How long has she been like this?" Hegai asked.

"The household says she has never screamed like that before. But she does not sleep."

"She weeps a lot?"

"She does at night, master, and Lura says she hardly seems to know where she is some of the time. Her mind is far away."

"Her mind will go completely if this doesn't stop. Get the physician."

Parnakka, the physician, came and prescribed sleeping herbs. Esther found this a welcome escape from pain; she even began to look forward to nighttime. But when her body became accustomed to the sedation, she would wake long before dawn; she would then ask Armis for more. Armis, knowing Esther was Hegai's special protégée, was caught between her love for the girl and her well-founded fear of the eunuch. It became a battle of wills.

One day when the doctor was examining Esther and prescribing special foods to tempt her appetite, she asked him about the herbs in the sleeping draught. "What are they, Parnakka?"

"We do not tell our professional secrets, my lady. Besides, what good would it do you to know them?"

"None, I suppose," she conceded. "How much could one take—I don't want to be harmed," she added quickly. "Is it dangerous?"

Parnakka looked at her sharply. What was she thinking, this lovely, untamed creature who could not settle down to harem life? "It would take a very great deal of it to be dangerous," he said.

A few nights later Esther woke suddenly after a short sleep. It had been a bad day; she had wept uncontrollably and was exhausted. All the old fears, large in the dark, moved in; stationary things seemed to live.

I am losing my mind, she thought. Very quietly she got up and moved into the next room, carrying Siko, who snuggled his head against her shoulder in contentment. She paced on the thick rug.

"Siko," she whispered into the furry ear, "I'll scream again, and that upsets everyone. What can I do?" She cried into the little dog's fur. He whined. "Hush, little dog. We mustn't wake the household. But I *must* sleep."

In the room beyond, jars and boxes and bottles filled many shelves. She moved with great care; the eunuchs were just outside. Moonlight helped her search the shadowed room till she found the powdered herbs next to a ewer of water. Holding Siko in one arm, she poured the sedative freely into a goblet, drank greedily, and crept back to her room.

"Sleep, Siko," she whispered again. "I must have sleep."

The next day the household rocked.

At first, the girls were not concerned when they found it difficult to wake Esther. Often when they went to call her, they found her already awake; however, at other times her reluctance to face another day made getting her up a chore. But soon they realized today was different; she lay like something carved in alabaster. They called her name, they splashed cold water, they slapped her face. As long as they dared, they delayed informing Hegai, but eventually he had to be told.

He came with a swiftness that belied his size. Looking at Esther, at Siko, a wisp of furry misery, at the shrinking servants, his terrifying eyes left them in little doubt of their future if Esther died.

"Parnakka!" he ordered, and Siromus ran.

"How did she get like this?"

"We do not know, Hegai."

"You do not know? It is your business to know! Twelve of you! Your sole job the care of this one woman! And no one knows anything? Where were *you?*" He glared at the eunuchs.

"We were at our posts, master. We did not sleep; we swear this by Ahura Mazda."

"Ahura gets blamed for much," he snapped. He walked around looking at each servant. "Somebody either gave her something she should not have had, or she got it herself. I am going to find out which it was and when I do. . . ."

Esther lay still.

Parnakka arrived with the panting Siromus. After examining her, he said sharply, "Where do you keep the herbs I prescribed?"

Armis showed him.

"You fools! Look here!" Parnakka waved the powder dish. "Yesterday I left enough powder for twenty days; there is not enough here now for twelve."

Hegai's expression was awful. "Which? Which one of you?"

"Wait, Hegai," the doctor laid his hand on the eunuch's arm. "I am remembering something the little Esther asked me two days ago—about how much of this would be dangerous."

"And you told her?" roared Hegai.

"I told her one would have to take a great deal for it to be dangerous. And that is true. I do not think—"

Hegai's face was close to Parnakka's. "If she dies," he whispered, "if she dies, you will be impaled."

"She will not die, though that, no doubt, is what she wished for."

"Is this true?" Hegai glared at the servants.

No reply.

"Answer me!"

Lura, bravest of them, said, "No, master, I don't believe it is. My lady is often sad, often lonely, but she has great courage. I don't believe she would intentionally take her own life."

"Why aren't you doing something?" Hegai yelled at Parnakka.

"There is nothing to be done."

"What do you mean, nothing? You just said—"

"The drug will wear off. She will be weak and tired, perhaps ill, but she will be all right."

Hegai, looking doubtful, returned to Esther's sleeping room. Nothing had changed.

"I shall wait here, and so will you," he said. "The rest of you, do what you have to do, but none of you is to leave the house."

Siko looked up with sad, black eyes. The sunlight moved across the tiled floor.

"You surprise me, Hegai. You are not usually so concerned over your ladies."

"I do not usually have such a lady to be concerned about, Parnakka. In all my years as head of the King's House of Women, I have not seen one like this."

"She is certainly lovely to look at, but—"

"No, it's something much more than beauty. She has an extraordinary quality about her. I sense it somehow, though Angru Manyu knows she keeps it locked away most of the time. But in all her fear and sadness, I have never seen her cruel to another human being."

"Is she religious?"

"I would say so, though she never mentions Ahura Mazda."

"Perhaps she worships another god."

"Perhaps. What does it matter?"

Another turn of the water clock, and another.

"How long is this going to take, Parnakka?"

"I should think she will be conscious before long."

The sunlight moved to Esther's face, touched her eyelids. She opened her eyes, looked at Hegai, at Parnakka; she seemed puzzled.

Hegai's relief made him cross.

"No, Esther, this is not the afterlife; you are not dead. You tried to leave us, but you failed."

"Failed?" Esther's voice was thick with sleep. She cleared her throat. "Failed? How have I failed?"

"You and I do not play games, Esther. Remember? I am Hegai."

Esther looked even more puzzled.

100

"Hegai thinks," interrupted Parnakka, "that you took a big dose of the herbs to kill yourself."

Esther was dizzy, and her eyes had trouble focusing. This man was saying. . . . Then she understood.

For the first time in many weeks she laughed. It wasn't much of a laugh, but it reassured Hegai.

"I wasn't trying to kill myself, Hegai. I couldn't sleep. That's all."

"Then you admit you took the herbs yourself?"

"Yes, I admit that."

"But you were not intending to die?"

"Oh, no, I could not do that. I don't believe—it would not be right."

"Well," Hegai stood up, "never do this again. Now, I shall punish those who allowed you to do such a thing."

"No!" Esther sat up in bed. "No, Hegai. You must not punish anyone. I alone am responsible. You must not."

"I must not! Who do you think you are talking to?"

"Please!" She caught hold of his long sleeve. "Hegai, listen to me. It's not right to punish the girls or the eunuchs. I'm the guilty one; punish me. Whatever you think is just."

Hegai sat down, a crafty look on his face. He had worried about Esther, her thinness, her state of mind, her future. Worry for his own ambitious plans had become a genuine concern for the girl herself.

"I will make a bargain with you, Esther."

"Anything, if you will not punish my household."

"A dangerous sort of promise, young lady. Listen to me! If you will promise me that, from now on, you will stop shutting yourself off, will eat your meals, will stop prowling at night, will act, in short, like a normal human being—if you will do all this, I shall not punish one servant."

Esther hesitated. In her concern for her servants, she had momentarily come alive. Now pain and confusion and loneliness crowded back.

"Esther?"

"Yes, Hegai?"

"It is one or the other."

How could she act as if there were nothing to grieve for? But how could she allow her girls, her guards—? No, she must choose and abide by that choice.

"I see what I must do, Hegai."

"Then you agree?"

She nodded slowly. "I agree."

"Very well, then. We begin today. Up!"

"Not so fast, Hegai," the doctor protested. "She will need a day to recover. Her system—"

"All right," snapped the eunuch, "tomorrow then. I want you in the dancing class tomorrow. Do you understand? You will pay attention, and you will work hard. And a final promise, Esther! You will never, ever do this again."

Esther realized this was part of the decision she had made. "I promise."

From that time on there was a new dimension in the relationship of Esther and Hegai—trust and a deeper understanding. He spent more time with her, and she began asking him questions about the king.

"What kind of person is he, Hegai?"

"A very brave soldier, powerful, clever."

"No, no, I mean, what is he like as a man? I don't care what he is like on the battlefield!"

"You mean," he said with disconcerting directness, "what is he like in bed?"

Esther blushed and was furious with herself for blushing. By now, she considered herself too sophisticated for that. "Yes," she tried to sound nonchalant. "That and other things. What is he interested in, what does he like to talk about, what kind of women appeal to him most?"

"What kind of women? As far as bed partners go, he has a wide range of tastes, Esther. He likes excitement and variety."

"I hear so many stories about the king's bravery and some terrible ones about his cruelty—"

"This is not for you to discuss," said Hegai sharply.

"But at home, with his children, is he kind? Does he love them?"

Love? Hegai had never thought about that aspect of his sovereign's life. How should he know? "I am not the best person to ask that sort of question, but, yes, I am sure he loves his family."

"Has he many children?"

"Quite a few."

"Some are grown, aren't they? He must be *very* old!"

"Do your remember your friend Mordecai? He is a year or two younger than he is."

Near father's age? The man she would sleep with? "But, Hegai, that is old! Tell me about the queen, about Vash—"

Hegai stopped her.

"All right, but can't you tell me anything about her?"

"She was very beautiful, very independent, very regal."

"Did he love her?" Oddly, she found she was jealous.

"Yes, I think he regretted ever having sent her away. But having done it, of course, he couldn't change his mind."

"The law. Yes, I know. Do you think she loved him?"

"She understood him," he said cautiously. "She knew how to manage him."

"Manage him? Manage a king? I thought they did the managing."

Hegai laughed. "We have been trying to teach you that women, if they are wise, manage even kings without ever letting them know they are doing it."

"When I go to the king, Hegai, I am going to get to know him, make him talk to me, tell me how he feels about things, tell him how I feel about things."

Hegai looked into those beautiful eyes, at the intelligent mouth, and sighed. He was afraid it was going to be a difficult road for this independent spirit. Only if she became queen would she have any chance at all of realizing such a dream.

"Esther, has it ever occurred to you that you might be the one chosen as the new queen?"

Esther hesitated. "I suppose the idea has crossed my mind, Hegai. We girls do talk among ourselves. But I've never—" she shook her head slowly. "No, I've never really thought I would be chosen. There are lots of girls prettier than I—Rhasa, for one. She would make a marvelous queen. Why, Hegai, I should be terrified. What does a queen do?"

"Please the king, mainly—using all the arts and court etiquette she's been taught here. She does much entertaining, gives banquets for the wives of visiting dignitaries or important men in Susa. And Xerxes likes to have his queen dine with him fairly often."

"Has she anything to do with ruling the kingdom?"

"Not officially. But in Persia we have had some very strong queens; the present king's mother, for instance. Queens can exert immense influence through the eunuchs, through the harem, the House of the Concubines. She is a very important person." He saw that this held her attention. "Think about it, little one. You could do much for me, you know, if you were chosen."

14

The months went by. After Xerxes, his concubines, courtiers, their ladies, and thousands of attendants had left for Ecbatana's coolness, the breathless summer in Susa had somehow to be lived through. The untried, still "unfinished" virgins stayed on in Susa being prepared for their debuts. Battering down on the mud-brick roofs, the heat made their cubicles stifling. No air moved in the tiny rooms except when slaves waved palm fronds. Day and night the soft rattling sound went on. Fortunately, the walls and roofs were thick, but from the first hour after sunrise until the sun left the brassy sky, all suffered. Knowing better than to voice his displeasure, Hegai fumed inwardly.

The king wants these girls fresh and lively, in good health, at the peak of their beauty, then he leaves them here to be cooked. And me with them. I'd like to take him one on a gold platter. He swept off an imaginary lid: "There you are, my lord king, the best of our roasted virgins." He shook his long curling hair and drank some cooled wine. Daft. I'm getting daft. The heat has addled my brain.

Esther was keeping her word, although it was a struggle. Only Lura, her closest friend, knew how hard a struggle. She worked at the dancing lessons, singing lessons, deportment lessons, where, instructed by Hegai, the eunuchs in charge became more demanding.

She and her girls had good evenings in the garden when the sun was low and birds ventured out. All of them were young, and they played favorite games till they were tired, then threw themselves on the grass.

"What were your parents like, Esther?" Armis wanted to know.

"I hardly remember them. My father died when I was a baby. My mother—I remember my mother a little. There was a swing in our garden; I can hear her telling me to hold on. She laughed a lot, and she would sing to me." She twisted the gold ring she still wore.

"And then?"

"Then she died, too. I was about three, and I missed her terribly. I kept looking for her everywhere."

"Then who took care of you?" Lura was avid for any details that would help her understand this girl whom she had grown to love.

"Oh." To hide her confusion, Esther leaned down suddenly and picked up a bright skein of wool she had dropped. Dangerous waters here; Mordecai was well-known in Susa. "A cousin of mine brought me up," she said offhandedly. "A very kind man."

"What was his name?"

"That's my secret!" she laughed. "Come on! Catch me!" And she raced up the long garden over tiny bridges, jumping over pools and terraced cascades, splashing water on whoever came nearest.

Siromus came out. "Young ladies!"

The shrieks and giggles stopped.

"You forget where you are! You," he said to Esther, "are being trained for the Great King of All Peoples. What are you thinking about, acting like a six-year-old! As for you," he glared at the attendants, "Hegai shall hear of this."

"I daresay he already has," said Esther, looping her arms through those of the girls nearest. She was not afraid of Siromus. "Come, it's time for us to bathe."

Autumn came eventually, the air clear, the colors at their best, the flowers slow to leave. When winter arrived, it was very cold with torrents of rain.

Hegai considered his charges. Since Xerxes had returned to Susa, he had been requesting new girls fairly frequently. Nothing, however, was heard about a new queen.

There were all types of girls in the harem: some still weepy and frightened, some more haughty and proud every day. For one reason or another a number had been disqualified, and Hegai had sent them home; others he kept on as attendants.

It's time, he thought. Time to send the little Esther to the king.

One day he pointed out to her a doorway she had never entered. "Tomorrow you will report there and begin the course called the School of Love." In the past, she had noticed different girls being taken through that particular locked doorway, noticed they were in the room a long time and that when they came out they looked upset. But as they continued going there, they came out smiling slyly or laughing and whispering with others of the initiated. Esther, who had a normal amount of curiosity, asked Armis, "What happens in there?"

Armis shook her head. "I am not allowed to tell you."

The day Hegai ordered her there, she came out emotionally shaken, her lovely eyes dark with shock; she shut herself in her room and would not speak for the rest of the day. Huldah's teaching had not prepared her for her experiences there.

"Come now," said Armis as she prepared her mistress for bed. "It wasn't so terrible, was it? A eunuch can't hurt you."

"Don't ask me to discuss it, ever. It's ugly, degrading, perverse. And one day, one night—"

"But, Esther, perhaps you will love the king. Wouldn't that make a difference?"

"Love him?" Esther looked at her and frowned. "Love a pag— a man I have never seen, a man who has had hundreds, maybe thousands of women? Love? How can you use that word?"

Armis had not lived in the palace for three years without learning something of human nature. "Love is unexpected, Esther. The heart is strange."

"Not that strange," said Esther. "Not my heart."

Now, in the light of the new things she was learning, she tried again to imagine being with the king. No matter how she tried, she found the new ideas distasteful. She was not prudish. In his teaching of the Scriptures, Mordecai had included not only the moving love stories of their Jewish history—Ruth and Boaz, Isaac and Rebekkah, Jakob and Rachel—but also had read her King Solomon's erotic Song of Songs. But her ideas of love, the deep part of herself reaching out for a corresponding depth in another, had always been within her Jewish framework.

What was she, one of Adonai's chosen, doing in a pagan court, facing strange practices with a pagan king? She thought about killing herself. Wouldn't that be more pleasing to Adonai than these distortions of something he had planned but which these people denigrated? She paced the garden at night and considered it. Why not? What had she to live for?

But her ingrained sense of respect for all human life was too strong, her sense of adventure, her love of life too real for her to go very far on the road to self-destruction. And there was her promise to Hegai. Beyond that, Adonai was sovereign, and she was one of the chosen; suppose he had something for her to do here?

What? her rational mind scoffed. What can you do in the king's bedroom? In the House of the Concubines? But Hegai had said something

106

about being queen. Again, her rationality mocked her: You! Who do you think you are? Twenty girls more beautiful than you have gone to the king in the last month; none of them is queen. Why, he probably will send you away after the first hour.

The girls often speculated among themselves about those nights with the king. Overeducated but inexperienced, they talked endlessly. How frustrating not to have someone come back with a firsthand description! The ones who went to the king couldn't tell them, for they went to the House of the Concubines. They never returned. And the eunuchs weren't telling; their secrecy added to their prized sense of power.

The months had changed Esther. Physically, she was more ravishing than ever. The childlike curves of cheek and chin were gone, and the lovely bone structure showed through. Her skin had always been fine; now, protected from sun, polished with emollients, massaged and stroked and kneaded by skillful hands, it was perfection, her entire body like perfumed silk.

During the days she was cheerful, fun-loving, and worked hard. But she still had trouble sleeping. Lura, by Hegai's orders sleeping in the room with her, tried everything. She sang, she talked, she told stories until she herself would fall asleep, leaving Esther wide-awake, staring at the dawn.

Hegai scolded: "Dark circles do not enhance your beauty, Esther. You remember your promise? What is wrong?"

"You would not understand, my friend."

Hegai, rubbing his beardless chin, thought of the time long ago when he had been brought thousands of miles to the overpowering court to the bitterness of his castration, the loneliness, the fear. . . . "Perhaps, child, I do. Perhaps I do."

"I'm sorry, Hegai. Forgive me. Of course, you do."

Their friendship was her present consolation. In some ways he had replaced her father, her father who now seemed so far away. What did he look like? Of course, she remembered his features: eyes, hair, mouth. But sometimes it was hard to recall his expressions, ways he had looked at her, his smile.

She sat by the open window. A nightingale sang as if it would break its heart. *Sing for me, little bird. My heart is breaking too, and the songs I love I cannot sing here.* "How can I sing the Lord's songs in a strange land?"

The virgins in the large harem were not allowed much freedom. Communication was not encouraged, but the girls learned secret ways of sending messages and soon knew which eunuchs were open to little bribes. Although they had no money, the girls had special food and confections not allowed others; they had the occasional bibelot or trinket.

At first, Esther's preferred status caused envy in the harem, but her charm and generosity drew people to her. With more freedom than most, she managed to visit every girl in the harem. Adept at the art of listening, she forgot her own hurts as others poured out theirs. She was particularly fond of Rhasa, the Bactrian, sharing with her reminiscences of her friendship with David.

"And your Bhindi? You love him very much, don't you?"

"Oh, yes, Esther! We have always known each other, you know; we were betrothed when we were born. I can't go on living without him. I won't."

"Rhasa!" Esther spoke sharply. "That's wrong. That's murder you're talking about; God forbids murder."

Rhasa's eyes hardened. "Then he should not have sent me here."

"But it's not his fault," Esther was surprised to hear herself saying. "I'm *here!*"

"Yes, of course, but men brought you here, not God." She settled herself on the brilliant cushions. "God made people with the power to choose."

"I did not choose to come here!"

Esther's eyes flashed with interest. "No. Your being here was someone else's choice. But if God makes one person free to choose, he makes all free to choose. Don't you see? That means they can choose evil as well as good. Otherwise, what freedom is there?"

Rhasa wasn't listening.

Esther sighed, hugged her, and left, a little envious that Rhasa had a young man she loved.

Siromus, to his own surprise, had become devoted to Esther. One day as she sat in the courtyard of her house, he came along and began a seemingly pointless conversation with the slave who was gardening. "I saw that man again today on the porch. He walks there every morning." Siromus was careful not to look at Esther. "He's the man who wears a sprig of myrtle in his belt. Didn't you ever notice?"

Myrtle! Hadassah! Esther sat very still, eyes on her sewing.

"You never saw him?"

"I don't think so." The gardener shrugged; he looked confused.

"He's often there. I thought you might have noticed the myrtle." And Siromus walked away.

Esther felt as if someone had put an arm around her.

Another day Siromus talked to the gardener again in her presence. "I saw that man again. He's an odd man. He said something strange. It sounded like Epen . . . ? Eben . . . ? Ebenezer? Something like that. I wonder what it means?"

The gardener went on weeding around an apricot tree, not the least interested. "Some new language, I suppose. We hear so many."

Esther's heart was a singing bird. Ebenezer! The prophet Samuel and the marking stone. "So far Adonai has helped us." Courage . . . Ebenezer! Tears splashed on her sewing. She was not forgotten.

One by one familiar faces disappeared. The virgins who had been there when she first came were taken to the king. For this great night, the culmination of all their training, the girls were allowed to choose whatever they wished: There was a large wardrobe to select from; exquisite jewels from the royal collection to be borrowed for the night. Some girls were like greedy children in a sweet shop and moved as clumsily as pregnant women under the weight of draperies and ornaments. Their eyes were thick with kohl or antimony, cheeks and lips heavily colored. Esther watched them sadly, thinking they had been lovelier without so much adornment.

I suppose, she thought, it's significant in some way. They lose their innocence; perhaps it's right that they look so sophisticated when they leave here. And they never come back.

One night Esther was awakened by the sound of screaming. At first, she thought one of the girls was having a nightmare. She and Lura crept to the window, but they could see nothing except garden and, above the wall, the shadowy heights of the great Apadana. Then the wordless howls of anguish were smothered. The silence was worse. The two girls huddled together, Siko between them, till dawn.

When Esther tried to find out what had happened, the eunuchs shook their heads. "Do not ask."

Arunah came in, white and frightened. "It was Rhasa's friend."

Rhasa. Bhindi!

Arunah motioned the girls closer. "He was caught climbing up the side of the House of the Women. He was trying to get his love away from this place. They—" Her teeth chattered.

"Tell us." Esther spoke with the quiet authority she had developed lately.

"They cut—they cut off his ears and—and—his tongue and—"

"Go on, Arunah, we must know it all."

"They put out his eyes."

"He is dead?"

Arunah hesitated. "He is now, my lady."

"Does Rhasa know?"

"She knows."

"I must go to her."

"You cannot! The eunuchs and soldiers are everywhere. Everyone is ready to jump at nothing."

Esther knew she was right. It would not help Rhasa or anyone else to have more crises in the harem.

Just then Hegai appeared. He knew his Esther by this time. "You will want to show sympathy to Rhasa," he said. "I warn you, Esther, do not be so rash. It will accomplish nothing. Do you understand? Nothing. And it could do great harm, especially to Rhasa."

Esther nodded, but her mind was busy: *There must be a way. Perhaps after midnight, when everyone is asleep. . . .*

That night, Rhasa strangled herself with a scarf.

Esther was shocked, seared with guilt. Couldn't she have done something? Shouldn't she have disobeyed Hegai? What kind of demons were these people? Words from the Psalms, learned long ago, drifted through her confused thoughts: "My soul is among lions, and I lie even among them that are set on fire."

After this incident, she became quieter than ever, and the mischievous sparkle was seldom seen.

"You are getting too thin again," said Hegai one day. "You must eat more. The king does not like a girl's bones poking through her flesh. He says they hurt him."

"The king!" For an instant it was the rebellious Hadassah who stood there. She pushed her thick pigtail impatiently over her shoulder.

"Please, Esther, for my sake. What harm can it do you?"

She hesitated, then smiled. "For you, my friend, I might try."

At the beginning, she had thought about ways to escape. As she had grown accustomed to the vigilance in the House of the Women, the impossibility of her situation became clear. And now, realizing what would happen to her friend Hegai, she no longer planned. She still dreamed though; sometimes she was at home again with her father, talking, laughing, studying in the softly lit room she loved. Waking was awful: *Who am I? I used to be Hadassah, a Jewess. I was Mordecai's daughter, loved, with friends and servants. I ran a household. I looked forward to marriage and children. I was of the chosen. Now. . . .*

Across the room, Lura slept. She loved Lura; she loved all her girls.

But these were new friendships without deep roots. When she left, would they miss her for long? Would she miss them? *"I am a sparrow alone on a housetop."*

Gradually, however, Esther began to see herself more in perspective. What makes you think, the rational part of her mind would say, that you are better than other girls who go to the king? Do you think they want to go?

Some do, another part of her would answer.

Yes, but you know many do not; they are just as miserable as you are. Many of them come from very far away; they are in a strange land. You are in your own city.

That does me no good now.

Your father lives.

I shall never see him again.

Perhaps, but at least you know that he walks the porch a few cubits from here. Who are you that Adonai should give you special consideration? Have you even thanked him that your father is safe? That you yourself live better than most? Have you?

No, I suppose I haven't. At least, not often.

Didn't father teach you that all men are made in Adonai's image? That he cares for all?

But I am one of the chosen.

Chosen to love Adonai and obey him. You know something of his character; you have been taught his will. That makes you responsible. Remember the first commandment: "You shall love the Lord your God with all your heart and with all your soul and with all your strength and with all your mind."

Adonai has forsaken me.

Because he does not answer your prayer the way you think he should?

I do not feel him here at all; I feel alone.

He *says:* "Call on me in the day of trouble." He *says:* "I will deliver you and you shall glorify me."

Me? Glorify Adonai here?

The idea was startling. Did Adonai have something for her to do in this place? Was there some pattern to all that was happening?

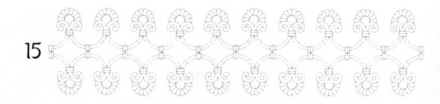

15

Esther was playing her harp for her girls, singing a song she had composed that day. It was a winter night, cold and still, but inside there was warmth from the coal fires in bright braziers.

Siromus stood in the doorway. This was unusual; they seldom saw him in the evening. There was something in his look, in the way he held himself. . . .

It is tonight. Esther's mind formed the sentence before Siromus said, "Hegai sends for you, my lady."

Esther's hand poised over the harp; the room was very still. Everyone understood the summons. Slowly, Esther put her harp down.

"Lura, you and Armis come with me." She saw the others' disappointment. "There will be time, girls. I'll come back so you can all say good-by."

She's going to need cosmetics tonight, thought Siromus as they walked the short distance to Hegai's apartments. She looks like a white spirit.

"It does seem to me, Hegai, you might give a little notice. This is inexcusable. Why was I not told?"

"Softly, little spitfire. The word has come that the Great King is in a good mood and wants company. When he is like this, he can be kind, charming, and considerate. It is the moment to—" He started to say "strike," but decided that might further antagonize Esther. "—the moment to take advantage of," he finished. "And this way you will not have so much time to be nervous."

"Time enough."

"Now, what would you like to wear?"

"Hegai! Surely I may have a few minutes alone?"

"The king—" He calculated: the king was dining; that would take several turns of the water clock; it would take time to get Esther ready. "Very well, but a short time only. I shall send Siromus for you."

Back at the house the girls clustered around her.

"You don't have to go?"

"What did he say?"

"Is it really to be tonight?"

"Hush." Esther smiled at them. "Wait here. I need to be by myself."

Accustomed to her "religious ways," they withdrew. She spent more time praying than anyone else they knew.

In her room, her hiding place, Esther drew the heavy curtains. Strange, not long ago she was complaining that she had no home, that this was alien; now it seemed as if she could not bear to leave it. What happened after tonight? She was nervous about her time with the king, certainly. Head knowledge was not experience. But what lay beyond was even more frightening. There would be a few women she knew in the House of the Concubines, but her own girls and Siromus and Hegai would not be there. She would grow old there!

Suppose she conceived tonight? *Conceive!* A child? Of this pagan whom she had never seen? Suddenly the brunt of the physical was abhorrent to her. She threw herself across the bed, disturbed by her thoughts of the king: old, repulsive, greedy.

"Even though I walk through the valley of the shadow of death. . . ." The words her father had whispered the last night they were together—more than a year ago. She got up and pushed back her hair. *I will go in the strength of the Lord God.*

She looked around the room, touched her pillow and the birdcage where the yellow songbird slept on his perch, kissed Siko, and went out. Looking at her girls, her family, she could not speak, nor could they. Though several were openly crying, Lura looked at her steadily, "Go in peace, my lady."

"Come now!" Siromus' voice was loud in the room. "This isn't a funeral; Esther goes to the king!"

"You will come back before you go? You will let us see you?"

"I'll come back."

Hegai took Esther into the enormous robing rooms. Rumors of their opulence had not prepared her for what she saw: great sheets of polished silver endlessly repeated the room and everything in it; before them, lamps burned among hundreds of vials of perfumes, unguents, jars of kohl; row after row of robes and dresses; jewelry flashing from silver and copper boxes.

The big man made an expansive gesture. "This is your night, Esther. It is yours to choose."

113

For the head eunuch this was the night of his dreams, his hopes, but a sad one too; he loved Esther and would miss her.

"I cannot trust my judgment."

"But your good taste is known throughout the House of the Women."

"No, my Hegai, not tonight. You shall choose for me. I'll wear whatever you select, take only what you advise."

This was too good to be true. Never had he had such freedom. And with this girl! He knew exactly what Xerxes liked, exactly what would please him.

"You are sure, Esther?"

"I am sure."

He swept past the glittering, over-trimmed robes and gaudy veils. Quickly he chose a simple robe of pale sea-green.

He stripped her and inspected her body carefully with the detachment of a doctor. He knew his own life could hang on details. He then handed Armis exquisite gold sandals of such fine work that they seemed to have no weight at all. Wrapping Esther in a silk sheet, he drew her to one of the mirrors and selected a pot of color.

"You are pale, little one."

Esther said nothing. She felt dead inside, like a doll being dressed and undressed. Skillfully Hegai massaged perfume on her body, smoothed color on her face, brushed the shining hair. He bound it up with a golden fillet, looping it up in the back in such a way that one pull of the golden band would tumble the whole mass around her shoulders.

Xerxes will like this touch, he thought.

He looked at the eye cosmetics, looked at Esther's eyes, and shook his head. "Pointless," he murmured. "There is no improving on nature here." He touched her pale lips with color and motioned Arunah to put the robe on her. It was of soft material that fell in clinging folds with long, full sleeves that moved like water. He handed Arunah a lightweight belt of gold links in a Greek design.

Jewelry? he asked himself. What would do? He tried this and that and finally shook his head. Nothing, he decided. Absolutely nothing. That will be a novelty, and by Anahita, she needs nothing.

He crossed to the veils and carefully selected one. It was a rich cream bordered with the belt's same Greek design intricately worked in gold. Carefully he draped it over her head and stood back.

"Look at me."

Esther raised her eyes, and the pupils were enormous.

114

"Perfect, my dear. Here, look at yourself."

He turned her to one of the tall silver mirrors. She gazed at a stranger. She looked a long time, very seriously.

It's as if she were saying good-by, thought Hegai. Well, in a sense she is.

"Come, Esther. I shall escort you myself." ·

"The girls?" Armis asked timidly.

"Yes, there is time; we will show the girls."

They walked the short familiar route. The last time, Esther was thinking, the very last time.

Word had seeped through the harem as it had a way of doing. At the entrance to every small room, every portico, there was someone: girls, slaves, eunuchs. All the house knew that this was Esther's night. They loved her, and they adored her beauty. There was fluttering excitement as she came, head high, with Arunah and Armis holding the ends of her long veil and Hegai himself alongside her.

"Esther! Esther!"

"Góod-by, Esther."

"May Mithra bless you."

Her own family was ecstatic. The irony of it struck Esther: It could be my wedding; they act as if I'm going to marry a man I love instead of—

She did not realize that among themselves they had agreed on no more tears, on a pretense of cheerfulness until she had gone.

She walked with Hegai up the staircase leading from the harem to the king's apartments. At the top, she turned and looked back at them. With no premeditation, she stretched out her arms in the most expressive gesture imaginable.

Xerxes' laughter ricocheted down the corridor. "What an evening, Harbonah! Angru Manyu, I'm glad that's over! The satrap of Bactria *or* the satrap of Sogdiana, but together—! I'm stiff with boredom!" He was hurling off his crown, his jeweled collar, his outer robe before the eunuch could assist him. "Now the evening really begins. Where is that woman I sent for?"

Hegai moved, holding Esther firmly by the elbow. "Remember," he whispered, "remember all you have been taught. For my sake, at least. The instant you are in his presence, prostrate yourself."

Entering the king's bedroom, Esther was not even aware which figure was the king. She had no difficulty prostrating herself; her legs would not have held her up much longer. Somehow she managed a graceful, fluid motion, her head touched the marble floor, her hands stretched out in front of her, all in the prescribed manner.

"Oh, there you are. It's about time! I—" Xerxes saw who was stretched out beside Esther. He came forward, his eyes quizzical. "Well! The master Hegai himself tonight."

At the king's gesture, Hegai rose from the floor.

"Get the girl up, get her up," said Xerxes, waving at Esther's still-prostrate figure. "Let me have a look at what Hegai thinks is worth his personal attention."

Hegai assisted Esther to her feet. She stood perfectly still, eyes downcast, hands wrapped in her veil as she had been taught. Xerxes walked around her, then pulled the veil off.

"Hmm. Well done, Hegai. She will— Yes, indeed. Now—" he put his hand on her shoulder, "look at me."

He was bending down as she obeyed him. The dark hair, dark lashes, winged dark brows had not prepared him for the eyes: green-blue as sea water and as clear. The contrast was breath-taking. He looked for a long time; then he saw she was trembling. He kept on looking but waved with his free hand to Harbonah and Hegai. "Leave me."

Alone, the man and woman regarded each other.

Esther was surprised too, though for different reasons. Here was no fat old man. Not young certainly, but tall and lean and very handsome. Without crown or outer regalia he looked almost vulnerable.

Hegai is right; he's not much younger than father. The thought made her smile.

The smile undid Xerxes. He pulled off the fillet, and the glorious hair cascaded.

"Come, little one." He took her hand and led her toward the big bed.

Her eyes widened; he did not seem like Mordecai now. He put his arms around her. "Don't be afraid. What is your name, beautiful one?"

"Hada— Esther."

Her nervousness was palpable, but there was something so courageous about her, such an aura of—he could not find a word, but he was strangely moved.

"Esther. Star. You are my star for tonight, Esther. Come, I will be good to you; I promise you that. Do you believe me?"

She looked at him steadily. "I—I do not know, sire. But I am sure,"

116

she added quickly, "that if my lord the king says he will be, he will be. The King of All Peoples cannot lie."

Xerxes laughed and went over to a golden ewer. "Some wine?"

"Yes, my lord, please. I should like some wine."

This was the night her life had been focused on for a year. She had been carefully trained for the hours in bed with the king; there should not be too many surprises. But what then? Suppose she failed to please him? Suppose he never sent for her again? The idea of being chosen queen had never seriously dominated her thinking; now that she had seen the dazzling splendor, now that she was in the actual presence of the man who controlled nations, the idea seemed ridiculous.

Xerxes handed her the wine with his own hands and mocked her gently: "It is good wine."

When she had drunk deeply, he drew her to him. "I promise I will be gentle with you," he said again.

Surprisingly enough, he kept his word.

Later, Xerxes waved lazily toward the harp that lay on a low table. "I see Hegai brought a harp; is it your own?"

"Yes, my lord. It is a very nice one."

"You will play for me and sing. What will you sing for me?"

Esther caught the green robe around her as she crossed to sit on the gold-draped couch and leaned back against the wall to steady herself. "What sort of song would my lord the king like?"

Xerxes looked at her with an odd mixture of lust, amusement, and respect. "You choose. I should like to hear the sort of taste you have."

It was good to feel her own harp in her hands. She sang him the song she had composed and sung to her girls that afternoon—a lifetime ago.

Xerxes listened. When she had finished, he stretched luxuriously. "Charming. Your own? But it is sad. Sing me something cheerful."

Esther's repertoire was extensive, and she sang for a long time.

Genuinely fond of music, Xerxes appreciated the girl's gift. "I will have a harp specially made for you with ivory and gold."

"My lord is most generous."

He joined her on the couch. Later, he sent for more wine and fruit.

"Dance for me, Esther."

She rose and began a slow graceful movement. "No, no! Not in that robe; you do not need it."

Mordecai would not have recognized his guileless Hadassah as in one flowing motion she obediently dropped the robe and swathed herself in the cream and gold veil.

"This dance, sire, is one that needs a veil."

Bewitched, Xerxes could only wave assent.

Esther loved to dance, and she became poetry and fire. For the jaded king, who thought he had seen all the dances there were, this was something new. Here was no hetaera's dance; there was no seduction in her movements. When she had finished, with her head bowed on her outstretched hands on the floor, the room was absolutely still for a while before Xerxes said, "That was more beautiful than any dance I have ever seen. Now come here again, my Star."

Toward dawn, when Esther lay wide-awake, weary, wondering about all that had happened to her and about all that lay ahead, Xerxes awoke. Soft light still burned in the shadowy room.

He looked at her, this little girl in his bed, and he felt his own vulnerability. "Esther, I love you." He kissed her. "I love you, do you hear? I never say that to my women. Never. I have never said that to any woman from my harem before."

Esther looked at him questioningly as his finger traced her eyes, her lips, her cheek.

"Listen well, little one. You will come back to me tomorrow night, tonight that is, and—"

"My lord wishes me to come again tonight?"

"And the next and the next." He was kissing her with tenderness and passion. "I love you! I must have you with me every night."

So night after night she came from the House of the Concubines. The king's love freed something in Esther, and she found herself responding with genuine warmth, able to communicate new ways of gentleness. She was no longer just the well-taught bed partner, trained by knowledgeable eunuchs.

Xerxes sensed the change, and it set him on fire. But it was not just sexual pleasure he was finding. He began to talk to Esther, to share his thoughts. He found her gentleness soothing to his wounded vanity, to the horror that even yet clung from all the humiliations of the Greek campaign, to his sense of failure concerning Vashti.

All Esther's skill as a listener stood her in good stead now; besides, she was genuinely interested.

Each day became filled with expectation of the night ahead; she looked forward to his gentleness, his flashing charm, his skill in arousing her. Sensing his growing dependence on her, she became convinced that here was a man who had never before been understood. Compassionately, she decided *she* would not fail him; *she* would bring him healing and comfort and genuine love.

True, there were times when her Jewish conscience asked her uncomfortable questions, but these she pushed down, telling herself that this was her mission in life. For this she had been born.

Early one morning after a particularly satisfying night, Xerxes had his great idea; he had found the answer!

"You will be my new queen!" He whirled Esther around the room. "You are the one, Esther; I know it. Harbonah!"

Esther burrowed under silken sheets.

"Harbonah, get a council together in the morning, this morning. I have chosen my queen."

Not a flicker of surprise crossed the well-trained face, though inside the man a storm churned.

"And, Harbonah, see to it that the Keeper of the Concubines House himself escorts the lady Esther this morning. Go now, in fact, and tell them to prepare a suitable apartment for the queen-to-be, a temporary one. The Queen's House is to be completely redecorated." He turned to the astonished Esther. "Have you any special slaves you want with you, little queen?"

Esther breathed a silent prayer of thanksgiving. "Oh, please, my lord! The seven girls who have been with me: Lura and Arunah and Armis and—"

"Never mind," laughed Xerxes. "Go and attend to it, Harbonah. At once."

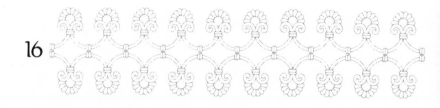

16

For the refurbishing of Vashti's luxurious house Esther was consulted by designers, chamberlains, and craftsmen who carried out every wish in detail. Carved chests and closets of cedar held an enormous shimmering wardrobe; gold caskets held jewels from many lands. Hatak, Xerxes' own appointee over the queen's household, personally screened the retinue of new servants.

When everything was ready for Esther's coronation, Xerxes sent a smaller replica of his own portable throne with a deep purple canopy, silver-fringed. With it came an honor guard carrying his other gifts: jewels, robes, golden dishes, exotic pets.

Wearing cloth of gold, pearls, emeralds, and turquoise, Esther was carried to the Apadana, flanked by her attendants. The Seven, who had not yet seen the fabled lady, stood impassively by the king but burned with curiosity. Lord Memucan himself held the controversial crown in its gold casket. At least, he was thinking, he didn't drain the treasury of more darics for another crown! This one had hardly been warmed by Vashti's head.

To the sound of singers and lute players Esther's throne was set in front of the king's. As Xerxes extended the shining sceptre, she knelt and touched its end, and when he himself took the crown from its case and placed it on the dark mass of hair, she flashed him a smile long remembered by those who watched.

"From this day onward, I proclaim you my queen. I have granted pardons in every satrapy in your honor, and I have distributed gifts worthy of the Achaemenids. People everywhere rejoice today because of you, Queen Esther."

The king and queen were carried to the banqueting hall. As the royal procession swung left, a movement caught Esther's eye. Down the right hallway the archers were changing guard with a crisp precision that never entirely conquered the fluid line of soft robes, the swish of flowing sleeves. Solemnly, spears were raised, there were brief nods, and the relief guard was in place; the others moved soundlessly away in their soft, pointed leather shoes.

To most they were a moving part of palace design, of little more interest than the ceramic figures representing them. But to the young Jewess all people were interesting. She watched the retreating backs, the curved bows, the spears alternately shadowed and shining as they passed through the pillared portico on the way . . . where? What were their names? What did they do with their free time? She must ask the king.

Now, she saw the inside of the building whose exterior had awed her that first frightening night. Caught in colored tiles, ceramic figures decorated the turquoise walls. Fantasy-animals, curling horns spiraling from their ill-tempered heads, snarled from one wall; on another, good-humored bulls curled their mythical wings and pranced.

During the lavish meal, the Seven watched the couple with interest.

"He's caught at last," whispered Meres. "Even Vashti was never able to make him indifferent to every other woman in the room."

Shethar yawned discreetly. "It won't last, I think."

"Who knows?"

For the afternoon the king had planned something unprecedented: a coronation procession. This had caused guarded mumblings: the great hegira which moved the whole court to Parsa for the New Year was not far away. So much work!

Through the night people had been gathering in the streets. Families sat huddled around braziers and small charcoal fires, fearful of losing vantage points. The weak were pushed rudely by the strong; old people stayed at home, hoping for a view from a rooftop or doorway.

Gradually the stars winked out; a crystal dawn held a new moon, and the great day was here. People who had rolled up in blankets and rugs began to stir; food was passed; a quiet hum grew louder. Near Mordecai's house a thick crowd gathered as rumor said that the queen might be coming down this street. It seemed a little odd; why this street? Of Mordecai himself there was no sign.

The sun had not been up long before great clouds foamed from the horizon; a chilly wind sprang up. Anxiously the crowd looked up: a bad omen! The downpour was sudden and drenching, leaving women with clinging robes, men with beards uncurled, and children shrilling and splashing in the racing gutters. The sun came quickly, and things began to dry; they also began to smell. People held their noses, laughed raucously, or moved to other places.

Soon there were no other places. Guards shoved people back, and excitement rippled as the first mounted soldiers came, then musicians, then more soldiers. This was better than when the king had returned from Greece! The crowd chanted, swayed, waved flowers, veils, scarves, even curtains.

As the queen's carriage approached, there was a great roar. Masses of flowers were in her carriage, and she tossed bouquets and small presents to the people. The opaque curtains screened her, but there were glimpses of beauty and a radiant smile.

As the procession approached the Street of Oleanders, it slowed. The crowd gasped: the queen actually leaned out and for a long moment looked up at a figure on one of the rooftops—a woman peering down and waving. The queen handed a bouquet to her nearest guard, who tossed it up to the old woman.

The procession moved on.

On top of Mordecai's house the small household surrounded Huldah as with shaking hands she pulled the flowers apart and found her child's message: a small headcloth which Hadassah had made as a child of ten. Huldah remembered the glow of pride when Hadassah had showed it to her. Nothing could have said more plainly: I love you; I have not forgotten. She threw on her heavy veil and pressed her way through the crowds to Bilshan's house.

"See what my Hadassah threw me from her carriage!"

As the family shared her joy, David alone seemed quiet. He went out into the garden, his place of refuge. This tangible token to Huldah and the way it had been given underscored the fact that his path and Hadassah's had diverged and would not meet again.

For Esther, the journey back to the palace seemed endless; she was grateful when they ascended the great staircase. She had looked everywhere for Mordecai. Had he ridden in the procession? Was he displeased with her? Where could he be?

Mordecai had not only ridden in the procession, but had ridden resplendent in the regalia of his own recent promotion: he had been elevated to the King's Gate. The gray streaks in his hair and beard had whitened over the past year; his mouth was a proud, hard line. As the queen approached the acropolis, he maneuvered his horse to a good vantage point. Her chariot stopped and an attendant drew back the curtain a little.

Esther looked at every face nearby. With a shock that shook them both, their eyes met. A thousand messages were in that look. Then Esther inclined her head slightly and the attendant dropped the silver curtain.

Lura wondered why the queen cried so long when they were alone.

Mordecai continued to gather all the news of his daughter that he could. He vacillated between pride in Hadassah's position and despair that he might never speak to her again. Questions jostled in his mind, keeping him awake at night. Was the king good to her? How long would the royal favor last? Was she remembering what he himself had taught her in those evenings in the now-too-quiet house? Had he taught her enough? Did she remember to pray? True, he had cautioned her never to betray her Jewishness, but he had good reason for that: He was aware of racial antagonism simmering below the city's surface tolerance. To put into anti-Jewish hands such a tool as either the queen's race or her connection with him was unthinkable.

Surely she would not forget the faith of her fathers, would not become a worshiper of Ahura Mazda. Would Xerxes require this of her?

Xerxes would not. Although a self-proclaimed follower of Ahura Mazda, one who had killed the evil daeva worshipers, the religious preferences of his women, even of his queen, concerned him not at all. When he sent for Esther, they discussed many things, but so far religion had not been one of them.

He became more and more enchanted with this girl-queen who seemed to know so well how to please him in any mood. With her, far more than with Vashti, he was able to share his inmost self, and she responded with the protectiveness the weak draw from the strong. For the young Jewess, he possessed the fascination badly flawed men often have for good women.

Catapulted into grandeur, the young queen was dazzled by the pomp, bewildered by the deference to her every whim. Excited at first, she found the very immensity of choice—clothes, jewels, food—eventually cloyed. With the coronation festivities over, she became restless. The endless round of beauty treatments bored her. How many perfumed baths, she fretted, could one take? She did needlework, practiced her lute and her dancing, entertained wives and sisters of important men, but her mind was not challenged.

She missed Hegai and occasionally sent for him for brief conferences, but their worlds were far apart now; she could best show her gratitude for his past consideration with handsome gifts. Hegai was content.

The one person who could talk intelligently with her was Hatak, the king's chamberlain in charge of her household.

A part of Babylon's yearly tribute to the Great King had always been five hundred castrated boys; one year in Darius' reign Hatak had been one of those boys. Now, over fifty years of age, he was stocky, gray-haired, gentle, and wise in the ways of court life. In his loyal company Esther found relief from the banalities of her life. He brought her news of the outside world; with his help she was able to surprise the king with her grasp of Persian history, court policies, and empire affairs.

Xerxes could hardly believe that a woman who gave him so much satisfaction as a beautiful female could be so stimulating to talk to. Till now, he had experienced such communication only with men, and since his position isolated him, even that was rare. He began sharing with her problems of government, new appointees, conflicts between satraps. As he himself found these matters irritating, he relied increasingly on her judgment.

"Tell me what to do, Esther. Two of my satraps are fighting over the same woman."

"Do you know her, my lord?"

"Only by reputation. I hear she's strong-willed as an ox."

"Then throw your influence toward the stronger satrap, my lord. If she takes the weaker one, she will dominate him. A strong satrap is easier to control than a domineering woman."

"Sound reasoning!" He yawned. "These problems bore me, little one. More all the time. I'm much more interested in my new buildings in Parsa."

A small frown showed between her eyes. Even in her short time as queen she sensed a weakening in Xerxes' sense of responsibility. Or was she imagining it? After all, what did she know of kings? But kings, she reasoned, were people too.

One morning Esther sent for Hatak.

"I want to learn about the craftsmen in Susa, how they contribute to the empire's economy, what their working conditions are, how they think. Where would you advise me to begin, Hatak?"

Hatak was no longer surprised by his lady. "Perhaps the queen would care to begin with a carpet-maker?"

A master carpet-maker named Mul was summoned. Trained in one of Haman's great ateliers years before, he was monkey-legged, thin and wiry. With him came Dola, his chief artisan—lumpish, but an expert weaver. There were also two slave girls followed by male slaves carrying the upright loom. Hatak sent for carded skeins of dyed wool from the palace storerooms, and the procession started down the corridors.

Mul was jumping like a doll on a string. "It is a great honor, Hatak, a very great honor for me to be invited to the palace—palace, malice, chalice—I love rhymes, you know. They are like the rhythms of the design-counting. And to perform before her majesty, Queen Esther!"

Hatak moved along silently.

"You do know that I am the most gifted master carpet-maker there is?"

"I should hardly have sent for you otherwise."

"Yes, indeed," said Mul.

"Indeed," intoned Dola in a mechanical voice.

"Indeed, no greed, take heed. See? I am unique! There is no one like me."

Hatak decided this was a good thing.

"I have in my head, this head you see here," Mul peered round in front of Hatak and was cuffed by a slave for his impertinence. "I have in this very head one hundred fifty designs. One hundred fifty. All from memory. One hundred fifty, nifty, shifty."

"One hundred fifty," echoed Dola.

"I weave bees (for immortality, you know) and boats (they look wonderful in a carpet, and boats mean serenity)."

Hatak wondered what this chattering squirrel knew about serenity. He was beginning to regret his choice.

"The bull, master," reminded Dola.

"Yes, the bull," Mul smiled slyly. "The source of life, you know, Hatak, and—"

"The crescent for virginity," put in Dola.

Mul squirmed. "Perhaps not just the one for this carpet."

Hatak gave him a look that silenced him immediately. But not for long. "Palms for long life. Palms, calms, balms—"

"May my master live forever," Dola's reply was quite automatic; his attention was on the glories around him.

"Lizards for divine wisdom." Each accented word was accompanied by a chopping motion of Mul's hand.

"Possibly, Mul," said Hatak wearily, "you should study the lizard more carefully."

"Study the lizard? Does the queen then admire lizards? I make excellent lizards, Hatak. Lizard, gizzard, wizard."

Hatak winced. "You did mention divine wisdom."

They emerged into the sunlight of the garden where the demonstration was to be given. When everything was ready, the queen and her attendants arrived in the portico. A translucent curtain separated them from the artisans. As all prostrated themselves, Mul's difficulty in keeping still was aggravated by a fly crawling on his nose.

"Your subjects, the carpet-makers, majesty," said Hatak.

Esther queried Mul on procedures, had him describe his shop, and surprised him with her grasp of the problems that worried craftsmen. She wanted to know how long it took to weave a carpet, what sort of customers he had, where they came from, what transportation he used to send carpets to faraway places. The little man was so interested that he either forgot to rhyme or dared not.

"You shall weave me a carpet, Mul."

They chose the colors. Esther, as usual, had ideas of her own. "What about horses, Hatak, and stags and eagles? Something the king would like when he dines with me here at home."

Mul realized with delight that he now had scope for his creativity with no limits on how much he spent.

"This will be a carpet to last a lifetime, a hundred lifetimes. The colors will be like wine shot through with sunlight. So shining this carpet will be that it will be like silk; so thick that her majesty will feel she is floating on a cloud."

The loom was threaded, a long process enlivened by the accompaniment of court musicians. Esther watched, absorbed. Tying hundreds of knots, the hands of the two slave girls were like butterflies.

At noon, the queen and her attendants withdrew for their meal. When they had finished, food was brought into the garden in embossed silver dishes.

"No one will ever believe this," muttered Mul to Dola. "When I tell them at home that I, Mul, ate from silver dishes in the queen's garden! Even though I tell them, I, Mul, who never lies."

When the queen returned to watch again, Mul began his work by chanting, row by row, knot by knot, to Dola at the loom. The shuttle flew and clicked. Mul chanted rhythmically without pause. The pattern grew slowly, but it was exquisite. Esther's eyes sparkled.

126

Late in the afternoon she dismissed Mul and his group, instructing Hatak to set the delivery time and give Mul a bag of silver siglots.

As Mul bowed his way out of the palace, he mentally raised the price on every carpet in his shop. How fast could he spread the news that he was now carpet-maker to the queen? He ran his hands through the coins. "My fortune is made! I have a royal commission, position, condition."

And in the street, he capered, monkey-like. "Come, Dola, here is the Golden Bough wine shop. I shall buy you a cup of wine. No, I am a rich man; I shall buy you two cups of wine."

"But there are plenty of Jews in Jerusalem, Bilshan. They are busy rebuilding. What would you do if you went back there?"

It was a rainy winter night, and Mordecai sat with Bilshan close to the fire.

"Nothing, I suppose; I am too old. But it is a cherished dream—to die in Jerusalem. Even our great forefather Joseph wanted his bones buried—"

"Not in Jerusalem!"

"No, but he did not want them to stay in a foreign land either."

"Please don't say you are going to ask me to take your bones all the way to Jerusalem when you are gathered to your fathers."

Bilshan's eyes were wistful. "You would not do it, would you?"

"If you asked me to, of course I would. But what's wrong with being buried here?"

"It's just not Jerusalem," said the aged man stubbornly.

"Grandfather, I will take your bones back if that's what you want." David had come in from the storm, shaking the water from his hair. "Only please don't talk about such a dismal subject now."

Mordecai turned to Bilshan as David went upstairs. "He's a man now, Bilshan, a handsome one."

"What a pair they would have made, David and your Hadassah."

Mordecai smiled enigmatically. "It was not Adonai's will."

"And perhaps not your will either?"

Mordecai's anger flashed. "If you are intimating that I had anything whatever to do with Hadassah's being where she is—"

"I know better. You forget, we lived through that together. But now that she is there, tell me, what are your thoughts?"

Mordecai was quiet for so long that Bilshan thought he was still angry. Finally, "I don't know, Bilshan. I miss her every day of my life.

Often I wonder if she is happy. But again I ask myself why it has come about that she is there, that she is queen to this powerful king."

"What are you scheming, my clever friend? Do you think he does not know she is Jewish?"

"I know he does not. I told her never to reveal it. And even now, Hadassah will do whatever I tell her."

"How do you get your messages to her?"

"With bribery, of course. Money can get one most things."

"Why did you make such a request of her, Mordecai? Surely she would be in no danger."

"Partly instinct, I think. The palace is a strange, complex world; the intrigues never stop. It seemed safer."

"And your other reasons? You are not without ambition, Mordecai."

"I admit it. I mean to reach high places. But on my own merit, not as the queen's cousin. Not now at any rate. But there is something else: I sense in Susa a rising tide of anti-Jewish feeling, thanks to Haman for the most part."

"Haman? Who is Haman?"

"He is an Agagite."

"An Agagite? Our ancient enemies?"

"I believe so. That would not seem so important of itself; but he is ambitious, without scruples, a man who is gaining rapidly in the king's favor."

"Another ambitious man!" Bilshan smiled.

Mordecai ignored the thrust and went on. "There could come a day when I need the special advantage of my relationship to the queen as a neatly timed surprise."

"I wish I could feel that your devotion to your people and to Adonai were as deep as your devotion to Hadassah and, forgive me, to your own career."

"Be just, Bilshan; I send my tithe every new moon to Jerusalem. What else would you have me do?"

"A tithe is a good thing certainly. But in your position—"

"Bilshan," Mordecai interrupted, "I have been given a position of influence in a foreign land. I have important work to do here. Surely I can do more for my brothers this way, using my influence and money—"

"And being near your Hadassah—"

"I see nothing wrong with that," cut in David from the doorway. "If you will forgive me, grandfather. Surely you are not saying that Uncle Mordecai should leave Susa and go trotting off to Palestine?"

128

"No, I am not saying that. It is just that I feel our good friend here has great talents that might be put to greater use for the nation of Israel."

"Nation? We are not a nation now," said David.

"I misspoke, David. 'For the Jews' is what I should have said."

"What have you been doing today?" Mordecai asked the young man, switching to more comfortable ground.

"The usual things, sir. Archery, horsemanship. I am getting better with the javelin at last, since I've grown so tall."

"Good." Mordecai liked David. "What about languages?"

David laughed. "Try me, Uncle Mordecai!"

Mordecai asked him some questions in Elamite, and the three spoke for a while in that language, then changed to Greek.

"Excellent!" said Mordecai. "What about history?"

"I'm enjoying history more than I ever thought I would. That reminds me—have I your permission to leave, grandfather? I have a lesson in history with Torbal tomorrow, and he's a hard master."

Excused, David went to his room but could not concentrate. Seeing Mordecai had brought Hadassah to mind again. It seemed so strange—his lifelong friend remote in the palace. What kind of life did she lead? Did she enjoy it? What did the king mean to her? He remembered the night of her capture. He missed her laughter; and she had always been more interesting to talk with than any girl he knew. But for those who loved her, she might as well have died. He thought of his own future. What did he want? A home and children certainly. Law? Business would be too dull. The military? Oh, well, that could wait. He turned to his scrolls.

Esther and her attendants walked in her gardens. Above the painted roofs, the stone crenelations seemed impregnable, symbolic of the power that held her.

Esther found herself thinking of Vashti and wondering how she had dared pit her strength against Xerxes. And how could she hurt him? She herself could never—would never do such a thing. What possible reason would she ever have for disobeying her love's command, risking his displeasure? She moved toward the house. "I am my beloved's and my beloved is mine." The ancient Hebrew love poem sang in her heart. She remembered that this night was the full moon and hoped he would send for her.

He did send for her. And in the silver sheen of the Persian moon, with the heady scent of a thousand roses drifting through the thinly curtained windows, their love swept them into their private paradise, and the night was long and rapturous.

In the morning, as the faint breeze shook new fragrance from the rose petals and birds murmured about the dawn, Esther kissed the sleeping king and left the bedchamber, escorted by the eunuchs who had waited outside in the court all night.

17

Vahush, treasurer of Parsa, blinked in the bright light and swore. "Look at them, Artatakhma, look at them down there. Like a swarming line of ants going for a honeycomb."

"Where will they all stay?" asked Artatakhma, master bronzesmith.

"Thank the gods that is not my problem, nor yours, but I do wonder. Surely the New Year festival last year was not so crowded?"

They were standing high above the ceremonial city of Parsa by a tower of the mudbrick wall that crawled up the side of the Mount of Mercy and guarded this newest of Achaemenid centers. Below them on Darius' colossal platform, preparations were being made for the yearly visit of the Great King and his court.

Gold and color flashed on the finished buildings. In the unfinished sections the sounds of stonecutters, woodcarvers, and masons formed a background to the cries and shouts of men. Chips of stone flew, ropes creaked, column sections were swung into position. Artisans of many nationalities shouted in their own languages, while the military were everywhere.

"It looks like Susa on market day," said Artatakhma. "By the way, what on earth are you doing up here taking your ease instead of looking after your treasury?"

Vahush adjusted his high fluted hat. "Surely you know that the best executives give the orders and someone else does the work? Isn't that the way you handle your deputy and your own underlings? You sketch the designs for your bronze ornaments and then come up here for a quiet talk with me."

Artatakhma laughed. "But you have to make room for all the tribute coming in: gold and silver, wine and oil, horses, sheep. Why, weren't there even camels last year?"

"Don't remind me," groaned Vahush. "The outlying provinces are sending more and more exotic gifts, jostling for royal favor. The gods alone know what we shall get this year."

"Word has it that there is a new queen at last. It will be interesting to see who has caught the royal eye."

"It doesn't take much to catch the royal eye; it's snagging the royal crown that's the trick. I wonder whose daughter she is."

Artatakhma glanced apprehensively at the tiny windows above them in the fortification tower. Taking Vahush by the elbow, he moved him away. "Haven't you heard?" he whispered. "It seems she is no one's daughter."

"What? You can't mean the king married a—"

"No, no. Nothing like that. But she is not a daughter of one of the Seven, and you know that has been a law for as long as one remembers. The law—"

"The law is flexible where the royal beds are concerned. Cambyses managed to marry his sister, don't forget."

"Well, if Xerxes chose her just for looks, she must be a rare one. I must leave you, Vahush. My workmen need encouragement. Those bronze-trimmed doors for the Gate of All Nations must be done for the king's arrival. If not—" He grinned as he made the immemorial gesture for heads coming off, but they both knew it could be reality.

Slow to leave, Vahush looked past the city over the plain of Parsa. It was late afternoon, and the clouds laid enameled shadows of blue and violet and gray. Off to the right, sharp against the sky, stood the two strange hills one always associated with Parsa. Directly below lay the green-black of Darius' fir woods, thick rugs thrown on the dusty plain.

Back in the warren of activity he drew a breath of pure pleasure; this was his world. Over a hundred rooms! Mounds of jewelry were piled according to kind: inlay or stones in one place, plain gold or silver in another.

"That pile there," he said, pointing to one of the latter, "none of the workmanship is anything out of the ordinary; melt it down and pour it into the usual vases; ingots are easier to store."

Gold dust in leather bags, bullion, and heavy rings were being weighed on scales of many sizes. Vahush did not stay long, but the workmen knew he had not missed a detail.

The next room was crammed with gold-and silver-plated furniture, precious carved woods, and inlaid pieces. The foreman was wringing his hands. "The place is like a thicket. You can see for yourself, master. The room is full, and with all the new tribute coming—"

Vahush walked through the room. "This is inferior. This we can do without. Let this go."

"Go! Go where?" wailed the foreman.

Vahush raised his eyebrows. "Surely you have a little place in your home, or a relative or two?"

"Do you mean it, master?"

"Of course I mean it."

Vahush walked out into the bright sunlight. Here in the gravelly court long lines of men collected their pay. Sitting at rather crude wooden tables were scribes recording as each workman brought his tally of time; the shekel value was then converted into merchandise.

"Gigis, worker in bronze. One month's wages, one-half shekel."

"Wine or oil, Gigis?" asked the paymaster wearily.

"Oil."

"Half a jar of oil to this man." He gestured toward the man in charge of the pointed jars set in wooden frames on legs.

"One jar of oil," said the man, reaching for a large jar.

"*Half* a jar, you donkey. Why don't you get your wife to clean out your ears one of these nights? Next!"

"Menosanes, worker in gold, one month's wages, three shekels." The scribe read from the parchment chit handed him. Menosanes threw back his shoulders; he was a member of the most honored group of craftsmen.

"What will you have, Menosanes?"

"A sheep; my flock needs replenishing."

The paymaster gestured toward the sheep enclosure which was some distance away and bellowed, "One sheep to Menosanes."

Gigis was waiting as Menosanes came away carrying his sheep. "How do you manage it?"

"Manage what?"

"I know you goldsmiths get much higher wages than we poor bronze-smiths, but I heard you were away half this past month checking up on your properties, or flocks, or women. I certainly didn't see you here."

Menosanes laughed. "Caria is a long way from here, even with the help of the Royal Road. But you forget that my wife is a skilled artisan too. When I am away, she works, and her wages are the same as mine."

"Are there many like you?"

Menosanes looked back at the long lines of men. "I would guess that at least a third of the goldsmiths in these lines are collecting for their wives."

Gigis tried not to feel dissatisfied. He was a good bronzeworker, son of a good bronzeworker. That was his trade, and bronzesmiths did not make what goldsmiths did, and that was that. It had always been so, time out of mind. He swung his half-jar ruefully though; it would be nice to have a whole one sometime. Maybe he could speak to Artatakhma about more hours.

As the festival time neared, work went on all through the night. Day workers, sheltered in rude houses on the plain below the great platform, could look up and see the orange flares, smoke-bannered against the sky. Many parasangs away travelers on the plains and on the mountain passes saw the strange glow on the night clouds and made the sign against the evil eye.

With no more work to do for the day, Gigis still could not tear himself away. He loved Parsa: the thrum of activity, the good-natured banter in many languages, the quiet conversations when the sweating men sought a smidgen of shade in which to eat their bread and goat cheese and drink cheap wine. He walked past the staircase leading to the palace in which Darius had lived—a staircase alive with serenely moving figures, depicting in stone what happened at the New Year's feast. The singing stone curves of the stylized plants decorating the porch wall were like the clean twang of a lute. He began swaying, balancing left and right.

"Ho there, Gigis! Sun got to you, has it?" He stopped as another workman came by, grinning broadly. "Or are you just a little drunk? Here, let me have some of that."

"Not on your life; that's a whole month's wages, that is."

Good-naturedly they scuffled till Gigis said, "Stop it! Between us we'll break the flask, and then where would I be?"

They separated, and Gigis went on admiring Parsa. "It's almost a city in itself, and all for the New Year's festival!" He looked again at Darius' palace, now Xerxes'. The dark limestone shone like a thousand mirrors, polished by a special process the Persians shared with no one. He had heard that Darius had sealed inscribed gold and silver plaques in a box and buried it, but he knew even royalty was not that crazy! Everywhere there was opulence, order, beauty. Surely Ahura would be pleased, would look on the sprawling monarchy with pleasure for yet another year.

"Hello there." He placed his hand on a stone bull's head, one of an unfinished pair. Back to back, they would one day be atop a three-and-a-half cubit column in the Apadana, holding triple roof beams between them. "Someday you'll be wearing gold horns. I could live a year on one of your horns, you monsters."

134

He strolled on toward Xerxes' Apadana and stopped beside a work-man chiseling one of the bell-shaped bases that would support the porch columns. He touched the top of the base, shoulder-height. "Do any of these ever crack when you put the cylinders on them?"

"So far, no. They're very carefully inspected, you know. But some-day it could happen; I wouldn't want to be the man responsible if one did crack."

"But surely," protested Gigis, knowing better, "there are faulty stones, accidents?"

The man went on tapping. "In this place there are no accidents."

David moodily strummed his lute in the garden. As the reality of Hadassah's warmth and beauty and their close friendship faded, he tried to keep the romantic idea alive, seeing himself as a heartbroken young lover, destined to spend a lonely life with music and memories. . . .

"David!" Jakob and Ruth ran into the garden, flushed from some game, eyes sparkling. "What are you doing, mooning under the tree?" Jakob pelted him with a pear.

"Look out, you idiot!" David laughed in spite of himself and re-turned the shot. "Let me get my lute out of the way."

Soon they were chasing each other round the garden, in and out of bushes, up and down stone stairways, until, at last, Ruth slipped with a squeal into the shallow pool. David and Jakob collapsed with laughter, which increased as Ruth splashed about, a water lily dripping over one ear, her long hair streaming.

"Come on, you two! Get me out of here. It's all slimy on the bottom. Ugh! Come *on!*"

As they pulled her out, David was suddenly very aware of the girl's body under the wet folds of her light robe.

"Ruth!" Jakob was the big brother taking charge. "Go home and change."

Ruth giggled. "Through the streets? Like this?

David and Jakob started laughing again, and Ruth joined them. Their shrieks of glee brought Bilshan into the garden.

"Must you make so much noise? I'm trying to study. Ruth—my dear girl! Whatever happened?"

"I—I slipped, sir."

"Well, you must get dry clothes on at once. David, get one of your heavy cloaks for Ruth and see her home. She looks," his eyes twinkled, "as if she'd come out of the Red Sea—*after* the waves returned. Jakob, can I see you here in my study please."

It was only later that David wondered if the old man was as guileless as he seemed.

Wrapped in David's blue robe, Ruth walked with him to her home. The wet trail she left behind and her bedraggled hair set them laughing again. Waiting with her for the gatekeeper to come, David pushed back a strand of her hair. Their eyes met, and they could not look away.

Ruth took off the cloak and handed it to him, saying, "Thank you," demurely. Again he found himself intensely aware of her body. Unable to stop himself, he reached out for her—Jewish tradition or no tradition—but the latch clanked and the gate was swung open. He had time to notice the pulse hammering in her throat before they said good-by and she was gone.

He ran all the way home, blood pounding, every nerve alive. The pale, romantic dream of Hadassah merged with the rest of his boyhood memories. David ben-Bilshan was a man in love.

Esther had been looking forward to the pilgrimage to the secret shrine of Parsa to celebrate the New Year on the 21st Viyaxna. The royal procession was several parasangs long.

At noon the caravan paused. Except for scrubby, thorny bushes, there was little growth, and grooms and muleteers cursed the lack of fodder. The fortunate who traveled in wagons ate inside, but thousands ate in the burning sunlight. Impervious to heat, children screeched with glee and ran wild.

"Advance!" The order was passed from Xerxes' caravan. Slowly the behemoth wriggled its mighty joints and, blurred with dust, lumbered on across the plain. The royal carriages were in the center for protection. Nearby, the figures were distinct and colorful; toward the unseen ends, the color evaporated till only a dust cloud moving against the violent blue of the sky showed that there were men there.

About three days' journey from Parsa, the road curved upward and progress became very slow. A supply wagon crashed over a steep ledge and hurtled to the bottom of the canyon.

"No stopping!" came the order.

Esther was shocked. "Lura! There are men down there!"

"No one could live down there, my lady. Look at that tangled mass; you can see the mules are dead."

"But there might be someone. Send a slave to the king at once."

Xerxes was gambling with some of his courtiers and had not heard about the fallen wagon. "It seems my queen would like to delay the Monarch of All Peoples to see if a benighted slave or two at the bottom of this pit might possibly not have broken his worthless neck." He looked at Carshena, Admatha, and Tarshish, his companions of the afternoon. Although they gave no outward indications, he sensed he was on trial: was he so besotted that he would give in to this ridiculous whim of his girl-queen?

Xerxes spoke to the messenger. "Take this to your queen." He handed the slave an elaborate necklace he had taken off because of the heat. "With my regrets. The answer is that the Great King is not to be delayed." And he returned to his game.

"I don't understand," Esther said when the message came. "A man, several men, may be alive down there."

"Help will come to them," soothed Lura.

"Help? Where from?"

"From—well, surely people ride through from the town we've just left."

"Brigands, probably, who will just go down to plunder and finish them off."

"Well, don't worry," said Lura, "they are only slaves."

"Lura!" The girl had never seen her mistress so angry. "Never say such a thing to me again. They are *men!*"

Lura bowed and fought back tears.

"What is my lord Xerxes thinking of!"

"It is the way of kings, my lady."

For the rest of the day Esther remained quiet. What kind of man had she married? Was human life of so little value? And that necklace—she threw it into a corner. Did he think to buy off her concern with a gift? The stories of his cruelties which had reached her even in the harem crept back into her mind. She had tried to ignore them, made excuses for him. She made excuses now: after all, he had had a wickedly cruel upbringing, and surely he was no worse than rulers had always been. She recalled some of her own Jewish rulers. . . . "It is the way of kings," Lura had said. But it was not her way.

"Parsa! It's Parsa!" Once again the cry sang up and down the line. The road had leveled out, stopped its twisting, and arrowed for the platformed city.

Xerxes flinched. That cry always brought back his father's funeral. Then he, too, was caught up in excitement as his wagon neared the staircase and he caught the glint of watchmen's spears on the high battlements. His eyes snapped with excitement.

"My dream city! My father began it, but it is I, Xerxes, who have carried on and expanded and molded. Posterity will honor me."

He moved to the palanquin, and the carriers moved sedately up the wide shallow steps. Behind him, he heard the clang of hoofs as the Immortals ascended without dismounting. Up many steps, and then the mighty staircase doubled back on itself. The horses wheeled smartly. Up more steps, and there ahead of him was his Gate of All Nations, guarded by immense winged bulls with human faces.

The queen was taken to her quarters, which, while no match for her house in Susa, were charming. Soft breezes wound through the open courtyard; the painted wooden pillars threw long blue shadows in the portico. "So many tents! They are like a city by themselves."

Hundreds of encampments were scattered over the wide plain. Smoke from the evening fires was bluing the air, and the smell of roasting meat and cooking vegetables came up in warm waves. From the courtyard came the sound of orders shouted, arms clinking, horses stomping. Songs and instrumental music mingled as different nationalities celebrated their joy at being in Parsa.

In luxurious conveyances, wealthy satraps arrived with their courtiers, slaves, and women; local innkeepers vied with one another to accommodate them. Their prices were outrageous, but the festival season was short.

Esther sent for Hatak. "What happens now?"

"As soon as the king is ready, the presentation of tribute will begin."

"How far have the satraps come? From as far as we have come?"

"Some of these representatives have come from as far as India."

"India! Why, that must take weeks!"

"Months, Majesty."

"What tribute do the Indians bring to my lord Xerxes?"

"They bring gold dust, mainly; many hundreds of karshas of gold dust."

138

"And no one robs them on the way?"

"It would take a daring bandit to rob the Great King's emissaries."

"Where else do they come from?"

"From Bactria, Caria, Sogdiana, Media, Kush, Egypt, Nubia, Ethiopia, Scythia—"

"Stop!" laughed Esther. "I shouldn't have asked; I'll never remember them. Does the king remember them all?"

"He is very good at remembering them, I understand," replied Hatak. "But there are always Presenters to announce the chief emissaries. He has one named Haman who is reported to have the best memory in the entire court."

"Surely the king does not personally see all these people?"

"He will entertain the chief representative from each satrapy. And when the tribute bearers carry their offerings, he views the whole procession. After that, the privileged ones are brought up on the platform and presented to the Great King at a banquet."

"Will the procession be soon?"

"Perhaps in a day or two. He will start with the lesser satrapies. The greatest day, of course, is New Year's Day itself, the 21st Viyaxna."

Esther's mind was elsewhere. New Year's Day? But surely the year began with— No, this was a new calendar; she must not betray her familiarity with an older one.

"Shall I be allowed to watch with the king?"

Hatak looked shocked, then reminded himself that everything was new to the young queen. "That would not be permitted, Your Majesty. But I think we can find someplace where you can see at least some of the proceedings."

Esther sighed and flung her pigtail over her shoulder. Had she no rights at all? First her concern for the slaves in the accident had been ignored; now, it seemed she could not even sit beside her husband.

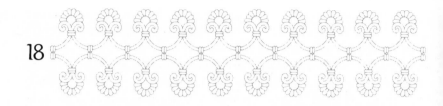

It was the 20th Viyaxna, the day before the vernal equinox.

Slaves carried the king to the eastern portico where he sat in isolated splendor two-and-a-half cubits above and facing the road below. An endless line of figures stretched down the straight road and filed down the roads branching to left and right. They came in orderly ranks, bearing their magnificent presents.

"Look at them!" Xerxes turned to the Seven who stood near. "There are even more this year than last."

"And the gifts are richer," Shethar nodded.

"That's a beautiful gold ewer!"

"And those Armenian rams are first-rate specimens."

Hour after hour the procession marched by. Xerxes, weary and dust-covered as the day wore on, kept the Achaemenean tradition established by Darius: only at sunset would he wave the day to an end.

"I hear someone has brought thirty thousand chickens," laughed Meres.

"By Ahura! I'm glad they won't be near my bedroom!" replied Marsena.

"Have the Babylonians sent their usual tribute?"

"Five hundred eunuchs? They had better; the king hasn't changed their levy."

"Angru Manyu!" Xerxes tried to sit still so that no one could see how excited he was. "Cilicia has sent white horses this year, and look at them! How many are there, would you say?"

"Two hundred?"

"Oh, more than that," said Meres.

"Three hundred?"

Tarshish was a practical man. As the others were speculating, he had been counting. "There are three hundred and sixty-five, one for every day of the year!"

"Give or take part of a horse," said Meres, a student of astronomy.

Xerxes was pleased. "I shall give them an award."

Below, the thousands passed silently, awed by the actual presence of a majesty so mystical, so intimidating that they would never forget it. Thus the Awful Royal Glory continued to exercise its mysterious hold on millions of disparate peoples spread over an immense territory.

In the evening the mood was joyous, and the encampments below went wild. Music and dancing, drinking and debauchery went on through the night. On the great esplanade some outer show of dignity was maintained; any excesses of the king or his courtiers were carried on behind closed doors.

Yet even in this festive spirit there was an underlying mood of solemnity. The emissaries honored the power that the king represented; they gave first to Ahura Mazda and then to his regent on earth.

The 21st Viyaxna dawned gold and blue. All night the palace cooks had been finishing the preparations for the banquet. Thousands of pheasants and partridges, hundreds of sheep, oxen, deer, even horses and camels, had been slaughtered and were now turning on spits. Mountains of fruit were piled by the kitchen doorways: melons of many shades and shapes, apricots, enormous clusters of grapes still attached to thick, twisted stems, peaches, apples, figs, pears.

A young slave recently brought from Sogdiana was watching, open-mouthed. One of the head chefs came by and shut his lower jaw so sharply he bit his tongue. "You stare as if you had never seen food before."

"I never have, master, not like this. Who is it all for?"

"The best is for the king, of course. His guests are allowed to take home all they wish."

The boy's mouth opened again, and his eyes were round. "And do they?"

"Do they! In Susa they prefer to come for breakfast with the king so that they can take home enough to have a dinner party for their own friends! Sumptuous parties they give, on just the remains of the king's breakfast!"

The boy's head went back and forth, not in disbelief but in wonder.

"And of course," the steward rose from the great wooden table on which he had been resting one well-padded haunch, "it's the way we, that is the king, pay some of the guard."

"In food?"

"Look at it, you young knave. Don't you think that's good pay?"

The boy, seeing the pastries and fruits, the meats and vegetables, the great jars of wine, could only nod. Wealth measured in food! He had never had more than the plainest food and a cup or two of sour wine in his entire life.

The procession of dignitaries began. Each delegation was led by a Persian or a Mede who often held the leader by the hand in a gesture both friendly and authoritative. From the courtyard a prize Babylonian bull was marched off to the abattoir while the officials carried less active gifts to the king. A Bactrian dromedary tried to look his haughty, two-humped self, but his eyes were frightened. Snarling and leaping on her chain, a regal lioness tried to reach for her two cubs, one of which was quite enough for its Elamite handler.

Meres and Shethar hurried through luxuriant gardens where water, brought up through the ingenious cistern system underneath, ran in cascades. Budding fruit trees looked like huge bouquets; low-growing flowers starred the thick grass.

Just then more slaves filed by carrying succulent roasts.

"Hurry!" said Meres. "I'm hungry enough to snatch one of these roasts as it goes by."

"A fine sight that would be! One of the mighty Seven gnawing on bones in the garden."

They moved up the stairs. Protocol was more relaxed than usual: men spoke to each other as they climbed, put a hand on another's shoulder, turned to see who was behind. But the granite-eyed Immortals were a reminder that this was still the court of the Great King. Those who forgot would be dealt with without a second thought.

"By the gods of my forefathers," breathed a Carian who had never been to Parsa before. "What is that?"

He stood transfixed before a carving taller than himself on the wall of the staircase: a muscular lion savaging the hindquarters of a bull whose head was turned to see if he could reach the charging cat.

"It—it's terrifying. What does it mean?"

"No one says. It represents something important to the Persians; what, one is never told."

The Carian shivered. "It's awesome," he muttered in a very low voice.

"It is meant to be."

During the stay in Parsa, Xerxes sent for Esther one day before sunset. After intense love-making, they lay on his couch spent and happy, quietly talking.

"Tell me," she said, stroking his hair, "why are you so good to me?"

He looked surprised. "Because I love you."

Esther could not leave it there. "But you have loved many women."

"Not loved, my Star. You know I have had countless women, but do you remember what I told you on that first night we were together? I had never before told a woman from my harem that I loved her. Never."

"From your harem. But—Vashti?"

He rolled away from her and sat up, eyes flashing. "You will never mention that name again. Do you understand, Esther? Never!"

This was Esther's first experience of one of the king's lightning changes of mood, and it frightened her. She caught a glimpse of the extremes she had heard about, and for the first time noticed the lines of harshness around his mouth.

He saw her fear and softened. "Never mind, my Star. I love you more than any woman in my life, more than I thought I could ever love. Is that enough?"

She nodded, but she did not smile.

He can't get her out of his blood. Why else would he flare up like that? Where is she now? He knows; I'm sure of it. What's to prevent him from tiring of me and recalling her?

"What are you thinking, little queen?"

Not daring to mention Vashti, she spoke of another subject that troubled her. "Don't be displeased with me, my lord, but please—tell me what happens when you get so—so angry."

"You have never seen me angry before," he teased.

"No, but one hears—" she stopped, wondering if she had gone too far.

"One hears! My queen listens to court gossip?" Then he grew thoughtful. "I'll try to answer you, my love. Sometimes it's as if an evil daeva takes hold of me—a blindness, a rage comes that I can't control. When I'm like that I—" This unaccustomed soul-searching did not come easily to the King of All Peoples. "I often feel very bad afterward." He looked at her quickly. "Swear to me you will never tell this to anyone."

"Of course."

"Sometimes I start something that I know is right—a just punishment, perhaps—but—but fury takes over, and I go too far. Then, because I am king, there is nothing to do but go on. My dreams are haunted—my memories—"

He stopped, and the queen stroked him as she would a child. "Don't feel so bad. You cannot help yourself."

She was so anxious to explain away his wrongs and too much in love to see the danger of absolving him of his responsibility for his cruel and unjust actions. She did not know that unwittingly she was contributing to the disintegration of personality that had been eroding since Salamis.

"My love," she whispered, "I give you all the love in my heart; I will heal the hurts of the past."

The Seven and other courtiers watched with amazement on the few public occasions Xerxes and Esther appeared together. No one could doubt the intensity of the queen's devotion to this man whom they knew to be erratic, self-oriented, and, when he chose, cruel.

In fact, what Esther was seeing was the man Xerxes was intended to be. Her love gilded over the faults; she seemed able to perceive what he could have been, stripped of his failures, and he was responding to her image of him.

As soon as the court reached Parsa, Mordecai had set up his network of informants and continued to pay well for news of the queen. With Esther safe and happy, he could concentrate on widening his own place in the sun. That his Hadassah had become queen still awed him. There seemed to be some pattern in these events, but he could not trace it.

The holiday season made a good time for him to entertain the Seven, whose preferences, weaknesses, and strengths he had analyzed with his usual thoroughness. They were scrupulously polite to him, but each was aware of the underlying power struggle. Memucan and Shethar admired Mordecai's brilliance, Marsena was suspicious, the rest simply wary.

As for Haman, Mordecai observed him with growing contempt. The nearest thing to a bond between himself and the Seven was their mutual dislike and mistrust of this rising favorite.

Walking one day from the Gate of All Lands, Mordecai was met by one of his most reliable informants. His heart tightened. "Is the queen—?"

"The queen is in good health, my lord Mordecai. But—"

Mordecai relaxed and put a friendly hand on his shoulder. "What has upset you?"

The man's face was shining with sweat. "My lord, you must believe me. Promise me you will believe me."

"Why shouldn't I believe you?"

"I'm—I'm afraid to talk, but I must, I must. Swear you will never use my name in this matter."

"Of course. Now tell me, what is this about?"

The man drew very close. "Bigthan—Teresh—the—the king—"

"The king!"

"Sshh! Do not speak! Just listen."

Mordecai was now all attention. "We must not stand here." He steered the man across the courtyard toward the Apadana.

"Not that way—too dangerous."

"All right, to the archives, then. We must look as if we had some business together."

They walked to the archives which housed thousands of documents in leather and clay. From here they could see the queen's house, white-hot in the noon sun.

"Now," said Mordecai firmly, "tell me what is wrong."

"Bigthan and Teresh—"

"The king's doorkeepers; I know them well. What about them?"

"They are very angry. They are insane."

"Angry? Why? With whom?"

Mordecai could just hear the scandalized whisper, "With the king, my lord!"

"With the king! Are they such fools as to let you—to let anyone know that?"

"More, my lord, they—they plan to kill him."

Mordecai swung the man around sharply. "Are you sure of this?"

"My lord, I heard them!"

"What did you hear?"

"I heard them say 'poison' and 'bribe' and something about 'cup-bearer.'"

"When is this to happen?"

"Tonight."

"Say nothing of this to anyone. I shall take care of it." And Mordecai walked rapidly toward the queen's quarters.

The sun had driven most people indoors. The chunks of limestone in the square, thick doorways were dust-white in the heat. He turned his ankle on a bit of gravel and glared at a snickering workman who lounged on his long branch-broom.

Of course there had been rumors of rows in the palace, of envy among the eunuchs over the king's preferential treatment of Harbonah, and other paltry affairs. Mordecai had shrugged them off; there were always rumors. Now it seemed that something more than petty jealousy was at work.

At the queen's house, Mordecai sent word to Hatak. "I regret disturbing you at this hour, but I must speak with you on a matter of greatest secrecy. At once. And where no one can hear."

Hatak knew Mordecai was no fool. Besides, his face was ashen.

"In here." He preceded Mordecai into a tiny anteroom with stone benches and no windows. When Mordecai had finished his story, it was Hatak who was ashen. Strike down the divinely appointed king? No more heinous crime could be thought of!

"You must take this message to the queen, Hatak."

"The queen!"

"They will have planned well. If they mean to kill the king tonight, we have no time to try secondary measures. Get this message to the queen and have her reach the king somehow. She will know a way. My Hada— the queen is clever."

Mordecai went home. He had done what he could.

Esther was terrified.

"What can I do, Hatak? I cannot go to the king unless he sends for me. I go to him tonight, but that may be too late. Besides, a woman's message? He would say I'm too protective and ignore it."

"Dictate a message to me, Your Majesty; we will send it in Mordecai's name. The king respects him. Just before we left Susa, you know, he elevated him to a position of honor at the King's Gate."

"Quickly, then; write it down for me. Oh, how can I find the words?"

She stood by the stone lattice of the window. Outside in the harsh light everything was still, but Esther was already learning that the order and luxury of palace life was yeasty with intrigue.

She began dictating: "To the Great King: May the King live forever. It has today come to the attention of your devoted servant, Mordecai, that there is a plot against the sacred life of my lord, King Xerxes. Tonight, two men whom the King trusts plot to destroy him. I beseech you, Great King, do not delay. Act at once against these—these monsters—"

"Wicked ones?" suggested Hatak gently.

"—wicked ones, even Bigthan and Teresh who guard the King's

146

door, who plan to lay violent hands on his Sovereign Person. I certify this to be the Truth and no Lie. —Mordecai, Councilor at the King's Gate."

Xerxes, at first, was unbelieving. Bigthan and Teresh? His chosen doorkeepers? He sent for the Seven and other advisors. Then the two culprits were brought in. They did their best to brazen it out, but knew they were dead men. It was a clever enough plot; unfortunately, for them, it had involved others, and these were the links that gave way under stress.

Xerxes' unbelief flamed into fury, then hardened into steely justice. "Take these two out," his voice was chilling in its quietness, "and hang them. This instant."

"Sire!"

"Great King!"

Their pleas were smothered as, faces covered, they were hurried from the chamber.

With due solemnity the case was written before the eyes of the king and became part of the national chronicle which would accompany the court back to Susa.

That night, high on Parsa's walls, there were two silhouettes swinging in the moonlight for all to see.

One who saw was Mordecai.

Another who saw was Haman.

Fools, he thought. *Bungling idiots! It serves them right.*

It would be good to be back in Susa where he could be in touch with things. He wondered what had been happening while he was away. He missed his sons, who had not been invited to the New Year's celebration. What new developments had there been in his absence? Was the trading going well? What new conquests had they made? Which led his mind to Zeresh. Was she still alive? He had never forgotten her, and now, walking under the moon in Parsa, he relived their times together during the campaign, forgetting the frustrations, remembering only her fascination. What a consort she would make! And she was a priestess. To the superstitious Haman, this made her a talisman for protection, an amulet against his many fears, even though they followed different gods. Perhaps if he could find her, she could even help during those nights he had come to dread when the evil daevas came.

The immense carving of the lion attacking the bull showed black and white in the moonlight. The corpses swung in the night wind.

In front of him something moved, and he nearly cried out before seeing that it was only the reflection of a guard pacing by one of the pools. What was happening to him when every shadow that moved seemed an enemy in the dark?

Angru Manyu! He was glad to be leaving the next day. The place was full of specters.

19

Shethar, approaching Mordecai in the King's Gate at Susa, was seething. "Lord Mordecai, I have been cheated, and I want redress."

"Cheated, my lord Shethar? Tell me about it."

"You know Parshandatha, Haman's oldest son?"

"I do, unfortunately."

"He has been buying up property lately. I bought a large tract of land from him for a huge price. Now I find there is no clear title deed, and I have lost both the land and my money."

"Which do you want back?"

"Actually, I am heartily sick of the whole affair. I have lost interest in the land; I want my money, but I want to make him suffer. I want vengeance as well as justice."

"I see. Let me think about this, Lord Shethar. Can we meet tomorrow?"

The next day, Shethar, bulky, impressive, returned.

After he had explained his plan, Mordecai said, "Leave everything to me."

The following day Mordecai called on Parshandatha. After the initial formalities had been exchanged, they talked generally about affairs in Susa, about business in various parts of the empire. Finally, Mordecai said, "I understand you are selling some land twenty parasangs west of Susa."

"It is my father's land, but he has given me permission to improve it. I am selling parts of it to carefully selected individuals, enough to make very pleasant estates."

"I think I should like to buy such a piece of land."

The price, a high one, was settled on and the deed signed. Parshandatha could hardly believe his good fortune.

"Now," said Mordecai, "I want you to show me my new estate."

Parshandatha shifted uneasily. "I think it would be better to wait awhile, Lord Mordecai."

"You are busy?"

Parshandatha grasped at the excuse. "Yes, today is very crowded."

"Very well," Mordecai said smoothly, "I shall be here tomorrow at sunrise. Be prepared to show me my land."

"But—but there are certain improvements—" Parshandatha looked anxious.

"I understand. Tomorrow at sunrise," Mordecai repeated.

The next day a very uncomfortable Parshandatha took Mordecai out to the land. It was good land cut through by a stream, shallow but very wide.

"There are poles in the stream" said Mordecai. "What are they for?"

"Those are markers showing the measurements of some of the tracts, the boundary markers."

"And mine?" Mordecai consulted the map sketched on leather which Parshandatha had given him. "If I read this correctly, mine extends from the fourth pole in midstream to the next, across like a square to the next—in fact, a parasang square I think you said. Nearly the width of the stream at one point. All under water. Is that correct?"

Parshandatha squirmed. "Yes, my lord. But you see, this is the reason I should have preferred your seeing it later. There is rich land underneath the water, good silt, fine for gardens. I propose to dam the water several parasangs upstream from here, diverting the stream, and then you will have some of the richest land in the province of Susiana. It is only a matter of time."

"Oh, no," said Mordecai.

"What do you mean, no?"

"I mean no. I bought this land; it is mine. I have the deed here. Is that not correct?"

"Certainly, but of course—"

"I bought it under water, and it will remain under water," said Mordecai. "You have no legal right to change my land in any way."

"But," sputtered Parshandatha, "all the tracts under the stream will be drained. There is no way to do that and leave yours under water."

"That is not my concern. *My* land will remain just as it is." The Jew's eyes were like agates.

Parshandatha knew defeat when he heard it. "Very well," he sulked. "Of course, you knew this would defeat my whole plan. How much do you want?"

150

"I want three times what I have just paid you for it."

Parshandatha howled, but Mordecai was immovable. Parshandatha paid. When Shethar heard the news, he and Mordecai roared with delight. Soon the tale went the rounds of Susa, and each telling made Parshandatha more of a fool.

"But I *love* David."

Rachel, Ruth's mother, didn't raise her eyes from her needlework. "All the more reason, my dear, why you two should not spend too much time together unless—" she looked up, and her eyes were warm, "or should I say *until* he comes to ask your father if he may marry you?"

"Oh, mother!" Ruth twirled around the room. "Do you really think he will? Do you? Oh, I never thought—I've liked him forever, but I was sure he'd marry Hadassah. She's so gracious and so talented and so very beautiful. But now she's a married woman and a queen and—and, well, he'll have to marry somebody!"

Rachel watched her daughter, golden hair swaying as it broke loose from the colored headband. A little plump perhaps, but her features were fine, her eyes dark and merry, her skin flawless.

"Well, I know I'm your mother, but I do think he could do a lot worse." She laughed with Ruth but was inwardly disquieted as she remembered Hadassah. Had David forgotten her? Would he consider her Ruth second-best?

These thoughts were interrupted by the entrance of her husband, Rabos. Under a mild exterior, this wiry little man had a keen business sense that had made him one of the wealthiest merchants in Susa. Outside the business world he was lost without his strong, sensible Rachel. She and her two children, Ruth and Jakob, were his reason for living.

"Jakob has asked if he may bring home a guest, Rachel."

"One of his fellow-students, I suppose. A boy from the school?"

"Oh my, no. A young lady."

"What!" exclaimed Ruth. "Our Jakob, the woman hater? Don't tell me it's that brazen flirt, that—"

"Ruth!"

"But, mother, she is!"

"Who is?" inquired her father with a man's vagueness about other women's failings, so apparent to his womenfolk.

"Rebekkah."

"But who said anything about Rebekkah?"

"But, father, you said— Rebekkah's been trying to get Jakob's eye for months, and he's not interested in any girl, so naturally I thought—"

"That's as may be, my dear, but apparently your brother has some interests you don't know about. This young lady's name is Judith."

"Judith! Oh, she's lovely. So quiet and pretty and such a lady." Then irrationally. "She's too good for Jakob."

"That's not very charitable, speaking of your brother that way."

"Well-ll—I do love Jakob, you know, but—Judith. And, father, mother, she's so young! She's only thirteen."

Rabos and his wife exchanged amused glances as they contemplated their aging daughter of fifteen.

"Well, perhaps, as you say, she is very young, but that does not seem to have deterred your broth— Hush. Here they come."

Jakob, curly-haired, stocky, laughing, came in with a tiny, birdlike girl, who, in spite of charming manners, had difficulty seeing anyone except Jakob.

Later in the evening when their guest had gone, Ruth and Jakob went into the garden.

"She's very lovely, Jakob. I must say, her daintiness makes me feel clumsy and wooden. She's so ethereal—"

"Nonsense! You're different types, that's all."

"Are you serious about her?"

"As serious as you are about David, little sister."

Ruth flushed scarlet. "Oh, Jakob! Does it show?"

"It does to me," he laughed. "And I think to David."

Ruth's eyes were anxious. Jakob pulled her close and whispered in her ear: "Don't worry. I'm sure he likes it."

At Haman's house, the doorkeeper brought word that there was a slave outside.

Haman yawned. "Send him away. I'm in no mood for business," and he reached for a slave girl who was arranging fruit. She shrank back; Haman had a reputation for being cruel to his women.

"But the messenger says he's from a lady named Zeresh."

"What!" Haman leaped off the couch. "Fool! Why didn't you say so?" He rushed to the door. "Where is she? Lead me to her at once."

The slave led the way down the shaded streets.

"Faster, faster, you idiot!"

Somehow Zeresh had found her way to Susa, hiding herself for several months while she gained back the weight she had lost, softened her weather-worn skin, worked the gloss back into her luxuriant hair.

Now, ushered into a cool and lovely room, Haman found her as fascinating as he remembered her. She was in an elegant setting, seductively dressed. Someone had taken good care of Zeresh. She held out her hand. "Welcome, my lord Haman. We meet once more."

He pulled her off the couch into his arms.

"Stop, my lord, stop!" she laughed breathlessly. "You will break my ribs. Do control yourself. Sit down."

His hard eyes never left her. "Where have you been? What happened? Why didn't you get a message to me? How long have you been here?"

"So many questions, my lord! Do have some wine. When Shishia died, I had to move very fast or I should have been killed. So I disguised myself as a eunuch."

"How did you get the clothes?"

"I killed a eunuch; it was my life or his. Then I lived any way I could. It was hard, hungry work. Finally, I joined the caravan of a wealthy merchant coming here."

"Did he discover you were a woman?"

"Eventually. What matter? I am here. I have been getting ready for my lord Haman."

"You will be my wife. Today."

"Come now, Lord Haman; you are a man of the world. These things take time. You surely don't think *your* marriage can be a hole-and-corner affair? I hear you are very prominent these days. There must be a great wedding, much preparation, invitations, feasts—"

"I have waited too long; I will have you, now."

But Zeresh had no intention of selling out cheaply. She would be Haman's wife—nothing less. Trusting no one—certainly not Haman—she would give him no opportunity to despise and discard her. She moved behind a chair and smiled coolly.

"Indeed you will have me, my lord. *After* our wedding."

Following their marriage, an ostentatious affair, they moved to an enormous estate with extensive gardens and a courtyard where cascades splashed. Both Haman and Zeresh had extravagant tastes, and their home became a showplace and treasure house. Zeresh reveled in her position as Haman's wife, especially when she presided with him at the feasts following his hunting parties when the king was his honored guest.

Early in the morning the party galloped out to hunt leopard, bear, fox, gazelle, or the king's favorite, lions. They returned, roaring drunk, with the arrow-spiked carcasses dragging behind in heavy nets.

At the banquet, Zeresh glittered. She amused the king, who would have been surprised to learn that she was a priestess of the goddess Astarte, or that the superstitious Haman always consulted her auguries.

There were other more intimate feasts without the king, at which the guests were treated to interminable monologues by the host. Subject: Haman. Haman and his wealth complete with detailed inventory of jewels, buildings, property, slaves. Haman and the number of important posts he'd been given by the king, a description of each, its difficulties and Haman's brilliant solutions.

Although time dragged, the guests dared not look away from the host. They stifled their yawns; to doze would have been disastrous. They stretched smiles wider and drank more wine.

Haman was at his most boring when he spoke of his children, especially his sons. One evening, he launched into the subject almost without preamble.

"Parshandatha, besides being a very successful lawyer and businessman, is the best rider in Persia. Such carriage! Such grace! Rather like his father, wouldn't you say, Lady Zeresh?"

"I would disagree with you on one phrase, if I may, my lord. Parshandatha is the second best rider in Persia."

Parshandatha, close to his father, narrowed his eyes.

"Second?" Haman feigned a slight annoyance. "Surely, Lady Zeresh, you trust my judgment on these matters?"

"As in all others. But so far my Lord Haman himself has not yet relinquished that first place." She turned to the guests, "I leave it to you, my lords and ladies, am I correct or not?"

A wave of applause broke out. Parshandatha had no choice but to join in.

"Dalphon is nearly as good as his brother on a horse. But Dalphon" Haman looked archly at the next son, "really prefers success with the ladies."

"Again like his father," murmured Zeresh.

"My dear Lady Zeresh! Still, I suppose I can hardly deny such a charge. How else could I have won you for my wife?"

More applause.

"Aspatha and Poratha are twins, you know. In the Greek campaign they were brilliant, absolutely brilliant. They seem—it is very interesting, but they seem to think as one man. Now there was a time before we crossed the Hellespont—" Aided enthusiastically by the twins, he retold a tale every guest had heard many times.

"My Adalia is not here tonight. There was not time enough for him to cancel one of his many social commitments. But that gives me a chance to tell you more about him." He laughed. "Adalia is particularly adept at, shall we say, being a father?"

"All my sons have many children, but Adalia—" He shook his head. "How many children do you think he has sired?"

"How old is he?" asked one courtier who knew very well.

"Twenty-three. Just twenty-three years old."

"Five?"

"Six?"

"Eight?"

The guests were glad to participate in this game. At least it helped them stay awake.

Haman paused dramatically, put his hands on the table, and leaned forward. "Twenty-three children, lords and ladies. Just the number of his age. He had his first at eleven, you know. A prodigy!"

"Like his father," chanted the guests.

"I sired Parshandatha when I was twelve. That's a fact. His mother was a charming girl. She—"

The guests, knowing he had five more sons to discuss, groaned inwardly. But Haman recalled himself. "I mustn't get started on my women, must I, Lady Zeresh?"

"My lord is a connoisseur."

"Quite true, and you are the prize of my collection, my dear. But I was speaking of my sons."

Aridatha, Parmashta, Arisai, Aridai, and Vajezatha—he eulogized them all. Never, it seemed, had there been such an exceptional group of young men.

"They are all grown now. The youngest is eighteen," he said ruefully. "I am fortunate to be able to have them come here occasionally. I have personally supervised the education of every one of them; they are thoroughly steeped in my own values. I think it is fair to say, lords and ladies—and I think you will agree that this is remarkable—I think it is fair to say that each and every one of them—given, of course, his special talent, his unique, outstanding personality—would conduct himself exactly as I would—at least, on any major issue. Yes, I think that is true. So you see, I feel I have not exactly been a failure as a father.

"As for my daughters, they are the most beautiful women in Susa and—"

He could go on for hours.

Haman worked like one possessed, driving his subordinates to exhaustion. But though he had captivated the king, he and the Seven, Marsena excepted, walked a tightrope of diplomacy stretched over a chasm of mistrust. The rest of Susa was divided between those who were mesmerized and those who hated; no one was neutral about Haman.

His anti-Jewish bias was his one secret from his wife. His amorous escapades, for instance, only amused her; besides, she had some of her own. But he knew that his venom toward a race she considered unworthy of any notice would arouse her derision.

"Is he very brilliant, my lord?" Esther was trying to discover her husband's feelings about the prosperous Haman. She herself had few confrontations with the Agagite, but had mistrusted him on sight; he was too smooth. Acknowledged by a courteous message of thanks, his lavish presents to her invariably were given to someone else.

"He is brilliant, my Esther. He's a better administrator than anyone I have ever known."

"Even," the queen approached the name cautiously, "the councilor Mordecai in your gate?"

"Mordecai? What do you know about Mordecai?"

She was about to remind him that it was Mordecai who had saved his life, when he abruptly switched the subject back to Haman. "He has taken a great deal of the burden of government, the daily trivialities from my shoulders."

"I should think the Seven would resent him."

Xerxes looked at her intently. "For a woman, you do think a great deal. The Seven are proved friends, the most important courtiers in my kingdom. But this Haman has great gifts. *And* the man has sired ten sons."

"Are they as clever as he is?"

"Oh, no, he's unique. But he has trained them, and I have important posts in mind for them in the future."

156

Of course Haman's wife had to be invited to Esther's banquets. Outwardly flattering, Zeresh watched the queen with contempt: *A child! Beautiful, if one cares for that type, but a little nobody made queen. No doubt a nice toy for the king, but no danger to us.*

"Your Majesty has exquisite taste."

Looking into Zeresh's sloe eyes, Esther thought: *The woman is a snake.*

"You are most kind," she replied smoothly. "Your own costume is—ah—" she let her glance move languidly over the ornate robe, the too-elaborate coiffure, the crust of jewels, "—is certainly unique. Where *did* you get it?"

"A marvelous seamstress made my robe and veil, but far too humble a person for Your Majesty to take an interest in."

Both attracted and repelled by this ruthless sophisticate who had come from such a different world, Esther remarked, "It is not exactly her humble station that would be of so little interest to me, Lady Zeresh."

Mordecai might not have been proud of his Hadassah that evening.

As time went on, Zeresh began to see that behind the queen's social graces a diplomat's mind was developing. She began to worry: It would never do for the queen to gain any real power over the king. She must warn Haman.

She might have been surprised to know that her concern was shared by the Seven, who, however, were even more disturbed by Haman.

Another royal banquet was in progress, a small one this time with only the Seven and Haman as guests. As the Agagite passed Harbonah, he stroked his own beard and looked significantly at Harbonah's smooth chin. He seldom missed an opportunity to underscore Harbonah's lack of manhood. Gradually insinuating himself between Harbonah and the king, Haman had taken over even the plans for court entertainment.

Tonight, Xerxes was in one of his mystifying moods: sly in manner, secret smiles lighting his face, a mood the Seven found both disturbing and irritating. Suddenly the king lifted his rhyton: "My lords! I make an announcement. Something I have been considering for a long time."

Memucan shot a look at Shethar; Meres eyed the others. What now? Familiar with Xerxes' moods and palace intrigue, they were still unprepared for what followed.

"I propose to create a new office, one my forefathers were not enterprising enough to create. You Seven have been with me through good times and bad; you are my friends and trusted counselors." He watched them closely. "I find myself in need of one man who will be my daily confident, who will—ah—distill the wisdom of all the others and bring it to me, so to speak, in one cup. I have decided to create a new office, that of Grand Vizier."

Another precedent gone! The Assyrians had Grand Viziers but not the Persians.

The Seven, however, began to assess the possibilities and each tried the new office on his own person. Memucan squared his shoulders and tried not to look self-conscious. Everyone knew he was closest to the king. The others were thinking: If Memucan is appointed, at least we can work with him. He is a loyal Achaemenean, and he knows the traditions.

"So, my lords," Xerxes continued, "I have chosen. You who are so dear to me—good Persians, good Achaemeneans who have upheld the tradition begun by my father and *his* Seven—you will remain together. I would never bring dissatisfaction and jealousy among my special group. Therefore, I hereby appoint as my Grand Vizier—Lord Haman!"

Even Haman, who had dreamed and connived for just such a moment, sucked in his breath sharply. The Seven tightened their grip on their rhytons. Not daring to look anywhere but at the king, it took all their control to keep their expressions blank.

"My lords?"

Marsena recovered first. "Huzzahs to Lord Haman!"

The other six joined in.

"Rise, my lords," commanded the king, "and drink to the new Grand Vizier!"

Somehow they managed the words of congratulation that the king expected. For once, the drinking went on far too long; they longed to leave the royal presence and be someplace where it would be safe to express their dismay, bewilderment, and anger.

"Grand Vizier!" steamed Memucan, safe at home where he had taken Shethar and Meres. "Where did he ever get such an idea? What possible use is a Grand Vizier? It's against everything Darius ever planned, against every pattern, every precedent."

"True, Memucan. But even had he chosen one of us, even you, my lord," Meres swept him a mocking bow, "we could have gone on much as before."

"You are too flattering," murmured Memucan abstractedly. "But this upstart, this Agagite—"

There was speculation in their glances.

That night the house of Haman blazed with light. Sounds of celebration went on till well past dawn. Zeresh was ecstatic. By sunup the news was all over Susa: "Haman is Grand Vizier! Haman is second only to the Great King!"

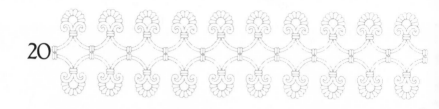

20

Esther walked in her garden. Five years she had been queen. Five years since she had lost her home, her innocence, her future. Now she had everything and—nothing.

In the beginning, when she had heard the celebrations of the Jewish holidays, she was overwhelmed with nostalgia. As time went on, those things became more and more part of a lost childhood. One day, when the singing and chanting from the Jewish quarter were particularly loud, Lura asked her what it was.

"Singing? What singing? Oh, that." She shrugged and then moved away from Lura, "Just some religious holiday, I suppose, from the—the Jews."

"Do you know anything about the Jews, my lady?"

Court life had not entirely deprived Esther of her truthfulness; she hedged. "Oh, a little but—come, this doesn't concern us. Let's have some music." And she whirled into a dance.

Little by little, the old ways, the old patterns of thought dimmed. The Jewish coloration of her thinking began to be dyed with other viewpoints. Along with poignant memories of home and Jewish friends, Adonai was pushed deep down. It all hurt too much. The colorful new life was like an overlay of bright enamel.

Power and riches had been intoxicating framed in love, but lately the king had been more and more preoccupied. A whole month had gone by, and he had not sent for her. A month! After being constantly together.

The perfumed baths, the massages and anointings, took on new importance. Each night her hopes rose; often she would stay dressed until nearly dawn. Finally she would call for Arunah to undress her—outwardly serene, even humorous; inwardly, humiliated and hurt.

Susa today was beautiful, and the scent of roses saturated the city. The tops of the trees were still gold, but in the gardens the shadows were cool. As color drained from the dome of the sky and settled in shimmering curtains, the sparrows came. Every tall evergreen, every fruit tree, each thick vine and lilac bush was filled with the crisp rustle and chatter of the little birds.

Esther loved the sparrows. They reminded her of the harem girls, all inconsequential chatter and light laughter. When she was a child in Mordecai's garden, the sparrows had been her friends. They talked to her and her alone, and she had stood, hands tight together, glossy little head thrown back, and laughed in sheer delight.

Now, the same excited rustlings reminded her of the contrast between her strange present and her carefree past. The sound began to hem her in; she covered her ears and went indoors.

From her bedroom window, she saw Haman hurrying along, colorful robes billowing around him.

I don't trust that man. Since he has been Grand Vizier, he has taken over more and more power. All his sons have been pushed into important posts. My lord seems quite blind to the kind of man he really is.

The great star called Salbatanu was a red ember in the sky. The lamps were being lit; music drifted in from the outer court.

What has happened between my lord and me? Have I offended him? A month since we slept together! There is someone else. A gold mirror showed that the startling eyes were wiser now, but the face she saw had no lines. *Ah, but he is fickle, and new girls flock into the harem. Who will be with him tonight? What is she like? Young, as I was young, but surely more sophisticated.*

She smoothed her robe around her thigh critically. Jealousy burned her. *Surely he has no cause for complaint yet. And who can understand him as I do? He needs so much understanding.*

Esther, too wise, felt old.

It might have surprised her to know her rival was not another woman but an extremely clever man.

Haman, warned by Zeresh that the queen's influence on the king was reaching alarming proportions, was doing his best to undermine it.

Poplars threw shadows on the tiles in the king's garden. Water splashed nearby. At Haman's orders, slaves brought cooling drinks; concubines lay on benches, by pools, on the grass. The king and his Grand Vizier were relaxing.

"The Great King's wife is dazzling, a fit consort for the King of All Peoples."

"Isn't she marvelous! And she's not only beautiful, Haman; you have no idea how intelligent she is. Why only last week—" and he launched into a lengthy account which only settled Haman's mind more firmly.

"You think this intelligent, my lord?" Haman injected a fractional shade of skepticism into his question.

"Oh, very. You cannot imagine how clever she is. Why, another time—"

Haman listened to panegyrics on her wit, artistic taste, even diplomacy in handling rival satraps. This was worse than he thought.

"How very fortunate you are, Majesty. My own wife, Zeresh, was rather like that once."

"Was?"

Haman laughed smoothly. "I was slow to see that I was beginning to look ridiculous."

"Ridiculous? You? What do you mean?"

"My friends, even my servants, were snickering behind my back."

Xerxes, never too secure, was groping for Haman's meaning. "I don't understand the connection between this and your wife and mine."

"It was a stupid thing; I should never have let it happen."

"What thing, Haman? Stop talking in riddles."

"Why simply that I was being unduly influenced by a—a mere woman. Of course, this could never happen to you, my lord Xerxes. No one would dream of doubting Your Majesty's manhood. Absurd."

"Of course it is!" Xerxes' reply was short. He went on. "She has a lovely nature."

"Indeed, sire, I hear it often in the palace: 'A lady who could charm Ahriman himself into doing her will.'"

"*Her* will? What are you saying? I was speaking of her doing mine."

"Forgive me, Great King. I was foolishly repeating words one hears here and there in the capital."

"They dare discuss my queen!"

"But I assure you, my lord Xerxes, it is a compliment. She has such charm that people have become devoted to her and would obey her slightest whim."

"Devoted to *her?*" The wasp that Haman had planted hummed in Xerxes' brain.

A word here, an implication there. Subtly, he implied that Xerxes should keep Esther guessing. "In my own humble experience it is never good to let a woman think she is indispensable; women cannot handle such privilege."

"Do you know," he moved forward confidentially. A guard stiffened; Xerxes waved reassurance. "I have found that if I am with my Zeresh too much it makes me unfit for affairs of state. You—understand, sire?"

Xerxes, mesmerized, nodded. "You are a wise man in these things, my Haman."

"Not nearly so wise as my king. All the world knows the Great King's prowess as a lover. Just look at those women—the way they look at my lord, the envious way they watch each other! That little light-haired thing over there—has the king noticed her?"

The king had not. Haman sent a slave for the girl. "My lord Xerxes is a connoisseur, and no connoisseur has only one example of what he collects, eh?"

Swiftly Xerxes and the girl disappeared from the garden.

In another garden, the queen sat with her chief chamberlain.

It had rained that morning. Pink blossoms fell thick on the grass like shredded silk; other petals made white water in the palace conduits.

"Tell me more about the king, Hatak. You have known him since—?"

"Since he was a young boy, Majesty. Part of his education was entrusted to me."

"What part?"

"In those days the crown prince spent a great deal of his time with the military: archery, spear and javelin throwing, horseback riding. Then they would send him to me for lessons in history and languages. I taught him to read and write in three languages."

"What kind of student was he, Hatak?"

"Not often an enthusiastic one; he has always been more for action than scholarship, if you will permit me to say so, Majesty."

"Of course I'll permit you. The truth is what I want to hear—what he was like. What he *is* like. There are still so many sides of him I don't know at all."

"Isn't that inevitable?"

"I suppose so, but I do wonder about so many things. Why does he flare up in these terrible rages, Hatak?"

Hatak looked quickly around the garden. This was not a subject on which he cared to speculate. "It is his nature, my lady," he whispered.

"Yes, but why?"

"The great Ahura Mazda made us all, Majesty; this is the way he chose to make the Great King."

The Queen looked at him thoughtfully. "You don't think we have anything to do with our characters?"

"I—I cannot say, Majesty. Are you sure you wouldn't like me to order some refreshment?"

"Tell me, then, of others the king has loved."

Hatak shook his head. "That would not be wise, Majesty."

She laughed. "In general then. Have there been more blondes? Has he preferred them fatter than I? Thinner? Does he seem to like straight, thick hair, or curly—?"

Hatak realized with a shock that this girl was not nearly as sure of herself as she seemed. He made some vague generalizations.

"One more question, Hatak. Then you may send for some fruit. Was Vash— the former queen more beautiful than I?"

Hatak's answer was quick and reassuring. "Oh, no, my queen. Never."

Esther's thoughts stayed with Xerxes. Where had she failed? Hatak had just assured her she was more beautiful than Vashti, but that could be a kindly attendant's consideration. Suddenly, for the first time in many months, she missed her home and Huldah, David, Jakob, Ruth, and Uncle Bilshan. And what wouldn't she give for an hour's conversation with her father! Why should it matter so much if the king discovered she was a Jewess?

Huldah carried steaming dishes to Mordecai's table, where the host sat with Bilshan and David.

Mordecai enjoyed David, who shared his grandfather's strong national feeling. His reaction to the rising anti-Jewish feeling was intense.

"It is getting to be too much," David was saying. "Today I was opposite the wine shop owned by one of Haman's sons—I can never keep track of their names—Poratha?

"Adatha," Mordecai said. "Poratha, besides his official position, owns all the rug shops."

"Well, Ruth walked by with her servant. I heard this Adatha say to a customer, 'There go two of those dirty Jews.'"

"We've never had such talk in Susa in my lifetime," Bilshan said.

"Nor in mine," added Mordecai. "It's disturbing. But let me tell you something that may cheer you: your prayers for me are being answered. This treatment of our people is turning me into a zealot."

In Mordecai's sensitive position at the King's Gate, he heard rumors almost as soon as they were born. Knowing that the anti-Jewish attitudes were fanned by Haman, the strength of his own reactions should not have surprised him.

"Then it will have achieved one good thing, at least," said Bilshan.

"Will we be a nation again someday?" asked David.

"Ask your grandfather. He is the student of prophecy."

"Yes, my son, someday, but who knows when that will be? The important thing now is that we stay true to Adonai and support our brothers wherever they are."

"How?"

"First of all, we can pray. Never underestimate the effect of prayer, you two men of action. Then we can send money and supplies to those working to rebuild Jerusalem."

"But what about here? Can't we protest in some way?"

"If there is such a rising tide of feeling as you describe, we will need our courage and our faith in Adonai. In any case, he will show us what to do when the time comes."

David's clear hazel eyes studied his grandfather and Mordecai. His grandfather's love of God challenged the doubts that had begun to erode his thinking when his father died and that had increased when Hadassah was taken. In Mordecai he found a combination of the militant and the intellectual he admired. When he talked about Haman, Mordecai looked as if he could set out with an army at once. David decided that if he ever did go, he would go with him. If Adonai existed at all, he would need scholars like his grandfather, but he would need soldiers too.

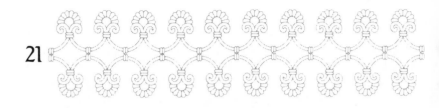

21

Memucan and Shethar walked along Susa's main road. The Hawk and the Lion, the other five called them. From the opposite direction came shouts and huzzahs; a trumpet blew.

"Angru Manyu! That's Haman!" Shethar pulled at his friend's arm. "Quickly! Into this wine shop!"

Memucan moved swiftly but had no idea why. Inside the shop Shethar led him to a couch and ordered wine.

"You have been away looking after your estates; you have not heard the new decree?"

"Another decree?"

"The Great King has ordered that whenever Haman appears, all are to bow."

"Bow? To Haman?"

"To Haman."

"But, look here, no one ever bowed to us."

"Not only that, but his seat at the king's table is above ours."

The implications were dawning on Memucan. "You are not telling me that *we* are to bow to Haman? In public?"

Shethar nodded. Memucan upset the wine ewer. "I will not!"

"Softly, my friend, softly. There are ears everywhere."

Memucan lowered his voice. "What do you mean, ears? Are there more than usual?"

"Many more. We have always known the king had his informers; that's as it should be. But now Haman has *his* spies. Everywhere. There is hardly a shop, a brothel, a business, or even a private home of consequence that does not have at least one of Haman's men in some position or other. And he keeps detailed records."

"What sort of records?"

"Who makes a bank deposit and how much; who sleeps with whom

166

and how often; who is perverted in his sexual practices; who grumbles over taxes . . . everything."

Memucan whistled through his teeth. "A cockatrice's egg has hatched. What's being done? By us I mean?"

"Tonight we meet secretly at my home."

"You have met before?"

"Weekly."

"What decisions have you reached?"

Shethar looked embarrassed. "So far, we have been unable to find one good plan."

"We must find one."

"I hope you'll have fresh ideas, Memucan. Our one hope is that eventually Haman will overreach himself."

"We must see if we cannot help him do just that."

When they left the wine shop, the procession had gone by. Seeing a group of servants in Haman's livery gave Memucan an idea. "I think we need to pay a call on the great Lord Haman."

"If we are going to visit him," Shethar answered, "we are going in the wrong direction."

"But his house is just around that bend in the road."

"His old house."

"You mean he has a new house? Why, the one he had was magnificent."

"Small," said Shethar sardonically. "Much too small. You have been away a long time. Come, you must see this showplace; it's on the citadel. We'll hire a litter."

When they sent in their names at Haman's gate, they were received immediately. Polished doors swung open; Haman himself met them. "My lords! Had I known you would do me this honor, I should have laid on a great feast—the finest foods, the best wines. As it is—" He clapped his hands for slaves.

"Do not disturb yourself, Lord Haman," said Memucan urbanely. "We have just eaten in our own homes. It is hardly the hour of the day for feasting," he added, subtly underscoring Haman's social error. "I have just returned from my Pasargadae estates—" This, too, was a calculated dig at the Grand Vizier, since only Achaemenids might own lands in Pasargadae. "—and heard of your new house. I felt the least I could do was make amends for not coming before. You will show it to us, my lord?"

Haman would. Here was his chance to impress men who seemed to despise him, whose good opinion he could not seem to earn.

Room after lavish room he showed them. Servants in Haman's expensive livery were everywhere.

"And now, my lords, my treasure rooms."

"*Your* treasure rooms?" Shethar was unable to keep the surprise from his voice.

"But of course! As Grand Vizier I am sent many gifts."

I'll wager you are, thought Memucan. With many strong suggestions behind them.

"In this room," Haman swept back fringed silk curtains, "are the special gifts sent me on my promotion. The king himself told the satraps what to send."

"But of course," said Memucan silkily, "the Great King would want honor done his own position. Yours is a reflected glory, is it not, Lord Haman?"

"As is your own," Haman flashed back.

Memucan bowed. "I have never thought otherwise, my lord." He gave the slightest emphasis to the first word. "And now we thank you for this tour. We are—" he hesitated, "—impressed."

As they were driven home in Haman's private carriage, Memucan and Shethar, aware that drivers have long ears, were silent. Once inside Memucan's house, however, they roared and slapped each other on the back.

"Elephantiasis!" chortled Shethar. "Haman has elephantiasis."

"Biggest is best! Did you notice that urn, that great, clumsy glob of gold? What could one possibly put in that?"

"Oil, my lord, oil to add to Haman's smoothness."

"Tcha! Any oilier and he would be a puddle."

"That set of rings—a color for every day, was it?"

"No, I think he said he wore them according to his mood!"

"And the Lady Zeresh! She looked like a rich prostitute."

"Can a leopard change its spots? Well, my Shethar," Memucan sobered, "we meet tonight?"

"Yes. Each comes at a different time and enters my home by different entrances."

"It's as bad as that? When should I come?"

"At sunset, and come by the south gate. Bring along a musical instrument. This must look like a social evening if anyone sees you."

"Till then."

"Make way! Make way for the Lord Haman, Grand Vizier of the Great King!"

Haman's retinue came across the vast space between the Apadana and the King's Gate. He sat his horse with fierce pride, his expression faintly suggestive of someone who smells something repulsive. A crier preceded him; attendants and guards surrounded him.

Standing at his accustomed place in the Gate, Mordecai watched the scene cynically. One of the king's scribes looked sharply at the Jew.

"He comes very close today I think, Lord Mordecai. Perhaps you should stop being so stiff-necked and bow like the rest of us mortals."

"Not I."

"Make way! Make way!"

The procession came almost to the Gate itself and then turned left. All the men at the Gate, men of prominence and rank, prostrated themselves. All except Mordecai. He stood as he had been, reading tablets. Unaware of anyone but himself, Haman failed to see.

"I assure you, Lord Mordecai," said another courtier, coughing as the procession trailed off in a film of dust, "you are toying with fire. Why won't you bow?"

"It is twenty days since the king's decree that all are to prostrate themselves before the Lord Haman," said the first. "We have been friends and colleagues for a long time, and you are putting us at risk by ignoring a direct commandment of the Great King himself. Tell us why you do it?"

"Why?" Mordecai looked up from his tablets. "I will tell you why, my friends. I am a Jew."

A soft murmur of surprise.

"We Jews do not bow for any man."

"But you bow for the Great King himself?"

"I bow for him because he represents the supreme authority in this land that has given me shelter. But this upstart Agagite—"

"Hush! Don't even think such words."

"I would not have harm come to you, my lords. I'll say no more."

"But you will not bow?"

"I will not bow."

The scene was repeated for several days. Each time the other officials grew more nervous.

"Why should we risk our necks for this Jew? We're not of his race."

"Praise Ahura for that!"

"I suggest we bring this to the Grand Vizier's attention."

"That might prove dangerous for our colleague."

"Curse Mordecai! He has not shown us much consideration, has he?"

"But from what I hear, the Grand Vizier is no Jew lover, and Mordecai is a fine man."

"No matter. We shall tell Lord Haman; that will clear us of suspicion. If he does not mind, there is no harm done. If he does, we will have showed him that we have no part in this outrageous attitude."

"Well said! Today we'll ask to see him."

Next day as the procession approached the King's Gate, their mission had made a difference. Haman was not riding in a state of oblivion but looked sharply at the men at the Gate. As usual, Mordecai was deep in study.

"Make way! Make way for the great Lord Haman!"

The men at the Gate swept a deep obeisance; Mordecai continued reading. Haman's eyes bored hard, but he took no notice. As the procession turned the corner, the Grand Vizier's face was set in implacable anger.

One man nudged a companion. "This bodes no good for Mordecai."

"The more fool he."

That night at home, Haman raged. Though his self-esteem was enormous, it was eggshell thin. Inside was an emptiness that frightened him. Any resistance to his will created fear, and what he feared he wanted to destroy.

"Me! *Me!* He had the impertinence, the absolute insolence to insult me!"

"Insult? What do you mean insult?" Zeresh was stroking his back.

"Don't you call it an insult? The king has said that all men are to bow to me, Haman, the Grand Vizier. This man didn't even look up from his tablets."

"My lord, this must be dealt with."

"And they tell me this has been going on since the beginning. He has never bowed."

"Why not kill him?" asked the practical Zeresh.

Haman swore. "Are you a fool?"

Zeresh looked at him coolly. "Sometimes when you act like this, I think I must be to live with you."

Haman hurled a dish at her; she ducked expertly and laughed. "You are very handsome when you are angry, my lord. Come here."

170

But for once Haman was not coming. "One man! One miserable, filthy little man!"

"As I said, my love, why not kill him?"

"Surely even a woman should know the answer to that."

"This woman does not." Zeresh swung her pretty foot back and forth. "Do enlighten me, great lord."

"The reason is that this is a civilized country. It is impossible to kill a prominent man just like that." He clapped his hands.

"Impossible for *you*, Lord Haman?"

"Even for me. Only the king has the power of life and death, and even he has to have two charges against a man. Not one—two. What can I accuse him of? He's a scholar, not a politician."

"Nonsense! All men are politicians. What's wrong with the edict as a reason? Isn't it a crime to disobey a royal edict?"

"It is, but that charge would make me look conceited."

Zeresh raised an eyebrow. "That would never do. But surely you can contrive a charge. It has not stopped you before."

"What hasn't?"

"Lack of evidence. You have always been very adept at, shall we say, *making* evidence."

He looked at her without seeing her and suddenly lunged out of the room.

All that night, fueling his anger with remembered slights and fancied offenses, Haman tried to think how to repay the outrage done him by Mordecai the Jew. His lifelong grievances about the race became concentrated in this one incident with a force that threatened to destroy him. Suddenly, he began to pray, and his prayer was to the god of darkness.

"Angru Manyu! Send me your wisdom. Show me how to avenge myself on this—this piece of offal. Send me a plan!"

Alone, he burned incense, sacrificed birds and insects, and drank strong wine. He continued to evoke the spirit of evil that he was convinced stood, mightier than any other, behind the power of the empire.

Late that night he had his plan: a strategy of vengeance that staggered even him.

In her quarters, Zeresh heard his laughter and shivered. "Astarte preserve me!" she whispered and ordered her slave girl to turn the lamp higher.

Early in the morning Haman called his chief steward. "Send me Azanes, the Magus."

The room was a shambles. The stench of blood and burned flesh mingled with the scent of incense and wine.

The Magus arrived, all in white. He did not bow; as a priest he was not required to.

"Azanes, I must know the exact date for something of the greatest importance. An event that will go down in history."

"My lord wishes to know when it is to occur?"

"No, no! *I* am going to make it occur. And—" he came close, "if a breath of this ever gets out, I will see to it that you die, priest or not."

"You wish, then, to know the auspicious day for this great deed?"

"I do, and it must be right."

"Then we must cast Pur."

"Cast, then!" snapped Haman.

"My lord! Something so important cannot be done here and now. It must be done with proper ceremony. There must be fire, the calendars, the sacred dice."

"Where?"

Azanes considered. There were no temples in Susa, only fire altars—great blocks of stone with steps cut into their sides.

"Tonight, at midnight, come to the eastern fire altar. If this is so important, it must be done in the presence of all the Magi of Susa."

At midnight, Haman and his chief steward went to the fire altar. Flames made orange fringes on the dark. Twenty-four hooded, white-robed figures stood in a circle, their shadows moving in a weird dance. A low humming sound rose and fell.

It was eerie, arcane. Haman found his palms sweating. What was beyond the darkness? Could this be a trap?

Azanes slowly mounted the stone steps until he stood silhouetted against the bright flames, arms outstretched. The other Magi circling the altar moved in slow, hypnotic rhythm; the humming grew louder. Azanes drew black and white dice from his robe. One at a time, the other Magi presented tablets, ancient Babylonian calendars, one for each month of the year.

"We begin by finding the right month," Azanes said, and solemnly they cast Pur. Day by day and month by month they cast. The Magi peeped and muttered; the stones clicked; the tablets were shifted.

Unable to follow the intricacies, Haman watched with mounting tension. The flames were dying; the shadows grew darker.

Azanes raised his hands and faced north, east, south, and west and then bowed to the fire.

"It is done."

Haman's throat was dry. "When?"

"The gods have spoken: the thirteenth of the twelfth month, the month Adar."

Involuntarily Haman gasped. "But this is only Nisan, the *first* month."

Azanes' eyes bored at him from under the peaked hood. "One does not quarrel with the Pur, Lord Haman."

Back in his carriage, Haman fumed. "Adar. Adar! Eleven whole months away!"

"It seems long," soothed his steward, "but it is important to have the day the gods approve!"

"You are right. Now I know I move under the sanction of the gods. And I will have time to—arrange things."

Early in the morning Haman presented himself in the king's outer court. He now had daily audiences with the king, although Xerxes often kept him waiting. During this morning's wait Haman had consolidated his scheme and arranged his words.

Harbonah came to summon him. "Oh, Harbonah, you'll be glad to know my youngest son has sired yet another child."

Harbonah compressed his lips and gestured him in.

The king spoke of state affairs while Haman surged with impatience. After a long time, Xerxes yawned and leaned back.

"Enough for now. I'm hungry. I'd like pheasant and a small lamb. You will dine with me today, Haman."

This signal honor was encouraging. A good omen?

"There is one other thing, O king."

Xerxes stifled another yawn. "Not more business?"

"Important business, Your Majesty."

"Surely it can wait until tomorrow?"

"I think this is a matter of the utmost importance, my king."

Xerxes laughed. "My hard-working lieutenant. Very well. If Haman thinks it is important, it is important. Out with it!"

Haman's lines were well-rehearsed, but he delivered them with convincing hesitancy. "I—I have not wished to disturb my lord Xerxes, knowing how much he has on his mind—"

"Get on, Haman, get on."

"Also, O king, I wanted to be very sure of my facts."

"A good idea."

"There is a people, a certain people in the king's empire—"

"There are quite a few!" laughed Xerxes.

"But this people is one that is scattered throughout your whole kingdom, and their laws are different from all other people's."

"You can't mean the Carians?"

"No, my lord king. These are a scattered people—diverse, but everywhere."

"They sound like nomads. Go on."

"They not only have their own practices—"

"Surely you know I don't interfere with people's religious practices," Xerxes said sharply. The Great King was hungry.

"No, sire. I mean, yes, I do know your great tolerance and understanding. But these people—" Carefully, he named no names. "They do not keep the king's laws."

"*What!*"

"It is as I say, sire," he lied. "After carefully investigating this matter, I do not feel it is to the king's interest to allow them to live."

Xerxes fiddled with his bracelets, concern and petulance making a strange mixture on his face. This might be serious, but he was tired of statesmanship today.

Haman went on. "If it please the king, let there be an edict that these rebels may be destroyed."

"Destroyed? Isn't that a bit strong?"

Gauging his means to the king's cupidity, Haman pressed on. "I am so concerned for Your Majesty's empire and for his personal safety that I myself will pay ten thousand talents of silver to those who have the charge of executing the king's decree, and they will bring it to the king's treasuries." He did not mention that he planned to get this huge sum from the Jews who had much of the empire's wealth.

"So much, my Haman? You *are* taking this seriously!"

The slaves arrived with platters of food giving off tantalizing aromas. Slowly the king drew off the great seal ring. Haman's heart thudded. Was his plan succeeding?

"Keep your silver, Haman. Whoever they are, they are in your hand." He handed him the ring. "Do whatever you think best. Now, by Angru Manyu, that is enough business for today!"

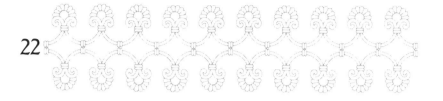

22

The eastern night had dropped its curtain of dark by the time the Seven were assembled at Shethar's house.

"Your food is superb, Shethar—and your wine!"

"I'll wager Haman's rivals it," said Shethar.

"Never." Carshena, the last arrival, was drinking rapidly to make up for lost time. "He has the wealth, but he'll never live long enough to acquire your palate."

"Or your figure either," said Marsena with unusual venom. The others ignored him, and slaves cleared the tables.

"Bring fresh wine and then leave us," Shethar told his steward. "Do not let anyone in the house or near this room."

"Haman's control of the king is increasing," said Tarshish.

"Unfortunately it is. To give the evil daeva his due, his intellect is not only more powerful than the king's, but far more subtle."

Meres agreed. "He's even clever enough to make the king think the great Hamanian schemes are his own."

"The Hamanian schemes, as you call them, are often very good," said Shethar. "It's his enormous personal ambition that makes him dangerous. I told you, Memucan, about his spy system. Our own spies have discovered that he has detailed notes on every person of influence in Susa. And he seems unduly concerned with Jews. One of his friends was discovered dealing with a Jewish money lender; another married a Jew. His reaction to both these reports was violent."

"What does he have against Jews?" asked Marsena, too quickly.

"The Jews are powerful and wealthy, and Haman would impale his own mother for one new estate."

"We need to remember that Haman has an enormous following," warned Tarshish.

"That fawning group of sycophants! They applaud every word of his; it's sickening!"

"It's strange," mused Shethar. "For such people his magnetism is almost supernatural."

"It's those huge eyes of his. They're almost frightening at times."

"Well, we can be glad he will never have power of life and death."

"He will not have it officially, but deaths can always be arranged, Meres."

"But that tool has a double edge: it should not be too hard for us to arrange an assassination."

"That's a strong word, Meres. And don't forget that Haman is the king's present favorite and Grand Vizier of the whole empire."

"I agree," said Shethar. "We have had years of war and unrest. Darius brought in a time of development; the present king is interested in developing Parsa and in general following Darius' pattern—or he was. Haman is so power-hungry that he will go too far. The king's blindness can't last forever."

"I'm not sure I agree with you," Memucan broke in. "The Agagite is clever enough to give Xerxes what he needs."

"You mean flattery?"

"Not just flattery, though Haman pours it on until I should think even the king would drown. No, I think Xerxes finds Haman the strong figure he has always needed. He had Darius and Atossa; he had Vashti. There has always been at least one person close to him who was stronger and wiser than he."

"Say it softly," said Shethar. "But perhaps you are right. In the war it was Mardonios. As for the queen—"

"We're drifting away from the matter in hand," interrupted Meres. "We're not exactly weaklings, and together we are as good a group of advisers as any Achaemenid king has ever had."

"We all know what a brilliant group we are," Memucan was mildly sarcastic. "But for the time being we are no longer close to the king. We have been deposed, in effect if not in fact."

"I'm not afraid of murder," said Meres, "but it would have to be done so that no suspicion falls on us."

"Harbonah might be a willing ally."

"Harbonah would be delighted to do the act personally, I daresay. But we can't trust him; he's much too emotional."

"The queen? *She* can't bear any love for Haman."

"As a matter of fact, it has seeped from the harem that she can't stand the man. But I'm afraid the lovely Esther would find murder unacceptable."

"I wonder if she realizes that it's Haman who has made the king so cool to her lately?"

"I doubt it. Wives, they say, are the last to know."

"You speak from experience, no doubt," jibed Tarshish.

Carshena ignored him. "What about Mordecai, the lawyer? A friend of mine in the King's Gate tells me that Mordecai refuses to bow when Haman rides by."

"Huzzahs for Mordecai, but it does seem a foolhardy risk."

"Mordecai," said Shethar thoughtfully, "is a steady man, quiet, unassuming."

"These quiet men are full of surprises. I think there is a great brain under that exterior. Suppose he has ambitions of his own?"

"In getting rid of Haman we mustn't go from a bad situation to a worse."

"What could be worse than Haman?"

They talked through the night. Every plan had some flaw. No one noticed that Marsena was very quiet. As dawn came, a cavalcade of horses galloped by. Shethar's house was on the main road out of Susa, the one leading to the north gate.

"What's that all about?"

They crowded to the windows and were about to pull the thick draperies back when Shethar stopped them. "Put out all the lights. These are queer times."

They saw mounted men tearing down the street and heading out of the great gate.

Shethar strode out the door. "Here, my man! What is all this about?"

Recognizing one of the great Seven, the courier reined in his horse. "A new edict of the king's, my lord."

"To be sent where?"

"Throughout the whole empire."

The man's restlessness at the delay was evident. Shethar waved him on and was about to stop another, then thought better of it and went back into the house. "There's a royal edict going out to all the empire."

"Without our being consulted? I find that hard to believe."

"You hear for yourselves, friends."

"But what is it? What does it say?"

"I started to ask one of the men, but I was ashamed to admit to a mere courier that I—that we—the Seven do not know what's going on in this kingdom."

"If we go to the King's Gate, we can find out for ourselves. It's sure to be posted there."

Ascending the long flight of steps to the King's Gate, they were aware of a sound churning through Susa accompanied by a flow of movement unusual for the hour. Men hurried in all directions or huddled in knots.

"There's something strange," muttered Carshena, "an undertone I don't like."

At the Gate the torches still blazed, though dimmed by the rising sun. Standing near one of them was a group of gesticulating men, while the king's herald read a proclamation: ". . . to destroy, slay, and annihilate all Jews, young and old, women and children, in one day, the thirteenth day of the twelfth month, which is the month of Adar, and to plunder their goods."

The Seven looked at one another in complete disbelief. Kill? Destroy the Jews? Their bankers? Their best merchants? For what possible reason? What could they have done to merit such injustice, such senseless cruelty?

Shethar drew Memucan away from the rest. "I think the king has gone mad."

"How could any Persian—even the mad Cambyses would not have destroyed his own empire!"

"Cambyses! That mad streak! Is it possible Xerxes has inherited it through his mother?"

The other five came over to join them. "It's signed in the king's name and sealed with his ring."

For a long moment nobody spoke.

"And this edict is being sent to all provinces?"

"To every satrap, in every language used throughout the empire. The scribes have been at work all night, I'm told, and all day yesterday."

"All day yesterday! And we were told nothing?"

"Women—children—in one day—" Meres was dazed.

"*Why?*"

"What was that date?"

"The thirteenth day of Adar."

"That's eleven months away! What evil daeva has bewitched Xerxes?"

"You know what evil daeva."

"All right, but what did the Jews ever do to Haman? What can he possibly hope to gain?"

"Oh, come now, Lord Meres, have you overlooked the clause that says their goods are to be confiscated? Some of the richest men in Persia are Jews."

"But Haman doesn't need wealth, and he *has* power."

"What will happen to our banks, our businesses, our trade?"

"Listen to me," Memucan motioned them closer, "when it is known that all Jews are marked men, the kingdom will become one vast slaughterhouse."

"Surely no one would dare kill before the day—"

"No one? Do not be naïve."

"We must see the king."

They went to the palace, but Xerxes was seeing no one.

"He is closeted with the Grand Vizier, my lords. He has threatened death to anyone who disturbs him."

Never before had the king been unavailable to his trusted Seven.

A sound had been growing in intensity while the men had been in the palace.

"The Jews!"

"They have reason to mourn."

Suddenly there was a sound that froze them where they stood, "Look! It's Mordecai!"

Memucan rushed to the foot of the staircase where the distracted Jew was throwing ashes on his head. "My lord! Lord Mordecai! Listen—"

But the terrible sound went on. He had sackcloth over his torn robe. As he started back up the stairs, Memucan took hold of him firmly. "No, Lord Mordecai, you cannot go up into the King's Gate in sackcloth. You'll be killed."

"Killed?" Mordecai laughed wildly but allowed himself to be led down the stairs. He went off into the streets, crying his bitter cry.

"I had not realized that Mordecai is a Jew."

"Nor I. He has much to lose."

How much, they did not know.

"Love you? Why should I?"

"There's no reason," David said cheerfully. "Why do you think *I* love *you*?" Ruth and David were walking in her garden.

"Oh," she twirled a bracelet, "I'm pretty and clever and Jewish and—"

"You could be all of those," retorted David, "and I needn't love you. Other girls have all that."

"Well!" Ruth splashed his face with water from the little cascade. "Why do you love me, then?"

He drew her to him quickly and kissed her, running his hands through the thick gold hair. "I have no idea why, but I love you as my life. I swear it!"

"David! You're a good Jew. Whatever made you do that?"

"Do what? I've done nothing wrong."

"You know you are not supposed to kiss me. And swearing!" She shook her head at him, but he knew she had enjoyed it.

He held her again, and his kiss was deeper.

Then the sound caught them: women's cries overlaying the deeper mourning sounds of men. They drew apart.

Ruth's mother rushed into the garden. "Inside, Ruth! At once! David, you must go home."

"Why, Aunt Rachel?"

"Just go! Your grandfather will need you."

"I'm sorry, Aunt Rachel, but you must tell me what this is all about. If there is danger, I will not leave Ruth."

"David, David! Go. You must!"

"But why?"

Then she told him.

He was shock-still for a drip of the water clock. Then he spoke: "Get inside, both of you, and stay there. Draw your curtains. Under no circumstances go outside or near the windows or answer any knocks. Where is Uncle Rabos?"

"At this hour? At work, of course."

"I shall find him. I'll come back as soon as I can."

"What will you do? What *can* you do?"

"I don't know, but Jews have always helped each other. We'll find a way."

Rachel watched him go. "I hope he is right. Oh, merciful Adonai, I hope he is right."

As David raced into his home, he found confusion. Weeping came from the women's quarters; all the male relatives had gathered and were in hot discussion.

As eldest, Bilshan spoke. "We will pray and wait on Adonai. He will rescue us."

180

"Grandfather!" David's voice was taut, "We can't just do nothing. We can't die like rats in a cage!"

"There are eleven months, my son. Adonai is all-powerful. We will wait and fast and pray."

"Adonai expects us to use the minds he has given us."

Voices became argumentative, strident. Bilshan remained imperturbable. "Adonai will protect us, my family. He will not fail."

Unnoticed, David slipped out, found Ruth's father, Rabos, and by a back route came to Ruth's home. The entire family was packing furiously.

"What are you doing?" demanded Rabos. "Rachel?"

"We're getting ready to leave," Jakob said.

"Where can we go? The edict covers every country in the empire."

"There are eleven months before it is in force." said Rachel. "We have a great deal of money. Go, Rabos. Quickly! Withdraw everything from the bank."

"We'll bribe our way," said Jakob. "Money will do what ordinary human decency and compassion would never do."

As Rabos left, David went across the room to Ruth who was packing a few things. "I am going with you."

"David! Your grandfather—"

"He has powerful friends and a big family. I'll go with you. When do you leave?"

Jakob clasped his shoulder in thanks. "You're most welcome, David. We go tonight at midnight."

"How will you get past the guards?"

"We have a plan—" He whispered it in David's ear.

In the insulated world of the palace, Haman and the Great King were laughing.

"Well done, well done, Lord Haman!" Haman had just assured the king that the nonexistent rebellion was being expertly dealt with. "You do carry things out with dispatch."

"O king, live forever," said Haman. "We have made the decision while sober. Dare I suggest that we now carry out the wise old Persian custom and—"

"And get drunk to see if we reach the same decision? An excellent tradition! Bring wine!" the king roared. And the two began to drink.

But Susa was perplexed.

The great Jewish banking houses closed and so did the shops. Mourning could be heard all over the city. Thousands of non-Jewish Susians who had friends in the Jewish community gathered together to discuss the edict, but they did so cautiously and few had the courage to go near the Jewish homes. The edict, written in Aramaic, Elamite, and Babylonian was posted in every quarter of the city. Around the notices stood hushed groups of those who could read; they passed on the information in whispers to those who could not. A great paralysis took hold of the lively capital.

At a few minutes past midnight the guard at the East Gate suddenly straightened.

"Hello. What's that cart doing coming along at this hour?" And as it came nearer, "Whew! It stinks to the moon."

"Ho! Stop! Where do you think you're going?"

A bent man with a ragged shawl over his head smiled toothlessly. "My master told me I must not be seen in the daylight with this load," he lisped. "He said it was of—offensive."

"I'll say it's offensive!"

The guard poked roughly at the pile of stinking hides. "What do you propose to do with these?"

"Bury them on the great plain, sir. They are, as you can see, too rotted for any use."

"Well—it's unusual."

He casually turned up his palm. The old man nodded and dug under his foul-smelling clothes. He brought up two silver siglots.

"Have you any use for these, sir?" he asked disarmingly.

Siglots? Where would this man get siglots? Then he shrugged, quickly slipped them under his robe, and opened the gate.

The wagon with its load of rotting hides creaked through and lumbered off into the night.

Holding his nose, the guard watched it go. "Getting rid of that is a good night's work." Whistling cheerfully, he locked the gate.

Out on the great plain, quiet under the stars, the wagon finally came to a halt.

"I think it's safe to come out now."

The pile of skins began to heave. Gasping, five people came out: Rabos, Rachel, Jakob, Ruth, and another pretty little girl.

182

"Hello," said David, dropping his lisp, "who are you?"

She looked shyly at Jakob who put his arm around her. "This is Judith, the girl I'm going to marry. I smuggled her in at the last minute."

David smiled. Who could understand better? But it does increase the risk, he thought. Somehow, the leadership of the expedition had fallen on him. Ruth's father, Rabos, was too shaken by events to do more than moan and clutch his head. His business acumen was no good to him here.

"We will all die," was all he could say. "That I should see such a day."

"We are *not* going to die," said Jakob firmly. "Now listen. You have a good friend in the satrap of southern Arabia."

"I *had* a good friend," moaned Rabos. "He will never acknowledge that friendship now. He wouldn't dare."

"Perhaps not for friendship's sake, father, but I seem to recall he has an enormous appetite for money and a wife who has nearly bankrupted him for jewels. We have both."

Rabos brightened a little. "That's true. Perhaps—yes, perhaps he would."

"Would what?" asked Ruth.

"Would smuggle us over his border into the part of Arabia that's out of the empire entirely."

"You mean, *live* there!" Rachel was shocked. "In such a desert."

"Perhaps you will be glad to be able to live at all." Jakob was impatient.

"Jakob! That's no way to speak to your mother."

"But he is right," said Rachel. "When it's life or death, one must forget one's dreams."

Far from forgetting *his* dreams, Haman, weaving home in the early morning, could hardly keep from shouting. *All the Jews. All the Jews! Every slinking, lowborn, highborn, rich and poor Jew. I hold the life of each of them in this hand.*

He looked at the king's seal. Who would have thought—?

In one day, on the thirteenth Adar, he would exterminate every Jew in the entire empire. And Mordecai would be last. I will break him with his people's suffering, Haman vowed. He will grow prematurely old, fearing how he will die.

And how he will die!

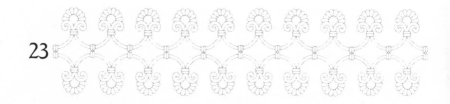

23

On the day of the edict, Esther woke with a sense of oppression. She was abrupt with Hatak and ignored the girls. Faint sounds washed up from the city. Suddenly her inertia was cut through by an eerie sound. Human? Animal? Who cried like that?

"Lura! Run. Find out what that cry means."

Lura ran. When she returned, she was accompanied by other attendants and three eunuchs. They had no details. They only knew that Mordecai, who walked outside the queen's porch daily, had not come today and was said to be crying in the streets wearing sackcloth and ashes.

Father! What has happened to father? A Jewish holy day? She tried to remember. She did not think so. An anniversary of a family death? None she could recall.

"Take him fresh clothes and destroy that sackcloth. It could get him into trouble with the king's men."

Soon the servants came back, carrying the clothing she had sent.

"Majesty, Lord Mordecai refused the clothes."

"He was told that I sent them?"

"Yes, but he would hardly stop his cries long enough to listen."

"Send Hatak to me at once."

The chief chamberlain arrived looking worried.

"Hatak, go to Lord Mordecai. I must know what has happened."

"He is ill, Majesty?"

"No. Yes. I don't know what's wrong." She told him what the slaves had found. "Hurry, Hatak."

Mordecai was stunned. The edict had come with slingshot force, and even though it came in the king's name over the imprint of the king's seal, he had no doubt who was the instigator. He asked himself guiltily if this would ever have happened if he had bowed to Haman. Were Adonai's people to be exterminated because of him? What he called faithfulness to Adonai—was it pride?

A chariot drew up. "Lord Mordecai! I bring you a message from the queen."

"She is safe, Hatak?"

"Safe? Of course!" *The man's demented! Look at him! And what has the queen to do with this?* "Her Majesty is concerned for you. She sent you clothes, and you refused them—a serious breach of manners, Lord Mordecai. She now sends me to find out what is wrong." Hatak spoke severely, his loyalty to the queen offended.

"You know of the edict, Hatak?"

"Who does not? Is this what distresses you?"

"I must speak to you alone."

Hatak dismissed his driver and attendants. Sitting beside Hatak in his carriage, Mordecai told the story of his feud with Haman, of his refusal to bow because he was a Jew.

"But the king's edict, Lord Mordecai—"

"It is not the king's edict; it is Haman's."

"How can you be sure?"

"He promised the king ten thousand talents of silver to be paid into the treasury to get this edict published. I know this to be true."

"But that is monstrous! Why?"

"Because of me, Hatak. Don't you see? Because I insulted him."

"But surely you did only what you felt was right."

"Whether my action was right or wrong, my people are condemned."

Neither spoke for a while; suddenly Mordecai straightened; his whole manner changed. "Send for a copy of the decree, Hatak."

When it was brought, Mordecai said, "You will take this to the queen. Read it to Her Majesty and tell her, from me, that she must go before the king and make supplication—"

Hatak started so that the light carriage jerked.

"—she must plead for her people."

"*Her* people!" Hatak felt his mental moorings coming untied.

"Her people. Swear on your life you will keep this secret."

"I swear, my lord."

"She is my cousin; I raised her. Now do you see how far-reaching this is?"

Hatak was beginning to see much more than he cared to. The beautiful Esther in danger. What would Xerxes do?

"Does the king know—about the queen, my lord?"

"He does not." Mordecai was climbing down from the carriage. "Take this to the queen and tell her that I say she must go before the king."

Hatak, in a daze, returned to the queen.

"No, Hatak! No! My father asks the impossible!" The queen and Hatak were alone in a heavily curtained room. She listened as Hatak repeated Mordecai's words over and over. That Mordecai had given away their secret was in itself all but unbelievable. But she could not go before the king unasked.

"My father does not understand. You know better than I what an impossible request this is."

"I do, Majesty."

Esther tugged at the thick pigtail of hair that swung down her back. Impatiently she untied its gold lacings and shook her hair free as if trying to escape bonds that held her. She turned decisively to her chamberlain. "Take this message to Mordecai: All the king's servants and the people of the king's provinces know that if any man or woman goes to the king inside the inner court without being called, there is only one law: all alike are to be put to death, except the one to whom the king holds out the golden sceptre. Besides—" Hatak, busy transcribing the message in cuneiform on clay, heard a catch in the queen's voice. "—I have not been called to come to the king—for—thirty days."

The last admission demolished her pride.

At the appointed place, Hatak gave Mordecai the queen's message. Mordecai pounded his fist. "She does not understand."

"I think, my lord, that it is you who do not understand."

"Tell Hadassah—"

Hatak sucked in his breath.

"—tell my daughter—did you bring writing materials?"

Hatak poised his stylus over the soft clay tablet he had brought, his dignity ruffled. Only because of the queen would he stoop to a scribe's tasks.

"Do not imagine that you alone of all the Jews will escape because you are in the royal palace." The queen's chamberlain could not believe what he wrote: "If you persist in saying nothing at this time—" Mordecai stopped, then his voice rang out with a sureness Hatak did not understand at all, "relief and deliverance for the Jews *will appear* from some other quarter, but you and your father's family will perish."

Before Mordecai's inner eye there was a picture of a young girl poring over the scrolls in their room at home, asking about Cyrus and Adonai.

"Besides," he added slowly, "perhaps you have come to the kingdom for such a time as this."

As Hatak prepared to leave, Mordecai added, "Bring me her answer here. I will wait for it."

Haman had called a meeting of his most powerful followers and a cluster of men who owed him favors.

"The gods have decreed it is to be eleven months till the proclamation against the Jews is in effect. In the meantime, we will make them sweat; they will bleed, smart, ache. We will ridicule them for trusting in their God. We can show people that all their misfortunes come because the Jews do not worship Ahura Mazda."

"You will have to work hard at that, you know," said a wise merchant. "Persians are tolerant; the Achaemenids have taught them well."

"Simpleton! We will send secret documents to the satraps stating that the Jews will debauch their women, that the Jews are diseased, that they are plotting to kill the king and overthrow the empire." In Haman's mind truth had become so choked that he believed most of what he said.

The man gasped.

"Of course, we won't be so crude as to put all these accusations in one document."

"But that sort of document needs witnesses, Lord Haman."

"For a merchant, you seem singularly unaware that with enough bribery, anything can be bought in Susa. Now, all of you, listen carefully. We must be sure the Jews do not escape."

"Where would they go?"

"There are not many places, to be sure; soon there will be none, but I want no loopholes."

"But how are you going to flush them all out? Surely there are Jews we do not recognize as Jews."

"I have thought of that." Haman looked like a self-satisfied camel. "We will require all Jews to register; even a little Jewish blood will qualify them for extinction. We shall offer a reward for any Jew pointed out to us who does not register."

"What about their women?" asked a wealthy lawyer.

"I doubt that you need direction on that score." He went on, "The Jews are a menace, a secret society whose net reaches across the entire kingdom."

"I had no idea!" murmured an inoffensive little man. "Imagine living with such dangerous people all these years! My neighbor seemed such a fine man."

"From now on," said the Grand Vizier, "I want a report on everything he does."

"Oh, you shall have it, my lord. I have been quite blind, but I shall soon prove my loyalty to you and the king."

Another sycophant spoke up. "The Jews have big libraries, my lord. They are learned men."

"Curse their learning! Their ideas must be obliterated! Every document they possess must be destroyed, burned, broken. Go home now, all of you. We have work to do."

Alone, he worried. The city was filled with powerful Jews; he must anticipate their every move.

After Hatak had finished reading Mordecai's message, Esther sat very still. When she spoke, it was quietly. "Go from me now, Hatak."

He rose obediently but felt he had to say, "Lord Mordecai waits for an answer, my lady."

Esther's smile was infinitely sad. "He loves me, Hatak. He will not mind giving me time to decide if I have the courage to die."

Darkness was around her—a deep inner darkness of spirit. Beyond the garden wall she heard the commands and responses as the guard changed. She was remembering Xerxes—smiling, tender, applauding her dancing, laughing, sharing his fears, his vulnerabilities. Until a month ago.

Breach all etiquette. . . ? Risk his anger. . . ? The coldness, the viciousness, the lightning shifts to violence—these, too, were Xerxes.

I cannot; it's madness to think of it! Father cannot ask this of me.

What was it Mordecai had said? ". . . you and your father's house will perish. . . " What would happen when the Grand Vizier learned she was a Jew?

"Esther the queen—Lord Haman wants Esther the queen—she is a Jew— She is a Jew! Kill her!"

She opened her eyes and looked around wildly. The garden was empty; beside the lily pool the flowers nodded gently.

Adonai? Where was he in all this? She had not thought of Adonai for a long time; it was longer still since she had prayed to him. But today's shocks were stripping the layers of Persian sophistication from her. The months of harem training, the nights as the king's consort, the years as queen to an alien people—like discarded robes, they fell away until she felt naked, defenseless, and very frightened.

Perhaps I could face a quick death. After all, if my lord no longer loves me there is only a purposeless existence in a household of women and eunuchs. She looked at her hands, white, delicate, competent. "Like water lilies, my Star—" But as she looked, Bhindi's cries came back across the years— Bhindi, mutilated for breaking the rigid court etiquette.

I can't . . . I can't. Father has it all wrong; there has to be another way. Even the king cannot change the edict. Why should I risk my life? Her father's voice seemed to answer her: "With Adonai all things are possible."

"Then let him find another messenger!" she said angrily and moved across the room. Mordecai's voice followed: "Perhaps you have come to the kingdom for such a time as this." *To die? How would that save a nation? And suppose the king did hold out the sceptre—I am a Jewess still—* She stopped pacing as the thought took hold; her panic lessened. *I am a Jewess. I am also a queen . . . their queen. Perhaps I have been sent here for this very purpose.*

"Oh, Adonai—help me!"

Slowly, the darkness began to lift and a clear idea of what she must do took shape.

She turned and walked straight into the big room.

"Hatak, take this message to Lord Mordecai: Go, gather all the Jews to be found in Susa, and hold a fast on my behalf—neither eat nor drink for three days, night or day. I and my maids will fast as you do." She paused, then added firmly, "I will go to the king, even though it is against the law. And if I perish—I perish."

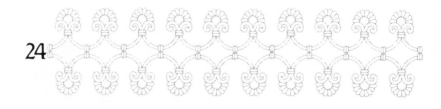

24

Mordecai sat in Bilshan's house, a lump of misery. "Did I do right? Tell me, *did* I do right?"

"You did what you felt you had to do, Mordecai."

"But if I had bowed to Haman—"

"Mordecai, it's too late for backward looks. I don't know what I would have done. Perhaps another Jew would have bowed. But it might have been more from cowardice than anything else. You showed the courage of deep conviction in refusing to bow."

"But it's one thing to pay a personal price for convictions; it's another to bring disaster on my people."

"Mordecai!" Bilshan's voice sharpened. "What's done is done, and we must go on from there. Adonai is good and understands our weaknesses. Even if some of our people are bitter and critical—he knows you did what you felt you should, for him."

"For him?" murmured Mordecai. "Or for my own pride?"

"Only Adonai himself can sort out motives. Now—you say the queen has asked the whole Jewish community to fast?"

"She asks that we do not eat or drink anything for three days and nights. She and her maidens will be doing the same."

"Her maidens? I wonder what those Persian girls think of that?"

"I only know it is said they are devoted to her."

"Well, we will fast and pray and uphold the queen. We must not fail her. Perhaps Adonai will hear and change the king's heart."

Mordecai walked to the window, then came back to Bilshan. "Are we quite mad? The king himself cannot change that edict now. What can be done by a small group, a group already under an interdict?"

"Nothing, my dear friend. But the God of that group is sovereign over all the earth. Solomon said, 'The king's heart is a stream of water in the hand of the Lord; he turns it wherever he will.'"

"Still—"

"Still, nothing," Bilshan's tone was sharp, unusual for him. "We will plead before him. There is not—there never has been—any power that could withstand his purposes. The Pharaoh's kingdom was as powerful as Xerxes' yet Adonai delivered his people as he promised Abraham four hundred years before."

Tempted to say that a deliverance four hundred years in the future was not very comforting, Mordecai replied, "But that was long ago. Here—now—with the blood hot in our veins—with the danger so real, with no escape—"

"Adonai is not held in time's limits, Mordecai. Remember our King Hezekiah and Sennacherib of Assyria. The men of Judah were a pitiful force against the Assyrians, yet Adonai made them victors. He is the same God today. It is hard to believe because it is *now,* it is *you,* and especially because it is your Hadassah who is involved."

"What have I urged her to do? What terrible death have I sent her to?"

"Nothing more terrible than she would experience if nothing is done."

"How can I know that? One woman against the power of Persia! What have I done?"

"Adonai has used frail instruments before. Come, we will get word to our brothers."

In the queen's house the air was thick with quiet, like a house of death. Refusing all food and drink, Esther had replaced her colored robes with mourning attire.

"Is this what she meant?" Hatak shouted at the slaves who brought back the untouched food. "She'll eat nothing? Can't her attendants make her eat? Lura?"

"They, too, are fasting."

"Fasting—fasting? What does this mean? What if the king sends for her? Mithra protect us all!"

Now from Esther's sleeping apartments came the sound of praying. The attendants heard her call openly on the God of Israel; they looked at each other in shock.

"Our lady is a Jewess?"

"That edict—she will die!"

"Don't say such things."

"She will!"

"The king would never allow it."

"It is the law."

Esther's attendants stood loyally by her during the three days' restriction. Armis, a religious girl, prayed intensely to Ahura Mazda; Arunah, encouraged by the queen's boldness, admitted that she, too, was a follower of the God of Israel; of them all, Lura understood most, but each in her own way loved the queen and wanted to help. Still, Esther spent most of her time alone indoors.

Her moods shifted. Occasionally, she went into the garden, where, during periods of exaltation she would look up at the night sky or at the sunlight pouring molten gold on the distant mountains and find a sense of Adonai's power. There seemed no reason to doubt his ascendancy over mere mortals. Then, her frailness, the smallness of her cause, the weakness of her people seemed opposed by might so vast that the whole idea of tampering with such a system seemed madness compounded with treason.

As a wife, her personal pain was deep. Her beloved did not want her any more. How, then, go into his presence at all, to say nothing of going as an intercessor for a hated race? Shamed in front of the whole court? She could endure that for her people. Banishment? Yes. Her Jewishness, something which had been receding into the background every year, had reasserted itself. But torture? There it was again. How could one *choose* to face the Persian methods of punishment?

If only she might plead her people's cause and then kill herself! But she knew no such easy escape would be allowed her. Her decision had been made; she had sent her agreement to Mordecai and, through him, to the entire Jewish community. But the temptation to withdraw assailed her viciously.

Gradually, her pain passed the boundaries of the personal, and she cried for her people. Never before had she felt so identified with them, yet so cut off. All the Jews she knew in Susa—Bilshan, Jakob, Ruth, David, Huldah, her father—what would happen to them? And to thousands like them?

"Adonai! You have acted before for your people. Don't fail us now. You have said that whoever touches us touches the apple of your eye; it is your honor at stake."

On the third morning Esther raised herself stiffly. Her head ached, she felt faint, and her throat was dry. Suddenly the thought was there: *This could be my last day on earth.*

Beyond her window the birds were commenting on the new day as if it were like any other. Siko stretched and woofed softly. Absently, she tousled his hair.

"Lura."

"My lady?"

"If I—do not return today—"

Lura left her bed and knelt beside Esther. "Oh, my queen, you will, you must! Your God will protect you, and you will come back to us."

"Adonai has mysterious ways, Lura. I might have to die. If I don't come back, will you take care of Siko?" It helped to talk of ordinary things. "It's time, Lura. Send for Arunah please."

For hours the two girls prepared their mistress as if for a celebration: baths, oils, perfumes, all too reminiscent of the night she had gone to the king for the first time.

"My coronation robe, Lura. And the crown." The girls were mystified. "And send for Hatak, please."

The chief chamberlain arrived; he could not believe what he saw. For three days the queen had been weeping and fasting in the drabbest of clothing. Now here she was, blazing with majesty. Why? Some message from the Throne? But that message would have had to come through him. Besides, the king was in the Apadana, holding court.

"I am going to the king, Hatak." Ignoring his look of unbelief, she went on, "You will prepare a banquet of wine for the king, Lord Haman, and myself. No one else."

Inviting the king here? Now? Should he warn her? But Esther's manner was remote; he could not.

In the palace it had not been a good day. Xerxes roared, cursed, threw things. With little reason he ordered the execution of a favorite slave. The Seven could not please him; Harbonah was a wreck; even Haman was treading softly.

As a matter of fact, Xerxes was not feeling too pleased with Haman at that moment. He longed for his queen, but Haman's wily insinuations had shaken him. Waiting his turn in the outer court, the Grand Vizier listened to the clangor of the king's rage, displeased that Memucan was admitted to the Presence before he was.

In the inner court, Memucan touched his lips and waited for instructions.

"I sent for you, Lord Memucan, because you are a wise man."

It had been a long time since the king's last compliment. What did he want?

"You are to make the arrangements for the audience today."

Since this prerogative had long been the Grand Vizier's, Memucan was both surprised and puzzled.

"And keep all fools away from me, Memucan." Xerxes' eyes had a light which boded no good for anyone. Oddly, the words of dismissal did not come.

"Salamis," muttered the king. "A stain on the shield of the Achaemenids. I had bad advice, you know. It never should have happened."

Greece now? After so many years? Memucan wisely said nothing.

"What good is all this," Xerxes indicated the shining room, "if I have to live with the shame of that defeat? Mardonios was a fool. If he still lived, I would impale him!" His voice rose. "And watch him die!"

The King sighed and in a different voice said, "Go and set up the court in the Apadana. I shall be there in exactly two turns of the water clock."

Two turns! That left little time to get the guards lined up, the bankers, lawyers, doctors, and other emissaries placed in order of protocol, the incense barriers arranged!

Xerxes, watching sardonically, was well aware of this.

Precisely at the second turn of the water clock there was a stirring in the throne room. The king was on his way. With the torches throwing strange shadows, the roof seemed higher, the columns more awe-inspiring. Memucan looked at the king's face. Mithra defend any poor suppliant today! He called the first emissary, a man from Lydia.

"But Your Majesty cannot go unattended."

"I am willing to risk my own life, Hatak. I am not willing to risk yours."

An unearthly quality about the queen silenced them all. The thick curtains swung behind her.

194

The guards could not believe their eyes. The queen! Alone? Those who had served Vashti and Atossa groped for some explanation, some precedent, but found none.

Esther moved along the narrow hall toward the entrance to the king's palace. On the other side of the door, in the grand palace itself, she began to tremble. The enormity of what she was doing struck her with almost physical force. Hesitantly, she moved on, her pounding heart shaking the sheer fabric of her robe. Never had she known such isolation.

Head high, she moved steadily through the halls and out into the courtyard. She stopped then and looked up at the Apadana's twin towers. As her eye traveled up and still up to the crenelated tops, she felt once more the terrified girl of fourteen who had stepped down from that curtained carriage. The Persians planned well; they knew how to confront mere man with his mortality.

The breeze stirred Esther's veil; a dark curl sprang loose and touched her cheek.

Line upon mighty line, the Immortals stood like statues. Figures crossed and recrossed the courtyard: emissaries going home, couriers hurrying on errands, foreign doctors, Susian lawyers. They stared in astonishment at the dazzling figure. Voices dropped; small knots of men huddled together and speculated.

Slowly Esther moved on. Up the carved staircase that doubled back upon itself, her robe cascading behind her like a waterfall of gold.

Now she was at the top, facing the forest of columns. High above her, lit occasionally by moving light, the formidable stone bulls stared down at her. Hundreds of torches wavered and smoked in the wind. Far, far down the pillared avenue she saw the door that led into the Persian holy of holies, into the presence of Ahura Mazda's representative who was her earthly lord.

The king's honor guard stiffened. Hands holding spears whitened at the knuckles. Did she know her danger? How could she not? Their queen was in deadly peril, and they could do nothing. Nothing but carry out the death order if it came.

She continued to advance, passing them, one by one.

As she faced the door to the throne room, her courage suddenly drained from her. She stopped. The gold-plated door seemed to lean toward her.

And suddenly life was very dear. She had been so preoccupied with the possibility of suffering that death itself had seemed a boon. Now it seemed nothing of the sort. An end to life? At twenty?

What folly had brought her here? Who was she, after all? A Jewish girl who, by a king's caprice, had become queen of Persia. Beyond that door was the figure who struck fear into the hearts of half the world.

All she needed to do was turn around. The guards were loyal; they would not tell. She must go now before it was too late—

"Perhaps you have come to the kingdom . . ." this awesome kingdom. . . . *How long does it take to die?*

"Your Majesty!"

She did not hear.

Adonai! If you are the God who does wonders, do them now. I don't understand, but if you have chosen me to plead for your people, give me strength. And if I must die, let me die bravely.

At a sign from her, a sign too compelling to disobey, the guard opened the door.

In the throne room, the king sat moodily under the canopy. Two tall incense burners blued the air with perfumed smoke, marking the boundary beyond which none dared come. Behind him stood his spear carrier, then Harbonah. The Seven were nearby. In the torchlight the gold fringe of the canopy moved and shone; the embroidery twinkled like stars. Xerxes grasped a stately lotus blossom in one hand, his long gold sceptre in the other, but he was paying little attention to the activity around him.

Greece—Salamis—whose fault? Mechanically, he conducted business, greeted emissaries, rendered decisions. He neither knew nor cared what impression he gave today. He looked down the imperial aisle—

A figure—unheralded, unaccompanied, and—it was—it could not be—it was a *female* figure!

Memucan, standing nearest him, felt his scalp prickle. He whispered, "The queen, sire."

Silence settled over the hall.

Steadily the shining figure came on toward the king who seemed carved in stone. His enormous black eyes blazed under the angled brows.

Step by step the golden figure came. Afraid to turn their heads, the Immortals slanted their eyes toward the king. Any moment now, the order would come.

"Stop!"

The word resounded through the vast hall, bouncing from marble pavement to ceiling, curling around the horns of the huge bulls.

Esther stopped. She prostrated herself before the king. Fear hung in the heavy silence. Fear and royal fury.

A moment passed.

Another.

Death was a breath away.

A hissing sound came from the king; the lotus snapped.

As he stared at the huddle of gold before him, the pounding in his ears lessened a little. His queen! He had forgotten how beautiful she was. The minx, the audacious little minx!

Suddenly he threw back his head and roared. He laughed until the tears ran into his gold-trimmed beard.

Shaking with mirth, he held out the golden sceptre.

25

Cautiously, Esther raised her eyes. There it was, stretched out to her, the shining symbol of absolute power.

Two of the Immortals helped her, trembling, to her feet, and she advanced as far as the tall gold incense burners to touch the sceptre's end. Her eyes met the king's in an indescribable look: his, amused, tender, curious; hers, a searching look of love and questioning. Neither looked away.

"What is it, Queen Esther? What is your request? It is yours, even to half my kingdom."

Steadily she answered him, "If it pleases the king, let the king and—Haman come today to a banquet I have prepared."

Risking her life for a banquet? "Send for Haman," he ordered. "Bring him quickly."

"I have your permission to go, my lord Xerxes?"

The king retained his dignity, but his lips twitched. "As you did not have my permission to come, Queen Esther."

The court hummed; speculation raced. Of course, the palace knew Xerxes and the queen had not been together lately; the palace always knew these things. Most felt the queen's action was a ploy to get back in favor. But why Haman?

"That was a very shrewd move, I should think," said Shethar, dining later with a bemused Memucan.

"What makes you say that? If she is just trying to get back into the king's bed, what has Haman to do with it?"

"The queen may be young, but she is not stupid."

"She's naïve."

"*Was* naïve," corrected Shethar. "Five years have not been wasted on that young woman. She must realize how close Haman and the king have become. Do you really think she would risk her beautiful neck just to get back into the king's favor?"

Munching nuts, Memucan shrugged. "Women are strange creatures. She is madly in love with the king to begin with."

Shethar shook his head. "I think there is something else."

"If there is, she's playing a deep game."

How deep, Esther was beginning to realize as she went over final details with Hatak.

Was she demented? Inviting her archenemy here before her relationship with the king was healed? The idea which at first had seemed brilliant now seemed dangerous in the extreme. But time was running out; already her people were being persecuted. If the choice was between the devious Grand Vizier and herself, how dared she think the king would choose her? Her lord had replaced a queen once before, but Haman was not expendable. Could she outwit the Agagite? Could she control her face, her voice? Perhaps already he anticipated her plan. She felt transparent.

"The king, Your Majesty!"

Esther swept into one end of her banquet room as the throne-bearers came into the other. Her smile was brilliant, her manner all grace and charm.

Xerxes complimented her on the flowers massed everywhere, the marvelous fragrances that helped diffuse the heat. With the court graces she had been taught, she replied with small talk at first, inquiries as to the king's good health and his children's. The New Year celebration was discussed, the gifts, the buildings at Parsa. Only gradually would she dare lead into the main issue.

Haman was transported. No victory had ever been sweeter. As he listened to an amusing tale the queen was telling, he congratulated himself that he always got his way with women. The queen was clever; she had never shown that her defenses were crumbling. But what a delightful way this was of capitulating, of recognizing his power and position.

The king thought his queen had never looked lovelier, not even on her coronation day five years ago. The soft lights emphasized the startling eyes; the wine warmed the pallor of her skin. Her skill as a raconteur sparkled. Never had there been such a glorious woman! Haman was a fool.

Finally, he felt the preliminaries had gone on long enough. "And now what is this petition of yours, my queen? It is already granted." His eyes promised her everything. "Even to half my kingdom."

He needn't go as far as that, Haman thought waspishly. It was a polite court phrase, to be sure, but suppose she took him literally?

Almost forgetting the awful occasion that brought the king here, Esther found it delicious to be near him again; the familiar magic was at work. Now his abrupt question brought her back to reality.

"My petition? My request?" Her small smile was enigmatic, but her mind was paralyzed. She played for time. *Now? How do I say it?* As required in the king's presence, her right hand was wrapped in its long sleeve; unseen, her fist clenched.

"If I have found favor in the sight of the king," she began, and suddenly her head cleared and her voice steadied. "If it please the king to grant my petition and fulfill my request—"

Haman thought, It has something to do with me. She is going to ask for some new honor for me.

"Let the king and Haman come tomorrow to the banquet which I will prepare for them, and tomorrow I will do as the king has said." Her smile had just the right touch of mystery and mischief.

Tomorrow she will do what the king says! Xerxes chuckled to himself.

"The queen's pleasure is our command. Until tomorrow, Queen Esther."

The throne-bearers carried him from the room, followed by a puzzled but still elated Haman.

Esther slept heavily but not for long. Waking abruptly, her mind spun with the events of the past three days: the agonizing decision, the long fast, the approach to the king, the fear, the awesome silence. At the banquet of wine had she missed her one chance? Had she done anything to alert the Grand Vizier?

One of us will fall. I never should have postponed the issue. By tomorrow Haman could hear all sorts of rumors.

Suppose he heard the story of the Jewish prayers? Could she trust her servants? She hadn't liked the way the Grand Vizier looked at her today. What was he thinking? What did he know?

She considered alternative plans. Surely she could make a plea for her people, for the Jews, without admitting she was one of them. That was it! She would present herself as humane, concerned, anxious that no injustice be done in the kingdom.

Her own Jewishness rebuked her: *You're a coward, Hadassah! You*

200

cannot plead for your people and deny them at the same time. No, it was all or nothing.

But this was a world of men; how dare she think she could outwit the brilliant Haman? Was there a better plan? Another way? She longed for her father's advice but dared not send a message; the balance was too delicate, and Haman's spies were everywhere. No, the die was cast, and she certainly could not withdraw an invitation to the king.

What was Xerxes thinking? In the banquet hall, he had seemed again under her spell. But he had not sent for her tonight. Why?

And Haman? With his network of spies, his access to the king, what was he doing now? Her delay could be her death warrant.

Haman strutted from the palace in his peacock mood. Litter-bearers jumped; guards saluted smartly. As his bearers swung toward the King's Gate, Haman sat in a haze of exaltation. Grand Vizier of the empire—and now honored by the queen.

And tomorrow! Today, caught by surprise, he had not had time to dress properly, but tomorrow! He considered his wardrobe. That tailor of his, a skulking Jew but a superb craftsman—not even he could produce something suitable by tomorrow. Never mind—there was his multi-colored robe with the elephant-shaped bracteoles with real ivory tusks and emerald eyes. And Zeresh had given him a new fur-trimmed coat. The weather was warm for fur, but he pictured it slung carelessly over his shoulders, the sleeves hanging free.

They were passing the King's Gate where all prostrated themselves, quite properly. All except one. There was that detestable Jew, reading his tablets as if nothing had happened. After the edict, he should be cringing. Why wasn't he?

Lacking neither political astuteness nor a sense of timing, Haman kept his expression in public impassive, but at home his silence was ominous. The servants kept out of his way. Real trouble was brewing for someone.

Summoning his chief steward, Haman ordered a huge meal and the attendance of his closest friends.

"I have invited you here to share something very important." He studied each face in the wavering lights. Satisfied that he had their full attention, he went on, "You will not believe it, but I swear by Mithra that it is so."

People became alert. They loved court gossip, and Haman was obviously bursting.

"The queen gave a banquet of wine today for the king—"

Eyebrows went up. The queen back in favor?

"—and I was the only other man present!"

He allowed time for this to be absorbed.

"Quite extraordinary!"

"Without precedent!"

"But that's not all," said Haman smugly.

"More?"

"What now?"

"Tomorrow I am invited again! Tomorrow it will be a full banquet. And again, there will be just the Great King and myself."

Applause was loud and long with cries of, "Fortunate man! . . . This is only what you deserve! . . . You are appreciated in the palace! . . ."

Haman beamed and bowed. Then his mood changed. "It's hollow; it means nothing—"

"What? . . . Lord Haman! . . . What are you saying?"

"It's tasteless wine, unsalted food, just as long—" A rush of blood knotted the cords on his neck. He banged his fist on the table. "Just as long as I see Mordecai sitting in the King's Gate!" With each word his voice rose until, at the end, he was bellowing and the goblets and dishes were bouncing on the table. "I hate him! I hate him!"

The company was stunned.

"He's robbed me! He's poisoned my joy!"

"Softly, my lord," cautioned Zeresh, a strange look in her topaz eyes. "This gets us nowhere. We must think."

Everyone looked at her.

"I have a plan," she continued.

Haman was petulant; he did not like being interrupted. "What plan?"

"You are the Grand Vizier. No one but the Great King himself has the power you have. Deal with this in a grand manner; that will appeal to the king. He has no time for little men, and this way—"

"What way?"

"Build a gallows, fifty cubits high." She threw in this figure randomly.

"For Mordecai?"

"Of course, for Mordecai!"

"But I can't impose the death sentence!"

"No, but you will persuade the king to."

"With your position," one of his friends said, "and after this token of favor from the queen—"

"—and tomorrow's invitation."

"Build the gallows!" They were all talking at once.

"Go to the king early in the morning and get permission to hang Mordecai."

"Then go to the queen's banquet in good spirits."

"The king will approve. He will do anything you ask."

They were like children planning a party.

Haman considered, probing the scheme for weaknesses. "Fifty cubits? That's very high."

"It will be a warning of what happens to anyone who dares dishonor the greatest man in Susa. Greatest except the king, of course."

"Where could I build such a thing? People will ask questions."

Zeresh, more than anyone else, had grasped the situation fully. She saw that it was much more than a question of one man's lack of respect. If Mordecai could insult the Grand Vizier with impunity, Haman's power was not absolute and her own position was at risk.

"Why not set the gallows in our own courtyard? No one will dare ask what the Grand Vizier is doing on his own estate. They will think you are making some revolutionary architectural change."

"Build a fifty-cubit gallows in my own courtyard? Why, everyone in Susa will see it!"

"That," said Zeresh evenly, "is the point."

Haman began to understand. What an idea! Now he need not wait for the thirteenth Adar to deal with Mordecai. And this execution would add to the terror of all the Jews as they waited for the great day. The general populace would feel freer to torment them. Magnificent!

"I will do it!" He sent for the chief steward. "Get me workmen—at once. I want a gallows—a strong, well-constructed one—set up in my courtyard. It is to be fifty cubits high."

"My lord! How—"

"How they manage to build it is no affair of mine, but it is to be ready, without fail, by tomorrow morning. They will work all night, of course."

His guests cheered loudly, and the drinking continued.

Zeresh looked like a very sleek cat.

26

Meanwhile, the King of All Peoples was having a sleepless night. He wanted Esther, but held back. Was Haman right? *Did* she twist people to her point of view?

Angru Manyu! but she was magnificent today. What courage, what spirit! And she was still the most beautiful woman alive. He had hardly had a night of real happiness since she was last with him. But was she sincere? Damnation! What did that matter in bed? He wanted her!

He lifted himself on an elbow to call Harbonah, then stopped. Haman's words came back: "I was slow to realize that I was beginning to look ridiculous to my colleagues."

But had Esther made him look foolish? Would she? He recalled the clarity of her look as they sat at the table today.

She is completely loyal. I cannot believe—

Haman again: "People became thoroughly devoted to her and would obey her slightest whim." Was she playing the ancient harem game? His queen? But kings had been duped before.

He found himself sweating. Haman was clever; he had proved himself a loyal friend. Or had he?

Suppose Haman had his own reasons for turning him against Esther? For one mad moment Xerxes wondered if Haman had designs on the queen himself. No. Haman would not dare lift his eyes that far. Whom to trust—his queen or his Grand Vizier?

He paced the room, tore the bedclothes from the great bed and demanded fresh ones. Harbonah, distracted, made suggestions.

"More wine, Your Majesty?

"Tcah!"

"A woman, surely?"

"I am tired of these girls. One is just like another."

"Perhaps the lovely Greek?"

"She is dull."

"The Lydian?"

"Stupid."

"Magrana, the—"

"Hopeless."

Harbonah wavered, caught between his concern for his king and his jealousy which had rejoiced in Esther's alienation. His loyalty won. "The queen, sire?"

It was the queen he wanted. He would send for her. But—

"No, Harbonah, not tonight." Their first night after such a long separation must be unique; tonight he was too restless, too racked with uncertainty. "Curse everything and everyone to Ahriman's realm! Why can't I sleep, Harbonah?"

"Might I suggest, sire—"

"Suggest *something!*"

"Let the Book of Daily Events be brought and read to the king."

Xerxes snorted. "That should be boring enough at this hour! All right, Harbonah, send for the chronicles, and scribes to read them. If anything can lull me to sleep, that should." Xerxes settled himself on the freshly made bed.

Two sleepy scribes came in carrying tablets.

"Where shall I begin, great king?" asked the first scribe.

"It doesn't matter—just so it's not too recent."

The scribe began reading detail after detail of palace life and court procedure. The droning was just beginning to make Xerxes drowsy when he heard, "This plot to kill the king, even the plot of Bigthan and Teresh, two of the king's chamberlains, Keepers of the Door, was discovered and reported by one Mordecai—"

Xerxes was wide-awake. "Read that again."

The scribe complied.

"Parsa! Those traitors! And Mordecai? What did we do to reward him?"

"Nothing is recorded, sire."

"Are you sure?"

The other scribe peered carefully over the first's shoulder; he shook his head. "No, Your Majesty, there was no reward made to this man."

"A disgrace!" The king was out of bed again. "My honor is at stake. We Achaemenids reward anything done for us—anything at all. This man saved *my life!* I must attend to this at once."

Dawn was filtering around the edges of the thick curtains. "Who is in the outer court, Harbonah?"

Harbonah looked and returned, masking his displeasure. "The Grand Vizier, sire."

"Haman? At this hour?" The king scratched his beard. Perhaps he could kill two stags with one arrow. Was Haman loyal or wasn't he? Why hadn't *he* told him that Mordecai was unrewarded? Such things were his business.

"Admit him."

Mordecai had considered his own position carefully: the decree had gone out and nothing could change it. Unless Hadassah's plea to the king worked a miracle, the Jews were doomed. As a leader among his people, he would encourage them by silent protest. Never give up, his posture in the King's Gate said; never give in.

Nevertheless, he could not keep his mind on his work that morning. He had all the proper tablets in front of him, but he did not see them. He was a deeply worried man. Yesterday was the third day—the fateful day when Hadassah had promised to go to the king. But the day had come and gone with no word. Mordecai became a plague at the door of the queen's house. Hatak, his ally, could not be reached; the house seemed to be full of scurryings hither and yon, yet he learned nothing.

Was Hadassah imprisoned? Deposed? Was she already dead?

Haman's attitude yesterday as he had come from the direction of the Queen's House haunted him. What had he been doing there?

Now, a great deal of noise came from the direction of Haman's house. What was that enormous shaft reaching above the housetops?

She had failed! Haman had won! And that spike—what would they do to her on that spike? "O Adonai," he prayed, "hear me: If she is to die, let her die quickly."

One of the clay tablets fell to the tiled floor, and the shards scattered. Some of his colleagues looked up.

"Lord Mordecai!"

"Look at him! He looks like death."

Then they heard the sound of hoofbeats. Tossing his great white head, the sun glinting on the gold interwoven in his carefully dressed mane and tail, the beautiful Jabor from the royal stables was coming their way. He wore a small gold crown on his head. Alongside the riderless

206

horse walked the Grand Vizier of the empire carrying garments that were unmistakably the king's.

Mordecai's head came up sharply. Here came the victor. What had he done to Hadassah? And what, he wondered, of their people now? He made himself stand erect, hold his head proudly. Haman continued to come forward, alone. Where was his guard of honor, his own horse? He did not even have a weapon.

Then Mordecai became aware of the great line of Immortals closing in toward them.

Haman, carefully groomed, had arrived as early as possible to petition the king. The gallows was nearing completion, pointing straight for the sky, the new-peeled wood shining in the first shafts of the sun. All that was needed was the king's permission to execute the Jew. He had been admitted to the Presence at once—a good omen.

Smiling he presented himself before Xerxes, his hand touching his lips.

"Good morning, Lord Haman. You are here early."

"If it please the king, I am happy in the honor given me yesterday and today. I am ready to do whatever the Great King requests."

"Good. I need an idea from that fertile brain of yours."

Haman was chafing to proceed with his request, but that must wait. "Anything I have is at your disposal, Majesty."

"What do you think should be done to the man whom the king delights to honor?"

I knew it! The queen's pleasure has opened every door to me. What shall I choose? What will give me the final accolade? I have it!

"May the king live forever. For the man whom the king delights to honor, let them bring a royal robe which the king has worn—"

Xerxes' look sharpened.

"—and the horse which the king has ridden, and on whose head a royal crown is set. Let the robe and the horse be handed over to one of the king's most noble princes; let him array the man and conduct him on horseback through the open square of the city, proclaiming, 'Thus shall it be done to the man whom the king delights to honor.'"

In the courtyard Haman spoke to the great horse, who stood still. He then held out the robe of the true scarlet that only kings wore. Mordecai recognized that particular robe: Xerxes had worn it at Esther's coronation. Grimly, Haman draped it around Mordecai's shoulders.

"By order of the Great King." He could hardly get the words out. He gestured toward the horse. "Mount."

The courtiers gaped.

Mordecai tried to make sense of what was happening. If this was a punishment exquisitely styled by Xerxes and the Grand Vizier, it had no precedent.

Beyond all speech, Haman gestured once more toward Jabor. Mordecai, moving like one marching to his death, mounted. Then, to the amazement of the gathering crowd of courtiers, Haman took the reins and began to lead the horse. He opened his mouth. Everyone strained to hear, hoping for an explanation of these strange events. No sound came. He tried again. "Thus shall it be done—"

He braced his shoulders and called out loudly: "Thus shall it be done to the man whom the king delights to honor."

Mordecai could not believe what he heard. To honor? Him? A charade, that's what it was. First, he would be humiliated, then— But, no, if this were Haman's scheme, he would never assign himself the role he was playing.

They headed out the gate and down the grand staircase into the city's square. A fresh detachment of Immortals had quietly lined up along the staircase and down the road.

"Louder!" snapped the captain to Haman. "By the Great King's order."

People were running now; the news traveled.

"Thus shall it be done to the man whom the king delights to honor!"

Ripples of laughter began and swelled. Men ran to their houses with the news; people appeared on the housetops. Cheers of "Mordecai! Mordecai! Praise to Lord Mordecai!" built a crescendo of acclaim.

"Thus shall it be done—"

"Long live Mordecai!" In the crowds and on the rooftops were many of Mordecai's Jewish friends.

"Thus shall it be done to the man whom the king delights to honor."

Two hours later, Haman, tired, dusty, and demoralized, brought Mordecai back to the King's Gate. Mordecai had said nothing the entire time. Now, dismounting, he took off the gorgeous robe, silently handing it back to Haman, who had no choice but to take it and move off with the horse. Moments later Haman was seen hurrying through the courtyard, his face completely covered by a thick veil.

Mordecai watched him go. What did all this mean? Xerxes was indeed a strange man. He wondered if this could possibly have anything to do with the assassination plot. But that was long ago. Why now? Besides, what did it matter? What mattered was Hadassah. What had happened to her? Fearfully, he looked toward Haman's house. Whatever was being built there was finished.

Haman's friends, having seen his degradation, flocked to his house—some to commiserate, others to gloat. White and shocked, Zeresh met him at the door.

"All Susa saw me, all Susa!"

The practical Zeresh was trying to get things straight in her mind. What did this mean? Haman, Grand Vizier of the empire, humiliated by the king in such a way? Xerxes made rulers and deposed them. He was capricious. But such a reversal to the man second only to himself? She picked away at the threads of the problem.

"What have you done?" she asked sharply. "What stupid thing have you done to get yourself out of favor with the king so suddenly?"

In all honesty, Haman could only shake his head. "I know of absolutely nothing."

"There must be something. Think!"

Haman was too distraught to think.

"Why was it Mordecai he honored?"

"The king did not say."

Down Haman, up Mordecai? Zeresh's unease increased. The auguries this morning had not been good.

"Haman!" There was fear in her voice. She remembered the edict. "If this man is a Jew before whom you have begun to fall, you will not prevail against him. You are finished."

Haman's face told her she had flicked him on the raw. *Mordecai a Jew? Why hadn't he told her?* All the stories she had ever heard of the ancient enmity between Haman's ancestors and the Jews, of the might of the mysterious God of the Israelites, came flooding into her mind. What if the auguries were predicting her husband's downfall? Mentally she prepared her private escape route.

Before Haman could answer, there was an imperious summons: "The king's eunuchs to escort Lord Haman to Queen Esther's banquet."

After the astounding events of the morning, Mordecai went home, a very troubled man. Later, he sent for his servant Shirik.

"Go up to the citadel. I don't want to be seen there just now. Watch Haman's house, and if you see him leave, report back to me."

Some time later Shirik returned. "The king's eunuchs came to Haman's house and escorted him to the queen's house, my lord."

No word from Hadassah, the mysterious events of the morning, that sinister shaft in Haman's courtyard, and now the Grand Vizier escorted to the Queen's House. . . . He could think of only one thing: Hadassah must be dead.

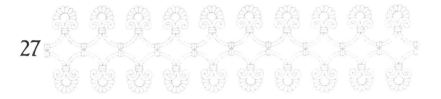

27

This is some strange dream, Haman thought. The same scene, the same players—the king, the queen, and himself—in the same room with the same gold service, the same servants, even the queen's same shining robe. He looked sharply from face to face but could read nothing. The king had welcomed him warmly enough; the queen's manner was, if anything, even less restrained than yesterday. He relaxed. Upset by the experiences of the morning, he was now reassured. This morning must have been one of the king's jests, and he must accept it as it was intended.

In the sunlight slanting through the interstices, the floating motes turned to gold while a stray wasp buzzed angrily before a slave crushed it. The royal pair did their verbal ceremonial dance toward the central question, and Haman exerted himself to be charming. Finally, Xerxes asked yesterday's questions in the same half-serious, half-teasing manner.

"What is your petition, Queen Esther? It is yours. Even to half of my kingdom."

Esther hesitated. *Very soon I shall know. Before that bar of light moves a finger's breadth, my life could be gone like that wasp's.*

Her mind went back to her first frightened day in the harem when Chersis had told her to come when the sunlight had moved a certain space. Six years ago! Another lifetime. Then a protected innocent, fearing the unknown, she was now an experienced woman, wife of this all-powerful man at the table. Was she also perhaps the pawn of the courtier opposite?

She studied Haman. The gaudy attire, worth more than some satrapies, the king's own ring flashing on his finger underscored just who this man was with whom she matched wits.

The king was growing impatient. Time had run out.

"If I have found favor in your sight, O King, and if it please the king—"

Xerxes waited out the formal courtesies.

The next words fell like small stones: "Let my life be given me at my petition—"

"Your *life?*"

"—and my people at my request."

Haman's mind was flopping about like a hooked fish. *What is she saying?*

"We are sold, I and my people, to be destroyed, to be slain, to be annihilated—"

The room became charged with fear, confusion, suspicion. Xerxes was speechless. His eyes bored into Esther's.

"—if we had been sold merely as slaves, I would have held my peace, even though the enemy would not be able to make up to the king the great financial loss."

In the warm, gilded room, Haman felt cold.

Thoroughly confused, Xerxes caught hold of the one idea clear to him: *Someone has threatened my queen.*

"Who? He? This one? And where? This one? He? Who has filled his heart to do this?" He was inarticulate with fury.

Facing her moment of truth, Esther spoke clearly. "An arch enemy, my lord, has done this." All fear left her. Looking at the rigid figure of the second greatest man in the kingdom, she knew such a sense of outrage at the injustice to her people, at the cruelty and cunning of the man, that her vision blurred. She lifted her arm and pointed, court etiquette burned up in the heat of the moment. "This man! This wicked Haman!"

Xerxes looked at his queen in shocked disbelief. As the import of what she had said filtered into his mind, his eyes moved to Haman. The appalling realization that the queen was herself a Jewess had pushed the Grand Vizier down into his chair; he seemed shrunken, skin taut over his cheekbones, eyes glazed with fear.

With a roar of profanity, Xerxes moved from the throne and swept into the garden, pushing aside two attendants who prepared to accompany him.

Haman? His trusted confidant, the man he had raised from nothing —*he* had done this? Done what? What was it he had done? *Am I a dog, a child, a fool? He has duped me. But how? And what has the queen to do with all this?* What could Haman hope to accomplish by a plot against the queen and her people? And who *were* her people? Xerxes realized he did not know who they were; it had never mattered.

"Destroyed . . . slain . . . annihilated. . . ." The queen's words sounded too extreme to believe. Was this some female trick? No, there was Haman's terror; she had uncovered something.

The edict! He stopped pacing. Haman coming only days ago with that story of a people who did not keep his laws, giving Haman his ring, telling him to deal with them as he thought best. Could it be? Angru Manyu!

"Harbonah!"

Uneasily the head eunuch came into the garden.

"That edict that went out three or four days ago?"

"Yes, sire?"

"It dealt with some small, odd group of people, isn't that so? Well, *isn't* it? Answer me!"

"It dealt with— with the Jews, Majesty." Harbonah could not understand why the king was asking about something *he* had authorized.

"*The Jews!* He said nothing about Jews!"

Treachery on treachery! Jews? There were thousands of them, hundreds in Susa alone. His bankers! His merchants! His most brilliant professional men!

"Bring me a copy of that edict this instant."

Harbonah bowed and ran. He came back with a scribe carrying a parchment.

"Read it!" thundered the king.

". . . destroyed . . . slain . . . annihilated. . . ." The queen's words!

So that was where Haman was going to get the money to pay ten thousand talents into the treasury! The Jews!

He began pacing again. How should he deal with this? No ordinary methods would do. The Persian law applying to someone in Haman's high position stated that even the Great King could not execute a man with only one charge against him; a second charge would be needed. A second charge before he could execute the lofty Grand Vizier. Damnation!

And my Esther! He would dare kill my queen! He strode back to the doorway.

In the dining hall, Haman had discarded all sham, all dignity. He had seen his sentence in the king's face; he knew it was not if, but only when and how. Unless—

He threw himself on the floor by the queen's dining couch. "My queen! Majesty! Save me! Have mercy! I did not know—believe me, I never dreamed—"

Her people's tormentor appealing to *her* to save his life! The queen looked at him with revulsion.

He scrambled up from the floor. "Majesty, please listen! You must help me. The king—"

The compelling eyes had no effect on the queen. She said nothing. Less sure than he about what the king was deciding out in the garden, she knew that her enemy was conceding defeat. But the judge had given no verdict, and should Haman recover from this attack, his vengeance would be implacable.

Forgetting everything but his fear, the Grand Vizier flung himself across the royal couch.

At that moment the king entered the banquet hall.

He took in the whole ugly tableau, frozen perhaps for the time of two breaths. Far too astute to misunderstand the motive for Haman's mad action, he saw what he needed. Here was his second charge! In a terrible voice, he roared, "Will he even assault the queen in my presence, in my own house?"

As the words left the king's mouth, the eunuchs moved forward and covered Haman's face.

Xerxes did not move.

Harbonah, small eyes bright with malice, spoke up. "O king, live forever—"

"Yes?" The king's eyes were on the departing Haman.

"The gallows, fifty cubits high, that Haman has made—it is in the courtyard of his own house—"

Xerxes looked at Harbonah then.

"He made it for the Lord Mordecai, who saved the king's life."

"Hang him on it!"

By the time the king's officers arrived at Haman's house with the doomed man, there was no one left inside the walls. Haman wondered where everyone was, how they could have heard the news so quickly. Then, under the death-covering, his mouth twisted in a grimace acknowledging the thoroughness of his own spy system. The news of his downfall had preceded him by time enough for his devoted family to run for their lives.

At the gallows, he knew a moment's desperate fear as the executioner removed the head cloth and slipped the noose around his neck.

And then he laughed.

"I've won!" he shouted. "I've done what no other man could do. I die, but all the Jews will also die. The royal edict can't be changed!"

Some premonition of disaster had made Zeresh keep the eunuch's disguise that had served her when Shishia died. Putting it on, emptying her jewels into a ragged pouch, she sighed. "You do not have good fortune with your men," she told her reflection in the mirror, and ran quickly down the rear staircase. Everyone else had fled.

Haman? No one but a fool gets caught, she thought. His ten sons had melted into the maze of Susian streets; where they went she neither knew nor cared. Let them get on with their many talents!

Outside the city gates, she turned for a last look at what had been her home. Swinging from the tall post above her garden was a form whose shape she knew well. She invoked Astarte and went on.

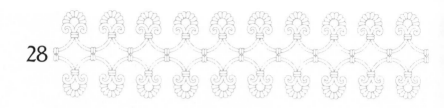

28

The Seven called a council meeting. Memucan took off his soft felt hat and sighed. "I still don't understand; too much has happened too fast."

Shethar nodded agreement. "First, we have the Grand Vizier leading Mordecai about—"

"Did you see Haman's face?" grinned Tarshish.

"It's not right," said Marsena solemnly, "to make fun of the dead." He was very pale.

"You're right, of course, Marsena. My apologies."

"—but then Haman is seen being escorted to the queen's house, and the next thing we know he's being marched to his death!"

If the king had so summarily executed his favorite, what was their own standing?

"Were Haman's sons executed too?" Meres asked.

"The report from the commander of the execution says they have all escaped and gone into hiding. Of course, the warrant is out for their arrest."

"What could have happened in the queen's house?" worried Shethar.

"The slaves who were in attendance have all been sent away; the palace is crawling with rumors, of course, but no one knows anything."

"Harbonah knows."

"Of course, he knows. He looks like a pet leopard who's just eaten a lamb. But you can wager your last shekel he won't say anything."

"Apparently the king has commanded complete secrecy."

Standing by a window, Memucan clicked his tongue. "Our newly honored friend is bound for the palace."

"Who?"

"Mordecai, escorted by two of the Immortals."

Shethar was thoughtful. "You don't suppose Haman's death is related in some way to the edict to kill all the Jews?"

"It's not possible. Although it's true the king was always friendly with the Jews until he issued that edict."

"That edict was Haman's dirty scheme."

"We've agreed on that, but it *did* go out under the king's own seal."

"Stamped by Haman!"

Memucan had something on his mind. "Suppose he did not tell the king that the edict was to be against the Jews?"

"That's preposterous," said Shethar. "You don't think for a moment the king would allow Haman to put out an edict to kill people he hadn't even named?"

"But keep in mind," Meres said, "Haman's influence over the king was hypnotic."

"It wasn't only the king. His effect on many people was inexplicable. He reminded me of one of those men who charm snakes."

"Memucan, you may be on the right scent at that," said Shethar. "It makes more sense if Haman duped the king into thinking it was some few rebellious outlaws he was putting down."

"Do you really think Xerxes would accept such a harebrained scheme?"

"It's no more odd than a lot of things he's been doing lately. The king hasn't been himself; he's gloomy, introspective, strange."

"He's never been himself since the Greek campaign."

"The Greek campaign! That was six years ago! He has always been temperamental."

"Temperamental, yes. But haven't you noticed how indifferent he has been during audiences lately?"

"He's certainly on the horns of a dilemma now: he's given Mordecai the Jew outstanding recognition, and now he finds himself committed to a Jewish slaughter!"

Memucan's eyes were slits. "If the rumor that reached me this afternoon has any truth in it, things are worse than that." He beckoned them closer. "The rumor is that the queen herself is a Jewess!"

Xerxes had sent for Mordecai. After Haman's betrayal, whom could he trust? The Seven? His confused mind fancied that they, too, might plot against him. All he was sure of was Esther's loyalty and that of the Jew who had once saved his life.

Mordecai arrived, looking puzzled. He expressed appropriate appreciation to the king for the honors bestowed on him that morning.

"The queen tells me you are her foster father."

"I have that privilege, sire."

"And you did not try to capitalize on it when she became queen; that's most unusual. I like that in you, Lord Mordecai."

For a while he said nothing more. Then, "Well, Lord Mordecai, it would seem you are now my father-in-law!"

"A very great honor, Majesty."

So far, the king was almost too normal. The cataclysmic events of the past few hours might not have happened. He spoke of various state matters. Haman was not mentioned.

Then the king's manner became confidential. "It's a strange thing, Lord Mordecai, to completely trust one person and then be betrayed. It has not happened many times in my lifetime. I chose Haman; I trained him; I gave him enormous power. I even placed him over my own Seven— Is it true that you never bowed to him?"

Recognizing what he risked, Mordecai said, "Never, sire."

"An astute man!" The king drummed his fingers on the shining armrest. "I created an office just for him, made him my Grand Vizier, and he betrayed me. Me, Xerxes, King of All Peoples." His color was rising.

Mordecai felt a twinge of fear; an angry Achaemenid was dangerous.

"I have given Haman's estates to my queen; she wants you to administrate them."

"Sire—" Mordecai started to protest. All too recently he had seen how a sudden rise in royal favor could end.

The king was not listening. He reached for his ring, the royal seal confiscated from the condemned Haman.

"You," he whispered, not taking his eyes from Mordecai, "you will be my new Grand Vizier."

"Majesty! I beg you—" Mordecai was shocked. The body of the previous Grand Vizier was hardly cold; he himself was a Jew under sentence of death. Ambitious he certainly was, but he had a keen sense of propriety as well as survival. "The Seven, sire—"

"The Seven are my oldest friends. I rely on them for advice; they carry out many duties. But I learned from—from Haman that I need a Grand Vizier." His eyes were strange. "*You* will be that Grand Vizier."

He put the ring on Mordecai's finger.

Was this legal? Was it even sane? Mordecai wondered. Considering Haman's fate, did he want the position? On the other hand, could it be the answer to the problem of the edict? But surely there should be witnesses!

Xerxes had thought of that. "Harbonah! Get the Seven here at once."

When the king's councilors had filed in and properly greeted Xerxes, he announced what he was doing.

"My lord king—!" Memucan dared to start.

Xerxes held up his hand. Unnaturally quiet, very controlled, he showed none of the hysterical excitement that had been evident at Haman's promotion.

"My lords, Mordecai is my father-in-law."

There were audible sounds of surprise, shock, disbelief.

"He has served us for many years; he is competent; he is loyal. In fact, because of him I am alive today. Surely you have not forgotten the plot of Bigthan and Teresh." He looked at each one with a bemused expression. It was as if he knew something they did not. "We will say no more of this now. The matter is settled."

As Mordecai left the king's presence, he felt his colleagues' displeasure. Holding power beyond his dreams, he knew he should feel elated. But he was under no illusion as to that power's temporary quality. Unless he found some way around the authorized massacre of all Jews, he had less than eleven months in which to live. And in subtle ways those months could be made very difficult by the envious Seven.

A sense of discouragement weighed on him. What had been accomplished was only a breathing space. Haman was dead, his house and lands confiscated and given to the queen, but his ten powerful sons were alive. Mordecai knew human nature too well to expect them to do nothing, wherever they were. No doubt Haman's spy network had rents in it, but the empire had hundreds of ambitious men more than willing to despoil Jews. Haman had seeded his plans carefully.

And there was still the edict; the *king's* seal had gone with that proclamation. Haman's death had not affected the terrible fate of the Jews.

And what of Hadassah? How, exactly, was the king going to escape the decree that *all* Jews were to be killed?

Left alone, Xerxes sat on his throne and stared at the floor. All the day's events swirled round him at last. The sleepless night, Mordecai's honors, the queen's astounding revelation, Haman's treachery, the real meaning of the edict. A mist formed in front of his eyes; it was like

Salamis. Dismayed, defeated, he had sat on a throne then, too, with chaos boiling below. A failure in judgment, Salamis. Someone's. Whose? The cries of his brothers—

"Mardonios!"

Harbonah rushed in. The king looked at him without seeing him at all.

And Vashti! Another failure in judgment. He had lost Vashti. Who caused that? The Seven. It was their advice. Her brittle laughter came back to him, her looks, her loving—

"Traitress," he murmured.

And now today. Haman, the clever man he had made his Grand Vizier, the man who understood him, who gave him such rich presents—!

He began laughing strangely. "Presents, Harbonah. He gave me presents. And all the time he was selling out my kingdom behind my back. That treacherous, lying Agagite!" He was shouting; then his voice became almost a whisper. "I killed him, didn't I, Harbonah?"

"He is dead, my lord king."

"Good, good." He gripped the arms of his throne. "He betrayed me, Harbonah." His speech was slower. There was sadness now. "Betrayed me. I gave him wealth, jewels, women, power. I gave him my trust." His eyes were dull and unfocused.

"And my beloved Star is a Jewess, Harbonah. You heard. What am I to do? This edict—I can't annul it. The queen— my father-in-law— Tell me." His mouth was slack, drooping a little to one side. "Tell me what to do."

"Your Majesty! You must get some rest."

"But the edict, Har—Har-bo-nah!"

"The edict is eleven months away, sire. Now you must rest so that you can think clearly tomorrow. Permit us to take you to your bed."

"Bed. Yes, Harbonah, bed." A faint, senile smile flickered and was gone.

The slaves carried him, still mumbling, to his sleeping apartments.

He did not leave them for two months.

29

For the little group of Jews escaping in the caravan, the journey to the border was long and frightening. They traveled as much as possible in the dark for safety and coolness. The days were gehenna; sometimes there was shelter, but along the great gulf they found long stretches of territory with none. Time after time, under the reeking hides, they gripped one another fearfully as the wagon was stopped and the toothless driver queried They bumped their hideous way across rocky roads in heat, sand, and gales.

David, in his disguise, was the one to go into the villages for provisions. He came back with stories he felt he could share only with Jakob.

"I saw them kick an old Jew today," he whispered. "And they spat on his wife. And two Jewish shops were burned."

When they finally reached the Arabian border, it was decided that Rabos would present himself at the satrap's palace and request audience.

Durakka, the satrap, having looked speculatively at the Jewish merchant, sent all his attendants from the room. A crooked man himself, he had the contempt of the devious for an honest man.

"You understand what I risk if I let you go through into that part of Arabia? I could lose my position. I have power, riches, a beautiful wife; I could lose them all, just for you."

Might it perhaps be worth the risk, he asked himself? After all, this man's bribe might end his wife's nagging for that necklace and bracelet she had seen in the jeweler's shop.

"How many people did you say?"

"Six."

"Six!" He clutched his brow dramatically. "That is asking a very great favor." He waited.

Rabos said, "I have hundreds of siglots. Even some darics. And many jewels. They're all yours if you give us safe conduct over the border."

Durakka put on a show of wrestling with his conscience.

"Very well." He called for a scribe. "I will give you six safe-conducts to cross the border, and you will give me everything you have."

Tears ran down the Jew's face. "My friend, you will never know—"

"Never mind," said Durakka, crisply, "I do not need to know. And don't call me friend any more; it's not safe, these days." He handed him the passes. "On your way, before I change my mind. My court treasurer will go with you."

Assessing the situation, the treasurer pushed Rabos aside and led the way from the room.

The Jews pressed their way through the crowded barrier. Their appearance was strange, and the transfer of the treasure to the satrap's cart had made their position clear. Jeers, ribald songs, and loud laughter followed them. Some of the hangers-on threw rotting vegetables.

But at last they were away from the gate, away from people. Ahead stretched the road to their freedom.

"Adonai is good," sighed Rachel. "We will find a good new life in this country. You will see, children. How much further do we have to go?"

"A day's journey more."

"We can survive that even in this heat."

They went on. Able now to travel openly, they had cast aside the revolting hides. This meant no protection from the glaring sun, but anything was better than riding below putrefaction.

When they reached the oasis near the town of Naktis, Rabos took his documents to Irtanka, ruler of that city. He came back smiling. "He says we are to wait here. He will send for us when he has the proper place prepared for us."

They slept peacefully that night, not hearing the sound of rapid hoofbeats traveling back the way they had come.

Irtanka's courier arrived at Durakka's palace the next morning. He presented his credentials and by afternoon was admitted to the satrap's presence.

"My master sends you greetings, my lord."

A slave handed the clay tablet to Durakka who could not read but could not bear to have anyone know it. He scanned the tablet carefully, then handed it to his scribe. "Read it aloud so that all can hear this interesting message."

The scribe read: "To the most revered satrap of Arabia, Irtanka sends greetings. What is this, my friend and cousin, that you have sent me? An impoverished family under the death sentence in your country? The man Rabos tells me he paid you well. Surely, you do not anticipate that I go unrewarded? If I do not hear from you, cousin, by the return of this messenger, I shall do what you would do under the circumstances: I shall send them all back to you. Greetings to your beautiful wife."

Durakka was thoughtful. What should he do? Give up some of the gold? Hardly. He chewed at his moustache. Suddenly he saw the answer. What a way to prove his loyalty to the Crown and keep the fortune!

"Tell your lord to send those people back here and give him my apologies. It was thoughtless of me to try to saddle him with them; we shall deal with our own problems."

At the oasis the family had become a spectacle. Children came in droves, dragging their toys, pulling at the hands of parents. Travelers stopped and pointed and laughed. Sensing an opportunity, fruit vendors set up small stands in the shade and hawked their wares.

"Jews, that's what they are."

"I hear they don't want Jews in the Persian empire any more. Why should we have them here?"

"They're all to be killed on the thirteenth Adar."

"Killed? Well, then, let's have some real fun."

Rabos was afraid. Why the long delay? Surely there were houses enough in this city. Surely his connection with Durakka and the vast amount of treasure had been sufficient to insure quicker action.

The mood of the crowd was getting ugly when the governor's courier rode up.

"Now," said Rachel, "at last." Rabos got to his feet, noticing that the man was followed by a contingent of armed men.

"How nice," said Rachel. "The governor has sent an escort."

The commander stopped. "Out!" He pointed to the road that led back to the border.

"I—I beg your pardon," stammered Rabos. "I don't understand. We have safe-conducts; I am the friend of Durakka, satrap of Arabia."

"I know quite well who you are. You are not in Durakka's territory now. This land is ruled by Irtanka, and he says— Out!"

"But there has to be some mistake. I saw him only two days ago. He said then—"

"Today is today, and today he says you are to leave and never return."

"But we cannot leave; we'll be killed."

"What happens to you is none of my business. I am carrying out orders. Back to the border, both of you."

"But our children," Rachel broke in, "they are in the town, in Naktis, looking at the shops and—"

"You do not seem to understand," said the commander. "If you do not leave this place and go back through the barrier to Durakka's territory at once, I have orders to kill you. And my contingent will follow you all the way to the barrier. On your way, Jews!"

Rachel, beyond tears, began picking up things and putting them in the cart. Rabos hitched up the mules.

"Go, Rabos, and fetch our young people."

"There is no time, woman," said the commander. "We will deal with them when we find them."

Rachel swung on him. "You would separate families, just like that?"

"Just like that." He spat in the dust at her feet. "Move. The others can follow."

"How? They have no transport."

"They have legs, haven't they?"

The crowd, watching in silence, now released its tension in laughter and jeered in earnest.

Slowly the cart with its solid wood wheels was turned around and headed northward, while Rachel kept looking back over her shoulder and calling, "David . . . Jakob . . . Ruth . . . Judith! —Jakob . . . my son!"

At sundown the oasis was filling with travelers and caravans drawing up for water, camels mumbling to themselves, people settling in for the night.

"They were right here!" Jakob said, coming up to the oasis.

"No, you dolt, they were over there."

"Well, they're not in either place now. Where can they have gone?"

"The governor has probably sent for them; perhaps they have left us a message."

They asked a family nearby who had just arrived, but these people spoke no Aramaic and merely shrugged. The young people went to another caravan.

"You know who we are talking about. Remember? You were here when we arrived."

"Yes," the man said.

"Then you must have seen our family leave. Which way did they go?"

224

Silently, the man pointed northward.

"That way? Oh, no, you must be mistaken. The city is the other way."

"They went that way, under guard."

"You mean an escort."

The man sighed. He was a kind man, and the whole episode with the Jewish family had upset him. "No, my son, I'm sorry. They went under guard back to the border."

"Back to— But that's impossible; they wouldn't do that. They will be killed."

"That's what your father said. They wanted to wait for you, but they were forced to leave."

At last, realizing they were homeless, moneyless, and horseless, Jakob said, "Sir, we have nothing at all to offer you, but we will have something one day. Can you trust us with a mule? Please?"

"You ask for a fortune, young man. Besides, what you ask is not possible. I have only two mules to draw my whole family, and we have many parasangs to go. I am sorry for you, but I can do nothing."

"In that case," David said shortly, "we shall walk."

It took them two days to reach the barrier. When they could see it in the distance, they sat down to plan.

"Since I'm the oldest," said David, "I will go to the barrier and see what I can find out. They won't remember me, and I look more like an Arabian than the rest of you."

Humming, for his own sake as well as theirs, he strode off through the dust to the barrier. They watched till they saw him go through the gateway.

After a long time they saw him coming back down the road and ran to meet him.

"David! What's the matter? What did they say?"

He stumbled to the ground.

"David," Jakob shook him, "we have to know."

"I was taken to the other side of the barrier, and—there they were."

"Fine. We'll get them out somehow."

"No— how can I tell you—?"

"David! Are they dead?"

"Both dead. They were let through the barrier, and your father asked to see the satrap. A crowd gathered and pointed to the edict posted on the gate. It seems there's been a great change since we left Susa: Jews trying to get away, lots of anti-Jewish feeling, plotting to get our lands, wives, daughters—"

"So the people—?" Ruth's question was a whisper.

"They mobbed them, tied them to the cart, and—set it on fire."

The four clung to each other and wept.

All David's doubts rode him now. *Adonai, where are you now? Two godly Jews dead. Their children left to starve. What kind of God are you? What do you want of us?*

Abruptly he said, "There is no more time for tears. We must get away from here as soon as possible."

"Where can we go?"

"You'll all stay in hiding. I'm going to Susa for help."

Ruth stared. A boy she loved had walked to that barrier; a stranger had returned.

"Jakob, you must take charge of the girls."

His friend protested.

"Jakob, I must go fast and hard and alone. Someone must stay to protect the girls. Find some kind of shelter for them."

"Food?"

"Forage for it, hunt it, steal it. We are facing a far worse situation than any of us realized. The thirteenth Adar is ten months away, but people are not going to wait till then to start trouble. I will try to get help."

He pulled Ruth to him and looked at her a long time. Such a different look than the first time they had really looked at one another, outside her home in Susa. Harsh lines around his mouth softened. "I love you, Ruth. I pledge you my life. I'll find some way for you to have safety and freedom." He kissed her.

"We'll pray for you, David."

"It's too late for that!" He turned and left them.

Jews, Haman's last directive had stated, *are no longer part of the empire; they seek your women, your positions, your wealth.* The propaganda affected even those previously tolerant. Perplexed by the edict, torn between normal compassion and fear, many simply cooled toward their Jewish neighbors and took their business elsewhere. As for the naturally greedy and those who always had had an anti-Jewish bias, they now had sanction to express these feelings. The Jews owned fruit groves, shops of all sorts, banks—rich plums ripening for the inevitable plucking.

Secretly, Haman's directive went on, *they are plotting against the Great*

King. Then why postpone the day of reckoning for eleven months? Only a few knew how Haman had depended on omens. The delay at least seemed tacitly to endorse the growing maltreatment of Jews, so the satraps winked at things they never would have permitted otherwise, while asking themselves, "What does this edict really mean?" Garden walls were broken down and plants ruined, trees were felled, animals maimed. Jews were shouldered off roads, into mud when possible. Night after night they were wakened by youths banging metal pots together and yelling. In the streets, in banking houses, behind chairs in wine shops, any Jew might hear a chilling murmur: "The thirteenth Adar." Like evil daevas, the whispers were everywhere.

"God-is-*an*gry-with-the-*wick*-ed-every-*day* . . . God-is-*an*-gry-with-the-*wick*-ed-every-*day* . . . God-is-*an*-gry-God-is-*an*-gry . . . God-is-*an*-gry-with-the-*wick*-ed-every-*day*." David marched toward Susa with these words drumbeating in his mind. Traveling mainly at night, he hid through the day. He had been on the road for days. His feet had blistered, and the blisters had broken, but he was too angry to notice.

Gradually the land grew greener; there were fields and gardens. Occasionally he saw a caravan in the distance, or a group of Jews trying to escape. He was in more danger now.

Assuming his old-man disguise when begging for food, he also picked up an occasional bit of news.

In one town a tall man who looked like a Jewish refugee came up to David. "Are you a Jew?" he asked.

"No, are you?"

The man nodded vigorously. "Oh, yes, I am."

Why such enthusiasm to share dangerous information with a stranger? David decided to set a trap. "You Jews need a good leader now, don't you?" he asked. "Someone like, er, Jonah who led the people out of Egypt long ago?"

"Yes, indeed, we do need another Jonah," said the stranger, walking into the trap. "Every night I pray for another Jonah. Ah, over there is one of my fellow Jews; I must go and talk with him."

Certain the man was a spy, David wondered how to warn his fellow-Jew. Suddenly in a querulous old voice he began to sing one of the tunes used only at Passover time. The Jew raised his head sharply. Behind the tall man's back, David gestured, then turned away. There was no more he could do.

Any town David entered had its mourning Jews, wailing aloud, throwing dust and ashes on their uncovered heads. Everywhere the Jews were going undercover. It was a pathetic attempt. Deep in their souls, they knew it could be temporary respite at best; the power of the edict was all-penetrating.

In some villages there was an eerie silence. Afraid to move, the Jews had either fled or were staying inside their shuttered houses. But David found kindness too: people smuggling food to Jews, taking in frightened children separated from parents, even hiding Jews in their own homes.

Finally, far in the distance, David saw Susa's gates. He waited to enter with a jostling, shouting group of merchants. Once inside, he went straight to his grandfather's home. Would his family be there? An unnatural stillness oppressed him; the long shadows of trees lay violet on the paths. The house was shuttered and dark. So they had gone! But where? Or were they dead?

He recalled a Persian friend of his grandfather's. He would start there. But—

Will they recognize me? he wondered ruefully. His hair was long and knotted, his beard matted; there was hardly enough cloth left on him to keep him decently covered.

Creeping to the Persian's gate, he was stopped by a sharp, "Who's there?"

"A friend of your master."

The gatekeeper's glance was derisive.

"See here," said David, "I have nothing to give you, but—"

"You insult me," snapped the guard.

"I assure you, I'm a friend of your master. Please tell him that David ben-Bilshan is at the gate. If he does not respond, I promise you I will go quietly."

In a few moments the guard returned. "You are to follow me." He led the way around the house. "In there."

The room which opened onto the garden was dark inside. David went in cautiously.

"David? Is that you, David?"

A dark shape moved against the darkness. He was enveloped in a bear hug. "We thought you were dead."

"My family?"

"All are here—all well," whispered the Persian close to David's ear.

"Let me prepare them—" he held him off, "—and a bath and some fresh clothes for you first, I think."

After a time, in a heavily curtained room, David sat with his family, their joy at being together muted by their losses.

The next morning David woke with a raging fever. He kept crying "Ruth, Ruth!" but when he was questioned as to where she was or how they could reach the three young people, his mind wandered irrationally. Finally, however, he rallied and nothing would induce him to delay one day longer.

With a close friend, Nathan, and several others, he slipped by rope over the walls in the darkness and found the horses that Bilshan's friends had tethered. Two nights of hard riding, made longer by their need to keep away from people, brought them to the area where David had left the three. There was no sign of them.

Desperate, David searched and called. At night they risked fires, hoping the signal would attract Jakob and Judith and Ruth. The fear that had filled David's first rational thoughts after his illness, that chilled his heart as he traveled, grew worse. Where would they have gone? Where would they look for water, for plant life, for animals to kill?

Ruth was alone when David crawled up over a rock in the desert and found her. They clung together for a long time. Then, "Where are the others?"

She pointed to two figures on the arid slope. He started toward them.

"David! Don't! Come back!"

He kept walking until he stood looking down at his dead friends.

"Who did this?"

"No one. I mean—they did."

"*They* did?"

"They were ill. We were crazy for water, so I went to find some. When I returned, they—were like this. Jakob must have killed Judith and then himself."

After burying the two young lovers where they were, the sad little party cautiously went back to Susa.

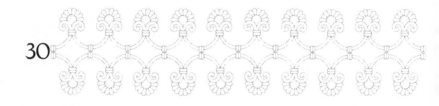

30

Word of Mordecai's promotion spread like flame.

"You are now Grand Vizier; you have powerful friends among the satraps," said his confidants. "Surely you can get them to control the outrages?"

"There is no *official* sanction for the persecution," he replied, "but what can we expect? The Crown itself authorizes the killing of Jews on the thirteenth Adar; of course the satraps will turn a blind eye. Besides, you forget my own precarious position."

Daily, messengers arrived reporting reactions to the edict. They came to Mordecai from Babylon, from Syria, from India, from Egypt.

In tiny villages where simple people lived, Jewish shepherds and their impoverished families huddled like their own sheep and were plagued by non-Jews. In larger towns, Jewish rug dealers, perfume makers, and jewelers were victims.

In Susa a customer wandered into a Jewish jewel shop and took up a valuable necklace. "Excellent. It will look good on my mistress's lovely throat."

"The price is many darics."

The customer laughed and flung the necklace down. "When the thirteenth Adar comes, you will be glad to pay me many darics for your worthless life. And I'll have the necklace as well."

The pressure increased. Jews who held mortgages were denied their payments, while any Jew unfortunate enough to have a non-Jewish mortgage holder was in danger of being foreclosed. Why have mercy on men already dead? The young were taught hate. "Jews are ill-omened; avoid them."

Night after night, when his day's work was finished, Mordecai retired to his home and wrestled over the edict. Ironic to have power he had never dreamed of and be helpless to use it for his people!

Every plan that came to mind had to be rejected for one reason or another. Escape? Perhaps a few might get away under cover of darkness, but where could they go? *Who wants us now?* he thought bitterly. Bribes? They had money, but it was pointless to think of bribing people who knew they could soon own all the Jews had. Some spectacular deed that would impress the king? But he himself had done that long ago, and, besides, it was not the king's personal favor that mattered now. He was too wise to act outside his own law and the Achaemenean tradition. On that stability the government rested.

Sometimes Mordecai called in trusted friends and they talked until dawn. There ought to be a way; there had to be a way. But every avenue of escape was barred by the inflexible law.

Among the satraps they counted as friends were a few, a very few, who might dare shelter some Jews. But then Mordecai would say, despairingly, "Of what use to jeopardize my position?"

"But even you will be killed on the thirteenth," one of his lawyer friends pointed out.

"That I understand. But until then, I can use what influence and ideas I have. I live for the chance that we shall be shown a way. But it *is* the king's edict. If I were caught plotting against it, my enemies would be delighted to use that to destroy me."

And they were back at the beginning.

Alone, Mordecai would relive the scene at the King's Gate in Susa when he had refused to bow to Haman. Such a short time ago! What would have happened if he *had* bowed. Would it have been so wrong? Yet he knew that a confrontation with Haman would inevitably have come.

Had their antagonism really been rooted in the ancient feud between his ancestors and Haman's? Knowing history as he did, that aspect of the situation had not escaped him. Searching his heart, he could not be sure, but that one man's hatred and vanity could incite vengeance on a whole people seemed beyond understanding.

A royal warrant was out for the arrest of Haman's sons. There would be no trial. Persian custom demanded the destruction of the offspring of condemned men; they were considered contaminated seed. But as reports came in, it became evident that the ten were using their father's contacts and stirring up feeling against Jews in Susa—not surprising, since Haman had so carefully nurtured anti-Jewish sentiment in them all.

Mordecai reminded himself that Adonai had brought his forefathers out of Egypt; had delivered them from the Hittites, from the Amorites, from many others. Surely he could deliver them again? But the present dilemma seemed hopeless. His people were scattered: they were in Susa and Ecbatana, Parsargadae, Babylon, Egypt—even the holy city, Jerusalem, was part of the empire. Where could they go? Who would be left? Adonai had promised he would bring salvation to the earth through the Jews. *How,* if they were wiped out like a plague of rats?

The capital was in turmoil. No one knew what had happened in the palace. The fearful edict stood.

Throughout the empire the news continued to spread, bringing wailing and misery. Although Haman was gone, his carefully laid plans continued to ferment like yeast in city and village. Informing neighbors were common; a few Jews cravenly informed on their own. The opportunity to exploit vast Jewish estates made a reasonably tolerant empire sick with greed.

Scattered, the sons of Haman eventually found each other and, in a dark ceremony, swore vengeance for their father's downfall. Hundreds in Susa who had been in Haman's pay followed the directives emerging from their secret headquarters. They had months to plan their revenge— months in which to make the Jews' lives a misery. Their personal vindictiveness centered, of course, on Mordecai.

"After all," reasoned Dalphon, "if the king orders Jews killed, he can hardly complain if we have a little fun at their expense, can he?"

In the palace's colorful corridors there was an unnatural stillness. The guards still stood in formal rows, but the courtyard was nearly deserted; even the street sounds were muffled.

The King of All Peoples was ill.

On days when he was well enough to talk a little, Esther would sit beside him. Then he would ask, "Why? What have I done to deserve so many traitors?"

Stroking his hand, smoothing back the rich black hair, now gray-streaked, Esther tried to comfort him. "Your father never betrayed you."

"No, not my father. What would he think of me now?"

"He would love you, as he always did."

Xerxes shook his head weakly. "He liked strong men—power, success. I am weak—"

"You are ill," she said firmly.

"Ahura Mazda has forsaken me."

"Why do you say that?"

"Surely," his speech was slow and thick, "it's clear. My fleet destroyed, my brothers killed, Mardonios, Masistios—gone, all gone." He seemed to have forgotten that he had once blamed Mardonios for Salamis.

"But that is life, my lord. Human beings are subject to disease and death and—"

"Betrayal?"

"Yes, even betrayal. That is part of life too."

His eyes searched her face. "There is something about you, my Esther. I don't know—a calmness, a serenity—"

"It is my faith, my lord. My faith in my God."

"And how does your god differ from mine?"

She took her time replying.

His illness had brought them closer than they had ever been. He demanded her presence constantly. Their former roles were now reversed: she who had catered to his whims, followed his every lead, was now the strong one, the one who had ideas, who made decisions, who instructed his servants. The sick king, no longer the demanding lord of the earth, was passive, almost gentle, with the Achaemenid temper seldom in evidence. He relied on her with the clinging dependency of a lost child.

"We both believe in a god who created all things," he prodded.

"Yes, my lord."

"We both believe in a god who helps us achieve victory."

"Yes, my lord."

"But you have something I do not. What is it? Is it just the way you are?"

"May I tell you how I see the difference?"

"Go on."

"Adonai is a God of love, of forgiveness—someone we can talk to."

"A god who *loves?*" Weak, he could still scoff. "How can you know?"

"One of our great kings—"

"*Your* kings? Oh, yes, the kings of Israel and Judah—*my* provinces now. There was a very wealthy one named—what was his name?"

"Solomon?"

"Yes, Solomon. You're speaking of him?"

"No, of his father, King David. He was a shepherd who was anointed king, and he sang many beautiful songs about our God."

"Sing one for me," he said feebly.

She sang:

> "Adonai is my shepherd, I shall not want;
>   he makes me lie down in green pastures.
> He leads me beside still waters;
>   he restores my soul.
> He leads me in paths of righteousness
>   for his name's sake.
> Even though I walk through the valley of the shadow of death,
>   I fear no evil;
>   for thou art with me;
>   thy rod and thy staff,
>   they comfort me.
>
> Thou preparest a table before me
>   in the presence of my enemies;
> thou anointest my head with oil,
>   my cup overflows.
> Surely goodness and mercy shall follow me
>   all the days of my life;
> and I shall dwell in the house of Adonai
>   for ever."

When she had finished, the king was asleep.

Mordecai met with Esther regularly; she was his main link with the king.

"The king is better?"

"Some better, father. Sometimes he says strange, wandering things. At other times he's more coherent. Today he talked of Adonai."

"Adonai! Xerxes?"

"Remember, he is ill and has much time to think."

"But do you think he cares about Adonai?"

"I wish I thought so, father, but I'm afraid he does not."

Seeing it pained her, Mordecai changed the subject. "The Seven are a closed group, Hadassah. They find it difficult to accept me."

"Well, from their point of view, one of *them* should be wearing that ring, not you."

"I understand. The point is, how can I improve relations between us?"

"It's time we had a dinner party."

"With the king so ill?"

"We'll have a small one, here in my house—the Seven, their wives, and you and me. It could be called a dinner of state, needed because of the king's health."

"And what do you propose to accomplish at this 'state dinner'?" he asked with his old look of amusement.

"Amity, father—good fellowship, understanding. If the men's wives can be won, the battle is half over."

Looking down the glittering table at Mordecai, Memucan fumed. *There he sits wearing the king's ring. Wrong, all wrong. He's not Persian, much less an Achaemenid. Worse, he's a Jew. That ring should be on my finger.*

Marsena looked at Mordecai only covertly. *Wretched Jew. What a pity Haman didn't get that smug head off before he died. What was the king thinking of? Some deep plan, I'll wager, and his illness changed it. Never mind, the edict still stands, and by the thirteenth Adar Mordecai will be gone, and one of us will sit where he's sitting.*

Shethar, more than the rest, appreciated Mordecai's genius.

"Lord Memucan," Mordecai was saying, "I need your advice about something."

"And what is that?"

"The administration of the royal estates of Pasargadae. I understand you have estates of your own there. Could we meet tomorrow? It would be of great help to me. I know nothing about that part of the empire."

Memucan bowed.

"At the third turn of the water clock, then."

Pleased at being singled out, Memucan was annoyed with himself for being so.

Giving each man special attention, Mordecai showed he appreciated their talents and planned additional ways they could be used. Meanwhile, Esther was charming the wives. By the end of the evening, the ice-wall had thawed a little.

"But what do I think I'm doing, Hadassah?" Mordecai said to her the next day. "What are either of us doing? Having council meetings, intimate dinners with the Seven, with the axe hanging over our heads? When the thirteenth comes, it will still drop."

"Have you ever discussed a possible solution with the Seven?"

"I have. They are all in favor of finding some way round the edict. All, that is—" he hesitated. "I've never fully trusted Marsena— In any case, we cannot find a way."

"Father, you taught me that Adonai is always the same."

"Who is, who was, and who will be. . . ."

"And that he will keep his covenant with us."

"But as a people we have failed him so often. *I* have failed him. Perhaps—perhaps he has forsaken us. Why not, after all? 'He will by no means clear the guilty,'" he quoted.

"Yes, father, but in that same place it says, 'having mercy upon thousands. . . .'"

Even in his distress, Mordecai was pleased that she remembered what he had taught her.

"Well, Hadassah, I have done all I know how to do. We must continue to pray, as Bilshan keeps reminding me. We shall have to wait and see which side of his character Adonai will show us in the months ahead—his judgment or his mercy."

They parted, and the light burned very late in Mordecai's study that night.

In her hours alone, Esther reviewed the situation. The elaborate plans, the terror of her appeal to the king seemed to have been for nothing. Nothing, in fact, was changed for the Jews, and she knew their enemies would not easily relinquish the prize of their wealth.

The demoralizing effect of the king's illness was apparent in the palace; rumors changed daily. And Esther's long nights and days with the sick king, her growing tension, were beginning to tell. She was edgy with the girls and often withdrawn. Even Hatak found her difficult. As for Harbonah, shaken with jealousy by her frequent visits to the king's bedchamber, he found her intolerable.

At home, Mordecai continued to wrestle with the problem. More and more he turned to the Scriptures for comfort.

Teach me, he prayed, *comfort me. I'm at my wit's end.* "Have no fear," he read. "Stand by and witness the deliverance which Adonai will work for you today. . . . Adonai will battle for you."

31

"The king holds audience in the throne room today, Majesty." Hatak brought the message to the queen. "He wanted you to know."

Hatak also brought her a cryptic message from Mordecai. She was to ask for audience with the king and make a certain request. The message puzzled her; still, Mordecai had told her to do it, so she would.

Sending her request to the king by Hatak, she had her maids dress her carefully.

Troubled as she was, Esther looked at them affectionately—the same seven who had been with her since the harem days. Lura especially had been more than a servant; she had been her loyal companion in the great crises of her life.

Xerxes, thin and with much new gray in his hair, read the queen's request and looked quizzically at Memucan.

"I'm not used to queens coming to the throne room. The last time—" He lost the thread of his thoughts for a moment. "Mordecai, what do you know of this?"

"I should be grateful, sire, if you allowed Her Majesty audience."

So again Esther passed the rows of Immortals, went through the great door, saw the forest of columns. There was no terror this time, but her spirit was heavy with fear for her people. And how would she put Mordecai's request?

Xerxes absent-mindedly extended his sceptre.

"My lord Xerxes, I come on behalf of my people."

Her people? Xerxes' clouded mind struggled with the idea. The sight of his queen kneeling before him brought troubled memories. *A kneeling queen in this same throne room . . . that was the beginning of . . . of . . . .* He frowned.

"Queen Esther, what are you asking?"

"If it please the king— if I have found favor in his sight—" She could not seem to get beyond the stilted court phrases: "—and—if I be pleasing to his eyes, let an order be written to revoke the letters devised by Haman." That was what Mordecai had told her to say. But surely this was simply posing again the problem that had plagued all of them for over two months. How *could* the order be revoked?

The king's expression puzzled her: blank, uncomprehending. Had he forgotten all the events of the past months? Surely, surely he had not forgotten Haman?

"Haman, the Agagite, the son of Hammedatha, my lord. The decree which he wrote to destroy the Jews. *My* people."

Shethar looked at Mordecai; was it he who had taught the queen statesmanship? Clever of her to lay the blame for the edict on Haman alone.

"How can I endure to see the destruction of my kindred?"

Here was the dilemma Xerxes had carefully avoided thinking about for weeks. Now, with his queen in front of him and the Seven and Mordecai beside him, he could no longer ignore it.

Aware at least that the thirteenth Adar would bring chaos throughout his kingdom, as well as endanger the lives of his queen and his new Grand Vizier, he turned to Memucan. "Have you found a solution, Lord Memucan?" He made it sound as if Memucan should have done so.

"No, sire. It is a grave problem. And," he twisted the knife a little, "there are thousands of Jews in your kingdom."

"I am quite aware of that," snapped Xerxes. "But Haman never told me he was talking about Jews. If he had, I would never have permitted such a thing."

Memucan did not remark on the fact that the king *should* have known.

"The edict, Majesty, strikes at some of your wealthiest and most influential men. If they are suddenly destroyed, the economy will totter—"

"Angru Manyu!" Xerxes shouted. "Do you take me for a fool? I know all this. I asked you for a solution, not a reprimand." It was almost as if he had never been ill. "Lord Mordecai, you are my new Grand Vizier; you are wise. What ideas do you have?"

"I have spent many hours in searching, Majesty. I have at last found a plan which I think might be acceptable: Might not the king send out a counter edict that Jews be allowed to *defend* themselves on the thirteenth Adar?"

Memucan gasped. But this was brilliant!

The king's eyes held Mordecai's as he weighed the possibilities. Wanting no repetition of his first error in judgment, he looked at the Seven.

Shethar, although irritated at Mordecai's secretive handling of the issue, realized it was the best solution they were likely to find. "May the king live forever—I believe this idea of the Lord Mordecai is sound. Although the first edict must stand, the Jews will be free of the persecutions they have been enduring and—"

"Persecutions? What persecutions?"

"Your Majesty has been ill. There have been, ah, incidents. With the death warrant issued from the Throne—" he left the sentence unfinished.

"But I gave no permission for any action before the thirteenth Adar! Have you men no control over this city? What sort of councilors are you? For two months I'm ill, and everything gets out of control. This must stop immediately! Go on, Lord Shethar."

"Under Lord Mordecai's plan, the Jews will be able to arm, and that will deter those who plan to kill them. Once a second edict shows where the royal will is, things will improve."

"What do the rest of you think?"

All assented. Only Mordecai noticed Marsena's reluctance.

Xerxes turned to Mordecai and the queen. In his royal trappings he looked small and a little pathetic.

"You may write as you please with regard to the Jews in the name of the king." He passed a hand over his eyes. "And seal it with the king's ring, Mordecai." He straightened, and with smoldering anger reminded them of what they all knew: "An edict written in the name of the king and sealed with the king's ring cannot be revoked. Send it to all the satrapies. Now!"

As his throne-bearers carried him from the room, he noticed Mordecai's plain brown robe and called, "Harbonah! See to it that Lord Mordecai does not leave the palace without clothes suited to his new status."

Immediately summoning the king's scribes, Mordecai drew up the new edict. It was the twenty-third of Sivan, over two months since the first edict had gone out. Using the identical words of the first edict, it declared that the king granted the Jews in every city the right to gather and defend their lives, "to destroy, to slay, and to annihilate any armed force of any people or province that might attack them, with their children and women, and to plunder their goods, upon one day throughout all the provinces of King Xerxes on the thirteenth day of the twelfth month, which is the month Adar."

Memucan, inspecting the new edict, whistled between his teeth. "Isn't your Jewish god supposed to be a god of mercy?"

"He is also a God of justice," retorted Mordecai, looking up from the parchment in his hands. "However, I must tell you that my hope is that this will avoid bloodshed and—"

"*Avoid* bloodshed? With that wording?"

"Yes, Lord Memucan. The original edict—" He referred to another document in front of him. "On the thirteenth Adar all in the empire are told to 'destroy, to slay, and to annihilate all Jews, young and old, women and children, in one day—and to plunder their goods.'"

"So now you are going to do exactly the same thing, is that it?"

"The new edict says that the Jews may gather and *defend* their lives—to destroy, slay, annihilate those who might *attack* them."

"A defensive action only?" Memucan was cynical.

"Look here, Lord Memucan." Mordecai was growing impatient. "There are thousands of men in this empire already plotting against my people. They have detailed plans for taking over the banks we run, the businesses we own; they have lists of all Jews in their towns. Do you deny this is so?"

"I cannot deny it."

"Very well then. It is imperative that this edict be made as strong as the original. Everyone in the kingdom must know that if they carry out the violence permitted in the first edict, the Jews have the king's permission to defend themselves; they can kill anyone who attacks them."

Meres broke in. "I suppose they need to defend themselves against children and women?"

Mordecai sighed; it had been a long day. "You are a man of the world, Lord Meres. Don't you see that if children and women are not mentioned, our enemies would take advantage of it? Don't you see how easy it would be to put weapons in the hands of women, firebrands in the hands of children? That clause is necessary. If they do not attack us, they will be quite safe."

"Are your people all so holy? Are you asking us to believe none of them capable of treachery and violence, even if not attacked?"

"No," said Mordecai, "I wish I could believe that myself. I'm afraid there are many among us who will go further than they should. All that I can do I will do."

The scribes were busily transcribing the edict into the kingdom's many languages. Mordecai, staying through the night, sealed each copy with the king's ring. Whipped by his uneasy conscience, Xerxes sent orders that the couriers were to go with the greatest possible speed.

In the morning, Mordecai, splendid in a golden headdress and flowing robe of fine linen and purple, as ordered by the king, came out on the portico. His appearance on the staircase set off a roar of approval from the thousands who had gathered during the night. The city of Susa shouted for joy.

For the Jews, the relief was indescribable. With all the passion and abandon of their nature, they threw themselves into wild celebration, feasting, singing, and dancing, embracing one another with tears and laughter.

After a sleepless night alone, Esther heard the celebration and sighed. "They are like children. Listen to them. There are people shouting out there who will never live past the thirteenth."

"It's naïve to think all our troubles are over," Mordecai said to Bilshan at the feast his old friend gave celebrating the new edict. With its publication Bilshan had moved his family back to the house in the Street of Lilacs.

"But surely no one will attack us now?"

"My dear friend," Mordecai laid his hand on Bilshan's shoulder, "Are you so unworldly? I wish all men were half as good at heart."

"But the edict says—"

"The edict says that the Jews can defend themselves."

Bilshan smiled his radiant smile. "Then everything is well."

"Everything is not well, grandfather."

David had entered the room, bowed to his elders, and joined the discussion.

"You, too, David? What a pair of cynics!"

"Grandfather, men whose greed has been growing for two months will not give up now. They've already persecuted our people—our friends died—"

"But this second edict brings an end to all that."

"This is just the beginning. Too many plans have been laid, too many greedy men have eyes on our money, jewels, businesses, estates."

Bilshan was listening at last, "You mean they would risk their lives, risk the king's displeasure—?"

"The king," said Mordecai dryly, "is caught in his own hunting net. The first edict has his seal as well as the second. He can hardly have men brought to trial or killed because they carry out his own injunction."

Bilshan sat down. "I see. Then, we must—"

"We must prepare our defense," said David sternly. "Uncle Mordecai, I am ready to do whatever you say."

"Thank you. In fact, I'd like to confer with you now. Bilshan?"

Bilshan gestured toward a curtained doorway. "You two go in there; my part of this action will be to pray. I want no part of your bloody schemes."

Mordecai paused at the door. "We value your prayers, but prayers seek an answer. We will be that answer."

The great empire shook. It was as if two tidal waves coming from opposite directions had swept over the land and had met with crashing force. The first edict had stirred the avarice of thousands; some had even turned it into a holy war for Ahura Mazda. But the wave carrying the king's endorsement of the Jews brought amazement: What god was this who could influence even Ahura Mazda's representative?

Throughout the kingdom hundreds became converts to the Jewish faith. Some were pragmatists; it was the safe thing to do. But many were genuinely convinced that if the God of the Jews could work a miracle such as this one, he must be the true God.

In Parsa, Vahush walked along the treasury road with Artatakhma, the master bronzesmith.

"Never before in our history have we seen anything like this. Any edict of the Great King has always been obeyed without question and was never reversed. And remember, I served under the great Darius."

"But this is not exactly a reversal, Vahush. It's a sort of countermand."

"Call it what you will, it's a change of heart on the part of the king—a public change of heart; it has no precedent. There is a power in this god of the Jews; I can feel it. Do you know their history? Many times their god rescued them in miraculous ways."

"Do you think the Jews will defeat their enemies this time?"

Vahush looked far out across the plain's colored layers. "I have a strange feeling they will. This man Mordecai has the stamp of greatness."

"Are you speaking of power? Haman had power," said Artatakhma.

"He wanted power for its own sake, and in the end it crushed him." Vahush pointed to the strong relief of the lion attacking the bull. "Power is like that; it can claw a man's vitals. No, Mordecai has more—faith, something that fires him more than life. I cannot define it, but it will make his name famous."

The satraps, their lieutenants and secretaries shook their heads and conferred. The king's preference was now obvious, no matter what the first edict said. Speculation ran wild. Jews had never been so well-treated by authority. They were offered help of every kind: influence, money, arms. At first suspicious, the Jews gradually realized the offers, if not the motives, were genuine.

David was in charge of the military preparations for all of Susa. With a hand-picked group of intelligent lieutenants he planned far into the night, spending his few free hours with Ruth.

"Where can Haman's sons be hiding?" she asked one evening.

David took her in his arms and kissed her. She had changed. Once almost plump, she was now as fragile as Judith had been, and her eyes were sad.

"You are not to worry your head, my darling, about those—" His expression altered.

Ruth put her fingers on his lips. "Don't, David."

"Don't what?"

"I know that look. I know where your thoughts were. Please, for my sake, forget."

"For no one's sake. Until their deaths are avenged."

"Have you forgotten? Adonai says, 'To me belongs vengeance and recompense; their foot shall slide in due time.'"

"It will indeed, and I'll help it slide. Do you think I won't hunt down those sons of darkness. I know every one of them. I don't know which one I hate the most."

"My love, they are under the king's sentence of death. You know the law. Why should you stain your hands? The Jews need help in planning their defense, and you're our best man for that. But defense, not murder."

"Your parents—Jakob and Judith—"

"They are gone. You cannot change that. And the sons of Haman will be dealt with legally. Save your energies for the defense of Susa."

David looked at her, all shining trust, and knew he must not voice his doubts. *Why hadn't Adonai stopped the tragedy?*

A young man dashed into the garden. "David! We think we have found—oh, excuse me."

"What have you found?" asked David. Ruth tactfully went indoors.

"We have word that Haman's son, Adalia, was seen going into that brothel down near the river."

"When?"

"Last night."

"Why wasn't I told sooner?"

"We just received the message."

They ran to their horses and pounded toward the river. Suddenly David reined in. Ruth's pleading hadn't been entirely useless. "This won't do. The king's guard wants to catch them all in one net. We have no plan. We can't act independently. But show me the place."

Once there, his eyes took in every detail of the large building, every balcony, every entrance. At home, he marked it on his map of Susa drawn with a quill on a large piece of leather.

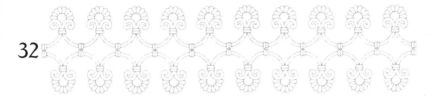

32

At last Mordecai had the scope he needed for his administrative talents. Invitations to the great homes along the Choaspes River flooded in, invitations which he refused; there was too much to do to prepare for the thirteenth Adar. Distant satraps, their governors and secretaries felt his impact and sent lavish gifts.

"The Lord Mordecai receives as many gifts as I do," Xerxes said one day.

"Never, sire. You see, they are testing out the new broom."

"And how is the broom responding?"

"He sweeps the gifts back, Your Majesty."

The Grand Vizier's prime concern was designing the Jewish defense. As the dreaded thirteenth approached, secret couriers were sent out carrying tactical defense plans, requests for money and supplies, orders for Jews in villages and hamlets to go to walled cities for safety. The courtyard on the acropolis was thronged with hurrying messengers, emissaries, servants. Prominent Jews poured in from every satrapy for instruction and advice; a few had even come from Jerusalem. They brought money, jewels, encouragement, and their prayers.

It was in Susa that Mordecai would need his best defense. Here the action would be murderous. The capital was a giant magnet: political agents, artists, engineers, philosophers, doctors, athletes, seamen, explorers, priests, and oracle agents came here. But a dangerous other world also came: tricksters, blackguards, thieves, murderers, perverts.

Mordecai placed David over the secret arsenals and the stores of food and water; he had spies in every corner of the capital. Little by little information filtered in; layer by layer the security that covered Haman's sons was peeled back.

The few Jewish traitors, thriving after the first edict, now found they belonged nowhere: their brothers spat at them; the non-Jews distrusted them. They rallied round the treacherous Marsena, the one member of the Seven who was a Jew-hater.

The other six were making the best of the court situation.

"It's difficult for me to admit," said Shethar one day as they gathered for a conference with the king, "but Mordecai is the most brilliant man I have ever known."

Meres laughed. "I suppose it's just as well to recognize one's superior, isn't it?"

"Particularly," Memucan said wryly, "when the Great King has already done so."

"Lord Mordecai," said Xerxes when they were all gathered, "what are your plans for Susa's defense?"

"Our plans, Majesty, cover every contingency; they can be shifted as the situation requires. David ben-Bilshan has trained our men into a strong fighting force."

"Are you in doubt of the outcome?"

"I am in no doubt whatever of the outcome."

"May your god be with you." The king turned to Memucan. "How is the population in general reacting?"

"For one thing, they are offering the Jews exhorbitant prices for their lands. Also, they are outdoing themselves to entertain Jews."

"All people not involved should stay inside their houses," said Xerxes. "They will have only themselves to blame if they do not. And mark this: none of my men, Immortals or regular soldiers, will take any active part in this—this brawl. I'll thank Mithra when this is over.

"Since we must go through with it, the day is to begin with dignity. At sunrise, trumpets from the citadel walls will signal the start of the fighting. At sundown, trumpets will sound again to end the day— *Damnation!*"

The Seven and Mordecai were alert. What now?

"That I, *I* should be brought to this by a traitor like Haman! May his memory rot! He would have branded me forever as a tyrant!" He looked at each man in turn. "Why haven't those treacherous sons been captured yet?"

The Seven looked uncomfortable, Mordecai impassive.

"They are exceedingly clever," said Shethar. "We believe we're on their trail in Susa."

"On their trail! I want them *found!* They are evil seed, and they'll propagate evil. I want the name of Haman cut from my world."

As the thirteenth neared, Susa became an armed camp. Houses were shuttered, and few people were on the streets after sunset. Relieved, if mystified, by the second edict, most of the city only wished to see an end to it all.

Esther wanted details of the dark affairs going on outside her walls, and Mordecai met with her frequently. He kept very little from her. One day, as they discussed many things, he asked about the king.

"Physically, he's much stronger, father. As you know, he is riding again. Even hunting occasionally. But there is an odd detachment about him—as if his mind is somewhere else, as if one part of him is there in the room with me and another part is faraway in a country of his own making. He often wakes up shouting."

"Bad dreams? What does he say?"

"He shouts his brothers' names, or his father's, and 'Salamis.' He curses Mardonios, and there's one name he often mentions—Pythius. When he wakes shouting 'Pythius!' he clings to me like a child."

What is on this man's conscience, Mordecai was thinking, *I would not have on mine for every bit of gold in his treasury.*

"What does he have to say about the thirteenth Adar?"

"Nothing. He will not discuss it at all. I have tried to talk with him, ask his advice. He cuts me off immediately. In fact, he has now forbidden me to speak of it."

They were sitting in the queen's garden. Above them, Haman's gallows speared the sky.

"Why have you left that dreadful thing up, father?"

"Didn't you turn over the administration of Haman's estates to me?"

"I did, and I'm sure you know what you are doing. But it's a horrid thing to have staring down on us every day. It must be visible all over the city."

"It's a reminder to Susa that this is what happens to traitors."

She frowned. "If you think it's necessary, of course it must stay, but I don't like it. At night when I want to look at the stars, there it stands!"

"One day soon we won't need it any more. Tell me, are you afraid of the thirteenth, Hadassah?"

"Certainly, I'm afraid." She answered with her usual directness. "It's going to be a terrifying day: people killed, maimed, bereaved. Horrible!"

"But not so horrible as a mass slaughter of defenseless people."

"But it's a terrible price—even for our enemies. Oh, it seems so senseless! Don't you think our enemies will respect the king's second edict?"

"I wish I did think so. But knowing human nature and the sort of men who will attack—" He shook his head. "Susa is infested with former Hamanites, hundreds of them. Some we know, but many we do not."

"But the king has made it clear he wants Jews left alone. How dare anyone fight us?"

"Human greed dares a great deal, my dear. Remember, those who kill and plunder our people will be within their legal rights. It's their own choice, Hadassah. They can stay indoors and be safe, but they will not. I am sure they will not."

"So our people will be forced to fight?"

"We shall defend ourselves."

"And take others' possessions?"

"Never!" Mordecai's mouth set in a straight line. "The second edict had to say that they could do whatever the first edict allows, but my orders are that they are not to lay a finger on the plunder."

"Some of our men will die."

"Inevitably. But we have the advantage: most of the population is aware that the second edict represents the king's *present* will; also, they fear our God. We shall have victory."

"Do we have enough men here in Susa to fight those hundreds of Haman-followers you spoke of?"

"I will not lie to you, Hadassah. The reports we have show that the enemy's strength is formidable."

Esther walked about restlessly. "I feel trapped in this gold cage. Here I am—embroidering, singing, playing with my dog, entertaining chattering women. There must be something I can do that *matters!*"

Mordecai took her by the shoulders. "Adonai put you here. There would *be* no second edict without your courage in going to the king—in exposing Haman."

"But now, father, now! There must be other things I can do. And don't tell me this is men's work and that there is nothing. I *am* the queen." There was a flash of majesty that others knew but which seldom showed when she was alone with Mordecai.

"The most important thing you are doing already—keeping the king calm. That leaves me free to get on with the task of planning Jewish defense. Try to discourage him from calling too many meetings. Convince him we are capable planners and have things well in hand."

"In other words, keep him out of the great Lord Mordecai's way?"

They exchanged a look of complete understanding.

"But there is something else. I think a message to the Jewish women should go out in your name asking them to store supplies of food and water, to arrange care for the wounded."

"I shall do it." She sent for Hatak and dictated the message. When he had gone, she said, "Now, tell me about David."

"That one!" Mordecai laughed, "He's my right arm."

"Is he so clever, then?"

"I've put him in charge of Susa's defense."

"Our nice, gentle David?"

"You forget—it's been six years since you've seen him. He's a man."

"What kind of man?"

"He's a fiery speaker. He has an innate sense of how to handle men; he knows when to change tactics and when to hold fast."

"Bilshan must be delighted with him."

Mordecai laughed again. "The old man is a bit bewildered by this bright lion his son sired. David moves too fast for him. Bilshan is a thinker, a philosopher, and, above everything else, a man who serves and worships Adonai. In other times, he might have been a prophet."

"I often remember that evening, that last evening, when you and Bilshan and I spoke of the Messiah." The sadness that always came to her at the mention of the Messiah was in her eyes.

"The filthy rumors going through this city can only come from those sons of Haman." David sat with Mordecai at his grandfather's table. It was the ninth Adar.

"What now?"

"You know the sort of thing, sir. 'The Jews are plotting the downfall of the king. They are guilty of usurious dealings. They are ruining the craftsmen. The Jews are fraudulent in their dealings.' And they sum it all up," he blazed, "by calling us parasites!"

"David, David—what did you expect?"

"It does seem to me, in view of the king's expressed sympathy, that they'd keep such lies to themselves."

"But lies like these make successful weapons. One can hardly blame them for using what comes to hand."

Bilshan joined in. "Adonai is our defender. Remember King David? He was younger than you when he fought the giant Goliath and told him, 'You come to me with a sword and with a spear and with a javelin, but I come to you in the name of the Lord of hosts . . . this day will Adonai deliver you into my hand . . . that all . . . may know that there is a God in Israel.'"

David was quiet. He wondered if Mordecai sensed the struggle inside him. Why couldn't he just have faith?

Bilshan, white hair and beard silvered by lamplight, went on, "Prayer is the answer. We must pray and wait upon Adonai."

"Prayer without action, when action is needed, is like fighting without a sword." Mordecai's deep voice had risen. "Adonai does not expect us to pray and *sit,* Bilshan. He gives us common sense to act as well."

Then he saw he had hurt the old man and went over to him. "You must be our Moses. You must hold up your hands in prayer while the fighting goes on.

"When Israel fought the Amalekites long ago," he said to David who was looking puzzled, "Moses prayed on a hill. As long as his hands were raised to Adonai, Israel had the advantage; when he lowered them, the Amalekites had it. This is your part, Bilshan. Can we count on you?"

"You may count on me," said the old man with his beautiful smile. "You may count on me."

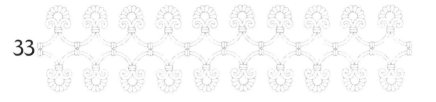

33

David, conferring with his first lieutenant Nathan, looked up in annoyance as a man burst into the room, breathless and wild-eyed.

"I'm sorry, sir, but—but—they've kidnapped Ruth from your house."

David became very still. There was no need to ask who "they" were.

"When?"

"It just happened, sir. It was fast and well-planned."

Suddenly, David was flashing orders. "You three—find out if anyone in the houses close by saw anything. You two—follow the river road. Nathan, come with me. I'm going home."

The household was upside down. Bilshan's eyes were swollen; the servants wailed.

"It was like an earthquake, David. They rushed in, and before we had any idea of what was happening, we were blindfolded and gagged."

"Could you hear which way they went? Or how many there were?"

"It sounded like at least six, and I thought they rode off toward the river."

David went out into the garden, looking for footprints or anything else that might show which way they had gone. Its peacefulness, filled with old memories, mocked him.

The hiss of an arrow made him duck. Landing near the pear tree, it quivered, pinning something to the ground. It was a message:

> We have your woman. If you wish to see her as you remember
> her, get amnesties for all of us and ten border passes. You have
> until sunset tomorrow.
>
> The Ten Sons of Haman

He leaped to the top of the wall; the street was empty. Racing back into the house, he nearly collided with his grandfather.

"My son! Stop! What is that?"

David showed him the note. "Are you going to say 'pray' now?" He snatched up his great bow and left.

When he arrived at Mordecai's headquarters, the Seven had gathered. He handed them the message, then picked up some arrows and started out the door, but a sharp command from Mordecai stopped him.

"David! I am very sorry for you, but—"

"I don't want your sorrow, sir. Suppose it had been the queen?"

"Listen to me. Your queen, your friend, risked her life for all of us. She hadn't a shred of evidence that she would not be killed when she put her life at risk. These men are treacherous; you can't trust anything they say. You know they're wanted by the Crown; if they were allowed to escape the king would hold us responsible. You cannot sacrifice your brother Jews for just one girl, no matter how precious she is to you."

David's reply was cut off by a smart rap on the door; one of the Immortals came in carrying a bit of blood-stained leather. "It was on a dead child's body, Lord Mordecai."

A token to remind you that the sooner you act and give us
what we ask, the more live Jews there will be.

"Do you see, David?"

"But, *sir*—"

Shethar interrupted. "We cannot stand by with a spear held at our hearts. We must plan. A wild chase will accomplish less than nothing. David! These men are wanted by the king. We're closing in on the entire group. You *must* trust us."

"I have trouble enough trusting my God at this point."

Another man rushed in with a girl from the brothel by the river, a place called The Forgotten. "This woman claims to have seen the group taking your lady away, sir."

"You *saw* them!"

"Yes, my lord." The girl looked frightened. "I saw them plainly."

"Where?"

"I was looking out the window—one of the ones facing the street where we—well, where we sit, you know, sir—and along came this group of men with hoods. Well, hoods in the daytime, sir—you don't see them very often, do you? I began to wonder."

"Were they carrying anything?"

"Yes, sir. They had a woman propped up on a horse."

"How do you know it was a woman?" Mordecai interrupted.

"Oh, sir, some of her hair had come out from under the blanket. Long, shining hair, it was."

David shut his eyes. "Did you see where they went?"

"Oh, yes, sir. Across the river and up that little rise on the opposite side."

"Could you show us the house?"

"I could, sir."

David snatched his bow.

"Wait!" Mordecai's voice was sharp.

"I promise I'll do nothing but get the lay of the land."

"Then leave that bow here. And go in my carriage. No one will attack that, and you won't be recognized."

As the carriage approached a large house with an enclosed courtyard, David marveled that Haman's sons had chosen such an exposed spot, then realized that was the genius of the plan. Who would think of looking here?

When he returned, Mordecai met him at the door, eyes hard. "Another note—on a woman this time."

So you are the one in charge of Susa's welfare, David ben-Bilshan? How fortunate! We will begin on Ruth at sunrise tomorrow.

It was nearly midnight. Wearing dark cloaks, David and ten of his best men went stealthily toward the river.

"Curse the moon!" said one. "It will make our task harder."

"Save your breath," said David shortly. "What is, is. If it makes things harder for us, it will make things harder for them."

In a short time they circled the house where Ruth was held. Some had ropes to sling over branches; some stood with drawn bows. Half a furlong away they had tied their horses.

"I can pick off that man on the roof now."

"Put your bow away, you fool! I'm in charge here," said David. "There is to be no unnecessary killing. You will wait for my signal. Once again: I'll climb this wall, swing over to the roof, gag the guard, and find Ruth. I'll bring her into the courtyard. We'll need to hug the shadows along the wall on the other side to avoid the moonlight." He looked for a place to anchor a rope. "Up there, Nathan. Knot it well, and I'll swing to the roof. When I have Ruth, we'll swing back. You bring two horses."

Poised on the wall, he could see one man standing guard on the roof opposite.

Hoping there was no one else, David waited until the man's back was turned and swung, black in the shadow, silver in the moonlight, and black again. He struck silently and bound and gagged the man. Carefully laying the body down, he slithered down a staircase. Everything was still, the courtyard white with moonlight, the shadows like ink. Staying close to walls, he slid through a doorway into a dark hall. *Now if I were holding a girl prisoner, where would I keep her? How can I get inside their hellish heads? They probably have her in the dampest, foulest place they could find.* He went down a stone staircase.

"Ruth," he whispered. "Ruth?"

A cobweb brushed his face. Small scurryings preceded him as he inched down the hall. Abruptly he touched something warm and soft. He stood absolutely still and waited. Nothing happened. Then a remembered scent—the scent of hair he had buried his face in—

"Ruth?"

"Oh, *David!*"

"I've come for you."

"David, you mustn't. The house is full of terrible men. They'll take vengeance on our people You must go—*now.*"

Her hands were bound behind her back, her feet—what had they done to her feet?

"It's all right," she said as he cut the bonds. "My feet are very swollen."

"I'll carry you."

"David, listen to me. This is all wrong. You must leave me here. They have a plan—"

"Tell me later."

"But they plan—"

He put his hand firmly over her mouth, swept her up, squirming, and headed for the dark steps. She beat on him with small fists.

"Later, later," he kept whispering in her ear. "You are safe, love."

She shook her head violently, but he held on. Still keeping his hand over her mouth, he set her on her feet beside the stairway that led to the roof.

With stunning swiftness she twisted from him and stumbled into the brilliant courtyard. His heart stopped as her voice rang out into the night: "Go! Fly! They are at your house! They'll burn everyone in it. Go. *Please!*"

Arrows rained from every direction, hitting the slight body with dull thuds, pinning it to the ground. Against all good sense, David started toward her. Grabbing him by the shoulders, Nathan, who was much heavier than David, spun him around, and they were halfway up the stairs before he knew what was happening.

"It's too late, David. You cannot help her now. Don't let her death be for nothing."

They galloped off under a rain of arrows. Incredibly, there was no pursuit.

"We hobbled their horses," Nathan shouted. As they raced through the town, David's other companions thundered up alongside.

As they neared Bilshan's home, they could see men with torches moving toward the house. How many? Ten? Twenty? Thirty? David's men had split into four groups, all brandishing knives, swords, daggers. They looked like an avenging host.

"Stop!" David called out to the enemy. "Throw down your arms!"

Instead, the men threw their torches in various directions. David's men rushed to put out the fires.

"We're surrounded!" shouted someone. "Run for your lives!"

David suddenly recognized a familiar figure.

"Dalphon!" He yelled. "I've found you!"

"Where are you, you young fool?"

David stepped into the moonlight and Dalphon hurled his spear.

David ducked and swung to pick it up. "Here's your spear back, you son of darkness!"

But he, too, missed.

Whirling a sword around his head as if it were a rope, Dalphon came across the grass. He was twenty manas heavier than David, taller and far more experienced. But David knew this garden; he could move like lightning. For a few minutes they twisted back and forth, and then David maneuvered Dalphon toward the pool. Haman's son went over with a great crash into the shallow water, David on top of him. Nearly crazed with his grief, David kept stabbing until his friends finally pulled him away.

He looked around the once-beautiful garden; the pear tree was smoldering charcoal. The big house had not been touched.

"Your family is safe, sir. All is well."

All is well! And Ruth in the courtyard— "Nathan! Come with me."

They swung over the wall and galloped through the city.

"Will their soldiers still be at the house, do you think?"

"I hope so," said David grimly.

But the alarm had spread. Ruth's body lay alone in a pool that showed black in the moonlight. David pulled out the arrows as gently as if she could still feel, then lifted her into his arms and carried her home.

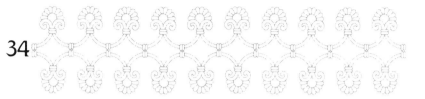

34

It was still dark on the morning of the thirteenth Adar. The great city was shuttered down for the siege, quiet with ominous waiting, though there were surreptitious movings, an occasional low call, muffled sounds from the river. Mordecai went up on the roof of his house in the Street of Oleanders. Above him swung those same constellations that had wheeled over Job's head centuries before as he pondered the reason for suffering.

Rich Susa. Small under the immensity of the sky! How many of its men now breathing, loving, hating would tonight be dead?

Had he left anything undone? Mordecai worried. Was there one Jew in the kingdom left unprotected?

Looking toward the palace, he remembered cursing the king the night Hadassah was taken. Then, it had all seemed futile, tragic; now the design was clear. Adonai had chosen her. What would their fate have been with a pagan queen?

"Adonai!" he prayed, "be with us. We are sinful, often disobedient and unbelieving, but we are the children of your covenant. We seek your mercy, O Most High. Be with your own in every city and town in all the empire. Lord God of Abraham, Isaac, and Israel, let it be known this day that you are God."

The last star faded.

With a zing like a giant wasp an arrow missed his head by a hair's-breadth and vibrated in the wood of the parapet.

"I am a fool!" Angrily he went down the stairs and called the servants.

"The king has ordered me to the Citadel before sunrise. None of you is to leave the house."

Huldah and his other servants huddled in the entryway.

"You will be safe. There are guards around the house and on the roof."

257

"May Adonai keep my lord," said Huldah. "Hadassah?"

"Hadassah was never safer." He smiled at the old woman. "And after this is over, I shall have you moved to the queen's house."

Outside there was clanking and clattering as his escort arrived. Forty mounted men from the king's own guard surrounded Mordecai's carriage, as he gave the order to drive to the Citadel.

Hot and still, the day was here—the day the whole empire had talked about, thought about, dreaded or greedily anticipated—the thirteenth Adar. For eleven months a kingdom spread over thousands of parasangs had braced itself for this day. In Ethiopia, tall black chiefs stood by early campfires; in Bactria, camels with armed men on their backs lined the roads. Half-naked Indians, bodies polished by the heat, moved swiftly along dusty highways. Wealthy Lydians hid their gold. The Parthians patrolled their cities; the Scythians supplied horseshoes and bridles to the Jews.

As the sun rose, fighting began. Ladders were thrown up against walls; women poured down boiling oil. The attackers were vicious, the Jews wild to defend their own. Jewish fortunes surged and ebbed. Legally impotent to stop the yelling mobs attacking Jewish homes, shops, and banks, the satraps, like the majority of their citizens, stayed inside their shuttered houses.

In Susa, as the morning trumpets shrilled, there was a stirring. A figure moved, an arrow arced. A cry. Another. Over a house wall a body hurtled. Two figures struggled in a street. A puff of smoke was followed by a sheet of flame.

Mounds of fruit disintegrated, spewing out men; chickens squawked and scurried while Jews below their roosts sprang into action. Piles of rugs suddenly grew legs; heaps of refuse erupted. There was a rising volume of sound: men racing through the streets, swords clashing, arrows thudding, the iron ring of javelins hurled and missed.

In his gilded room, Xerxes was in a fury. "None of this should have happened! I will have heads if every one of Haman's sons is not brought in today." Shouting above the cacophany in the streets below, he asked

Memucan, "What kind of men *are* they down there? My second edict should have been enough to stop this war against the Jews. My will was clear."

Memucan was not a diplomat for nothing. "Live forever, Great King. All the important men of Susa are safe in their homes with their families; it is the rabble who are attacking."

The king was restless. "Come! We'll go out on the platform and watch."

The air was opaque, the sun blinding on cameos of violence. On his portable throne in the great north porch, Xerxes might have been at an entertainment. "Almost like Salamis, isn't it, Memucan?" He seemed to have forgotten that Memucan had not been at that infamous battle.

Memucan stared. Never before had Xerxes referred to Salamis with anything except bitterness and wounded dignity.

"Look there!" the king shouted. "That man climbing up on the house wall by a rope! Can't he see there are men on that roof? They are over by the edge now. Fool! Is he a Jew or—"

At that precise moment one of the men on the roof leaned down with a smoking torch and held it against the rope which tore away at the burning spot, and the man plummeted to the rocky ground.

"Neatly done!" Xerxes shifted his attention to two men fleeing from rooftop to rooftop, pursued by a group of young Jews. The men in the lead were hugging heavy wooden caskets. Making a flying leap across a narrow alleyway, one miscalculated his distance and fell to the street, where the box broke open, strewing jewels in glittering piles. Instantly two of the pursuers dropped down after him, and a violent hand battle began. Blood and jewels made a strange mixture.

The Susians were unprepared for the Jewish speed, daring, and intelligence. When the Jews avoided obvious traps they had set, they lost heart and became easy prey, bolting down a street straight into the arms of blockading Jews. They dropped valuable weapons as they fled, which the Jews were only too glad to have.

The air became heavy with dust, ashes, flying stones.

Far down the straight, main road the sunlight bounced off the bossing on a small military chariot and the helmets of its two occupants. As four horses churned up the roadway, the driver's muscles bulged with the effort of holding on, while the single rider jounced up and down as the studded wheels ground over the road.

"It's David! The young fool! Why does he expose himself like that?"

Stones and spears narrowly missed him or were deflected by his helmet and wicker shield. At the foot of the great staircase he leaped from the chariot and raced up the steps.

"Halt!" The squadron of Immortals stood like a wall.

"David ben-Bilshan, in charge of Jewish defense of the capital."

"Your business?"

"I must see Lord Mordecai."

"We have orders to admit you."

In the courtyard robed officials passed each other on the stairs, messengers raced back and forth with leather or clay tablets, foreign dignitaries huddled in anxious knots.

David strode quickly toward Mordecai's headquarters, taking off his helmet, shaking loose his sweat-soaked hair.

"Reporting, my lord Mordecai." He stood stiffly before the Grand Vizier.

"How does the battle go, commander?" Before the other men the formalities were kept, but Mordecai's concern was in his eyes.

"Things are going well, my lord. The fighting is heaviest in the eastern quarter of the city and in the wealthy areas on the banks of the Choaspes."

"That's to be expected."

"But the opposition is not well-organized, and we are. They go down like cut grasses, but—there are so many of them!"

"How many are attacking?"

"It's hard to say, my lord. Hundreds, many hundreds."

"Are our losses heavy?"

"There are a great many wounded."

"And their spirit?"

"Excellent. Better than I could have dared hope. It's nearly impossible to make a wounded man stop fighting."

"They are not to risk their lives foolishly; tell them these are my orders. You'll be interested to hear that the reports from the provinces are all good."

But the day had an unexpected end.

The trumpets blew at sunset as planned. The fighting stopped. The reports were brought to Mordecai, who took them to Xerxes. Studying them, the king glanced at Mordecai and back to the reports. He was stunned.

"Send for the queen!"

Like many of the common people, Esther had slept poorly the night before. The early trumpets had filled her with dread. Throughout the day, Mordecai had sent her brief reports, sharing his concern that there were still so many known enemies waiting to pounce from unexpected corners. The last report had been far from encouraging.

Pale from the strain, she presented herself to the king, who said, "Queen Esther, these reports are astounding. To begin with," his smile was not pleasant, "all ten of the traitor Haman's traitorous sons have been killed. The Jews have done my empire a great service by ferreting those—those adders from their holes. I shall reward them lavishly. But—the Jews have killed five hundred men in Susa today. Do you see what that means? *Five hundred men* in my own capital who would dare ignore my second edict, when I plainly expressed my wishes."

"There are still many traitors alive here, my lord," said Mordecai.

"Are you sure?"

"Our spy system is very good, Majesty. There are whole pockets of Haman's followers and his sons' followers still not cleaned out."

Xerxes looked from Mordecai to Esther; he seemed at a loss. "Queen Esther?"

Esther had prostrated herself again before her husband. She had caught the one word "Tomorrow" on Mordecai's lips.

The king spoke the familiar phrases almost absent-mindedly. *"Now* what is your petition? I shall grant it. You two," he said, suddenly alert again, "have more wisdom in your little fingers than Haman had in his whole traitorous head. Get up now, get up," he added petulantly, "and tell me what you are thinking."

"My lord, allow the Jews in Susa to do tomorrow according to this day's edict."

"Another day of fighting? Defend themselves as before? Mordecai?"

"If all these followers of Haman are allowed to live, it will only be a question of time before—"

"Enough!" roared Xerxes. "Have you other requests, Queen Esther?"

"The ten sons of Haman—"

"Didn't you hear? They are all dead."

"But if it please the king, their bodies should be displayed on the gallows." She was looking very stern. "They will be seen by all of Susa, my lord king, and it may shorten this awful bloodshed."

Mordecai quirked an eyebrow. His Hadassah was learning.

Xerxes considered. He seemed to have trouble keeping his mind on the matters in hand. He looked at Esther as if to draw from her the strength to make a decision. "We have done this at other times. It's always a sharp reminder. And those scurrilous sons— Yes! Yes! We will do that." And he dismissed them.

David oversaw the hanging of the ten corpses on the gallows.

"Traitors, every one," grumbled the captain of the guard as he swung the last body into place. "Let them rot!"

Soon criers were going through the embattled city. Up and down every street and alley the decree for the second day of fighting was shouted from men on horseback. Knowing how many of their enemies still lived, the Jews were grateful. In the river shops, meeting places for the attackers, the gloom was thick.

The city was a charnel house—men's bodies in the streets; horses, donkeys, sheep, and camels dead in ditches. The ravaged shops of sculptors, potters, silk-weavers, and metal workers were surrounded with broken javelins, twisted spear-shafts, arrows, and pottery shards. Fleeing for safety and anonymity, men had flung off helmets, boots, insignia of rank. The Forgotten, brothel hiding place for some of Haman's sons, was a smoking ruin. Flies and beetles swarmed; the stench of death was indescribable.

Up on the Citadel, guards were silhouettes against the smoky sky lit by campfires and signal beacons in surrounding fields; the afterglow slanted hotly back from the Apadana's golden turrets. An air of suspense held the atmosphere like taut wires.

In the Street of Lilacs, David, alone with his personal bitterness and doubt, tried to shut out the day's spectres: a little boy wandering alone with a broken cup in his hand, a dog huddled on the corpse of his master, a woman with her hair on fire. His thoughts edged toward Ruth, but always an inner door slammed shut. Dimly he felt some gratitude for the fact that tomorrow would take all his energies. After that . . . .

Sunrise again, trumpets again, fighting again, as wild as before. Again the sound of splintering wood, clashing arms, and shouting men. David had redoubled the guard at all gates; every exit was a fortress. Fighting continued all over the city as the attackers launched a last-ditch campaign. "All or nothing!" they howled. "Get what you can and run!"

"Where do they all come from, these men who attack the Jews?" Shethar wondered.

"Out from under the stones, like lizards. The dregs, that's what they are. Susa should be a cleaner city once this day is over," Memucan answered.

"Marsena's been caught and his association with Haman has been discovered," he went on as they walked toward the staircase. "He'll be tried for treason."

Shethar's expression was grim. "Serves him right, but I don't envy him the kind of death he'll die."

As the day went on, the tide began to turn in favor of the Jews, though many of them died that day. Toward evening David sent scouts to clean out any pockets where enemies might be hiding. He did not stop until every house in the city was checked from top to bottom, every street and alleyway carefully combed. Then he went to Mordecai's headquarters.

"Susa is clear, my lord. There are no attackers left." David ben-Bilshan stood at attention before his commander, his eyes desolate.

"Well done, my son. Well done." But Mordecai knew that here was one man for whom the price had been too high.

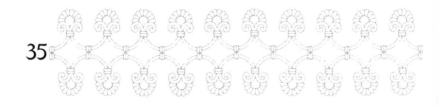

35

"The Jews are victorious! The Jews are free!" The king's announcement was carried over the city. The fighting was at an end.

As the couriers trumpeted the news through Susa at the end of the fourteenth Adar, shutters were thrown open, people rushed outside, threw their arms around each other, shouted, sang, danced in the streets. Laughter, the first for days, rippled through the capital. Music and psalms and shouts of "Victory for Adonai!" came from Jewish homes.

"I congratulate you," Xerxes said to Mordecai. "You have succeeded brilliantly. How do you explain it?"

"For months we lived and breathed, we ate and dreamed, we prayed and wept for this day, sire. This is no chance victory: our God has given us success."

"But you helped him—is that it?"

"We did what we could do. That, he would expect. But the victory is his."

That evening the king sent for Esther. Entering the bedchamber, she was surprised to have him meet her. He put a hand on her shoulder and said softly, "Look at me." They stood as they had done on that first night so long ago. "You are not trembling tonight, my Star. How long ago, my love?"

"A whole lifetime."

"Two lifetimes! Haman—my illness—how long was I ill?"

"Two months, my lord."

"So much that I don't remember—I am very tired." Then, "Why didn't you tell me you were a Jewess?"

Esther made a small gesture. "I—my father—I—"

264

"Ah, yes; he told you not to. I suppose it was best. Who knows? —I might have done something foolish."

"You might have sent me away?"

He pulled her to him. "Not so foolish as that, my Star—never that. I need you. I shall always need you." He went over to the couch and sat down. "Play for me. Play as you did the night you came to me."

She took up her harp and began singing.

Transported beyond time by the music, Xerxes found himself reliving the first night Esther had come. It was more than remembering; he was *there*—the younger king with the unexpectedly intriguing virgin. The same room, the same singer, the same emotions. When her present song ended, he was still faraway.

The silence grew. Were they, then, the same people? Esther still so beautiful, but changed—the spontaneous girl had become a woman of responsibility and influence. As for himself—that was better not thought about.

"You were singing, 'How can we sing Adonai's songs in a strange land.' That's a sad song, Esther—the very first song you sang me was a sad song. But why sad tonight? How can you *not* sing your god's songs on this night of his victory—you *do* see this as a victory for your god?"

Esther hesitated. "A victory—yes, of course. Adonai is our great God. But men have made it a costly victory. Susa is shouting and singing— Listen to them! —but there is weeping, too. Not just my people but yours—ours."

"Ah, well, you are young. You have always had too soft a heart. These are the fortunes of war. Come—dance for me, my love. Dance! Celebrate! This is a glorious night of freedom for your people, and you, my love, are safe!"

As before, she obeyed, dancing with poetry and grace, but her heart wept: for the dead, for the bereaved, for the nameless force that even now was drawing her lord far out into a sea of unknowing where she could not follow. When she had finished, the king was asleep. Looking down at him, she sensed the years ahead: Xerxes more and more in his land of shadows—Mordecai bearing the burden of government, healing the wounds of their people—herself sharing in that burden, that healing. That was her destiny.

Gathered below the wall of the acropolis, thousands of Jews roared Mordecai's name. Palm branches waved, scarves and colored garments fluttered, lutes, cymbals, trumpets, gongs made a victorious din.

On Jabor, the horse Haman had reluctantly led, Mordecai rode down the staircase. Had he really wept on this staircase in torn robes and ashes just months ago? Ignoring his gesture for silence, the crowd roared. They had moved so suddenly from the numbing threat of extermination to victory. Looking at them with affection, the Jewish leader knew it would take all his skill to guide them in the future.

Finally able to make himself heard, he said, "This is a glorious day, and we will recall it forever."

"Hosannah to Adonai!"

"His name be praised!"

"His steadfast love endures forever!"

Tired, bedraggled, bloodstained, the crowd cheered or sobbed with emotion.

Mordecai was too shrewd a diplomat to let this personal demonstration continue too long, and he gestured again for silence. "Our great king whose edict gave us the opportunity for this victory congratulates you all. He is mighty and wise."

"Great is Xerxes!" roared the crowd, following his lead. "Great is the King of All Peoples!"

Saddened by the loss of those he had loved, Bilshan did not hide the reality of his pain. Sorrow was an old acquaintance. But nothing could shake his serene faith in the wisdom and faithfulness of his God. Though the storms rocked his house, though the burning questions of suffering and evil continued as they had since the Fall, he did not attempt easy answers but fell back on the character of Adonai. As the shouting crowds surged into the street, he looked out over his charred garden and softly repeated ancient words of comfort: "'Adonai gathers the outcasts of Israel. He heals the brokenhearted, and binds up their wounds. He determines the number of the stars, he gives to all of them their names. Great is Adonai, and abundant in power; his understanding is beyond measure. . . . Adonai reigns.'"

36

Once again the King of All Peoples was giving a great feast. Once again Harbonah had overseen preparations and moved about muttering to himself. The eunuch's first responsibility of this kind was years behind him. Tonight he was smoothly accomplished, if even more fastidious. His resentment toward the queen would smolder to the end of his life, masked of necessity, but venting itself in increasing tyranny over his subordinates.

The stream of guests poured into the walled gardens. Saturated with perfume, sparkling with lights, the Persian paradaiso was again a dream world.

Glittering couches waited for their occupants. Guests looked eagerly toward the shimmering curtain. Behind it, the hall was a vast jewel, faceted with color and light. The rows of Immortals glittered; six of the Seven arrived and stood by their couches. By the king's order, Marsena's empty couch remained—a warning to would-be traitors. An unsmiling David took his place of honor.

The murmuring in the gardens swelled.

Gleaming with gold, Mordecai approached his place beside the two reserved for the king and his queen. The royal thrones were borne in and set down in silence, the reverent silence of a people who believed their king to be the earthly representative of their god.

Esther's eyes met Mordecai's. After the tension, the darkness, the fear of the past two months, the gilded setting seemed unreal.

As he had done more than six years ago, the king lifted his rhyton. "Drink!" he said in a voice husky with emotion. And the feast was officially begun.

Granted a special concession by the king, Jewish singers stood along the outside walls and staircases. Glorious sound poured like a cataract over the rejoicing city.

"Praise Adonai, for he is good and his steadfast love endures forever!"

Memucan looked across at Shethar. "Unbelievable," he breathed. "Two days of fighting and the world has turned upside down."

Xerxes brought the festivities to an early end. As he was carried from the hall, Esther and Mordecai walked on the platform overlooking the city. Torches, lanterns, lighted candles—the lights bloomed all over Susa like flowers.

"Blood, terror, death—was it for 'such a time as this,' father?"

Secure in his position as Grand Vizier under an ailing king, his mind alight with great plans for his countrymen, Mordecai was exultant. He had included Esther in his plans for the future, scheming how best to utilize her experience and influence. But now, with a pang, he realized that he had ignored her personal emotions and that at this moment her mood was very different from his own. This slight figure beside him with the wind ruffling her hair was the most powerful woman in the world, but also, perhaps, the saddest. She was twenty-one.

"My Hadassah!" he put his arm around her. "Through generations to come our people will celebrate this time. All the ends of the earth shall see the salvation of Adonai. He has kept his covenant; he has sent us deliverance."

She raised her eyes to his, searching for reassurance.

"The Lord our God," he went on, "will raise up a Prophet . . . there shall come a Star out of Jakob and a Sceptre shall rise out of Israel . . . for such a time as *this*."

AUTHOR'S NOTES

Like many other books in Scripture, Esther is a "bare bones" account, leaving room for many things that either happened or could have happened.

Who was the king? Xerxes has reliable historians who put his name forward, but others prefer Artaxerxes I or II. A scholar says, "This or this is possible, but, on the other hand. . . ." A novelist, in the end, has to come down on one side of the fence and stand by the choice. For me, Xerxes seems to fit the biblical narrative admirably—the times are right, the character very similar to the character of Herodotus' Xerxes.

While the Bible makes no mention of Xerxes' Greek campaign, it is established historically that the Persian king launched and lost his campaign against Greece in a period fitting roughly between chapters one (the third year of his reign) and two (the seventh year) of Esther. Because Herodotus and other Greek historians give us the only extrabiblical sources for Xerxes' life and character (except for the inscriptions and cuneiform documents found in Persia, which don't give us many details of the man himself) and since they concentrate mainly on the war, it seemed necessary to include this. The gory details of this encounter come from these accounts, not from my imagination. The campaign is important in another sense, too, since it contributed in a profound way to the dissolution that occurred in the king's character, bringing him to a tragic end.

Very little historical material is available for the other characters. Writing not very long after Xerxes' lifetime, Herodotus gives the king one wife, an unpleasant lady named Amestris. So where do Vashti and Esther fit in? For those interested in such things, J. Stafford Wright, in an article called "The Historicity of Esther" (see bibliography), suggests that this name Amestris is Herodotus' transliteration of the name Vashti, showing how it might have been done, letter by letter. (An overly simplified illustration would be translating the Italian Giovanni to the English John.) Should this have been the case, Vashti/Amestris could have returned to power after Esther's death or possible deposition. Rawlinson suggests this.

Although there is a tomb in present-day Hamadan alleged to be that of Esther and Mordecai, it remains unauthenticated.

As for Mordecai himself, an interesting detail has come to light: in the middle of this century a cuneiform tablet was found which mentions a Mordecai (Mardukkai) who held an important post in the court of Xerxes. This is too vague to be conclusive evidence, but its combination of the same name, same king, same position may be enough to suggest that "our" Mordecai is more than a Persian or Jewish fiction.

While in Iran, I met a Jewish doctor who said that early in his life the treatment of Haman's sons had turned him against his religion. (He called it fratricide.) That remark made me take a much longer look at the sons, and my resulting thoughts about them were a direct outgrowth of that chat in a hotel lobby.

Another stumbling block is the killing of so many people. At least two of the objections are: 1) who could take seriously such widespread villainy; and 2) there is no historical evidence. In regard to the first, Herodotus tells of the slaughter of the Magi in Darius' time, and Cicero accuses Mithradates of killing between 80,000 and 150,000 Romans in one day. It is also interesting to read commentators before World War II who found Haman's mad decree quite insupportable; but after Hitler's "Final Solution," it becomes much more believable if no less horrible. As for the second objection, many things once dismissed as untrue or improbable because of lack of evidence have later had to be accepted because that evidence was uncovered. To mention only one example: the Hittite civilization whose discovery in relatively recent times proved embarrassing to those who had written it off as a myth mentioned only in the Bible.

In Ezra 5 and 6 the Persian satrap demands to know on whose authority the Jews are rebuilding the wall of Jerusalem. When told it is by decree of the great Cyrus, the satrap hustles off to Darius, who, with the Persian respect for royal decrees, searches in Susa. Unsuccessful there, he sends to Ecbatana where it is found in the archives, and this settles the matter. Personally, I cannot help wondering what documents are buried deep under present-day Hamadan, erected over that ancient Achaemenean capital.

The imaginary characters (see list in front of book) come from my head and heart, but they are people who could have been there. Certainly, there were many more people involved in this complex tale than those in the biblical account, and the edict would have affected many lives.

Whatever opinions are held by writers on the subject of Esther's historicity, all agree that the writer was very conversant with the Persian court of the time.

The Book of Esther has always been a controversial one. It bristles with theological and historical problems. As I began my treatment of the story, I had to consider the question: could I accept Esther as I accept other portions of Scripture as dependable, authoritative, God-inspired? I came to the conclusion that since it had been examined by the same body of scholars that had accepted the other books of our canon, and since, in spite of the difficulties over its credibility, it was admitted to both the Jewish and the Christian canons, I who am not a scholar, had to trust their judgment.

One of the most frequently cited objections theologically is that the book contains no direct mention of God. But the presence of Adonai permeates the story. An example: There is no mention of prayer in 4:16—"Go gather all the Jews to be found in Susa, and hold a fast on my behalf and neither eat nor drink for three days, night or day. I and my maids will also fast as you do"—but I was assured by a Jewish scholar in Isfahan that fasting among Jews was and is always accompanied by prayer; thus, it is there by implication. However, this is not the place to discuss all the historical and theological questions, even were I competent to do so; I have tried to unravel some of them within my treatment of the story itself.

It has been my concern to be scrupulously faithful to the biblical account, using these facts as pegs on which to hang my story. Historically, my main source has been the Greek historians and later scholars who got their data from them. Herodotus, writer/traveler extraordinary from Halikarnassus, gives us the fullest account of the Graeco/Persian wars and the Persians themselves and is considered historically dependable even as he amuses with his vivid imagination and prejudicial reporting. When confronted with a conflict between his opinions and the biblical account, I have opted for the latter.

ACKNOWLEDGMENTS

Any writer is aware of much help in finally getting a book into print. In the case of this book, which took some five years of part-time work and trips to Paris and Iran for research, I am more than usually obligated.

I want particularly to express my appreciation to the scholars who, with enormous generosity, gave of their time and expertise in advising on historical details and suggesting bibliography: Dr. Donald J. Wiseman, Professor of Assyriology at the School of Oriental and African Studies, University of London, and Dr. ADH Bivar, Lecturer in Iranian and Central Asian Archaeology, University of London (SOAS). Dr. Jack M. Balcer, Professor of History at Ohio State University, actually volunteered to read through the whole manuscript during a short stay in London, even reading on his return flight to the USA, catching many a dropped historical brick. None of these scholars is to be held in any way responsible for my opinions nor blamed for any inaccuracies or flights of fancy.

While in Iran I was given valuable help and hospitality by Ron and Jessie Axtell in Shiraz, Iraq Mottahedeh (himself of Jewish origin) and his wife, and the Bishop of Iran and his family in Isfahan.

I am indebted to the readers who ploughed through the long manuscript in various stages and gave me the benefit of their careful—and sometimes searing—criticisms: Jim Boyd, Jr., Dr. Donald J. Drew, whose encouragement had much to do with my being a writer, Mary Endersbee, Evy Herr, Victoria Hobson, Patricia Jacques, Ann Rose, David Winter. In addition, there were others who not only read and gave suggestions, but who provided shelters in which to write: Jim and Helen Boyd, put up with me for months in the USA; OS and Jenny Guinness provided a retreat in Oxford; the Manfields on their farm in Cornwall; Max and Elly Blatt turned over their house to me; Roger and Marcia Lier allowed me to clutter their study; May Warburg provided a London refuge for several years; and I owe Daniel and Grace Lam a debt I shall not soon forget. Nancy Yuille stayed with me for the better part of a year in London, reading, making suggestions, and looking after the day-to-day routine. Diane Pugh was most helpful in typing the lengthy bibliography.

I sometimes hear of bad relationships between authors and their publishers. I know nothing of these. For ten years my contact with the staff at Zondervan has been a joy. Robert DeVries has for all that time been remarkably understanding and encouraging. Carol Holquist has patiently dealt with all sorts of requests for information and assistance. Finally, my warmest gratitude to Judith Markham, my editor, who put up with transatlantic phone calls, desperate letters, sheaves of last-minute corrections and quietly and wisely tried to keep me in line.

There are many others who encouraged the project from the beginning, who gave advice, enthusiasm, and their prayers. If I were to list them all, it would take pages, and I would probably leave out someone even then. So will each of you who had a part, however small it may seem to you, accept my sincere and deep gratitude.

PARTIAL BIBLIOGRAPHY*

ARCHITECTURE

Ghirshman, I. "L'Apadana de Suse." *Iranica Antiqua* 3 (1963).
Pope, Arthur V. *Introducing Persian Architecture.* New York: Oxford University Press, 1969.
Schmidt, Erich. *Persepolis.* Chicago: University of Chicago Press.

COMMENTARIES, ETC.

Buttrick, George A. *The Interpreter's Bible.* Vol. 3. Nashville, Tennessee: Abingdon Press.
Fuerst, W. J. "Esther, a Keystone of the Bible." *Cambridge Bible Commentary on the New English Bible.* Cambridge: At the University Press, 1975.
Moore, Carey A. "Esther." *The Anchor Bible.* New York: Doubleday & Co., 1971.
Streane, A. W. "Esther, Notes and Introduction." *Cambridge Bible.* Kirkpatrick, 1907.

COSTUMES, JEWELRY, ETC.

Beck, Pirhiya. "A Note on the Reconstruction of the Achaemenid Robe." *Iranica Antiqua* 9 (1972).
Calatchi, Robert de. *Oriental Carpets.* Rutland, Vermont: Charles E. Tuttle Co., 1967.
Goldman, Bernard. "The Origin of the Persian Robe." *Iranica Antiqua* 4 (1964).
Gregorietti. *Jewellery Through the Ages.* Translated by Helen Lawrence. Feltham, England: Hamlyn, 1970.

Houston, Mary. *Ancient Egyptian, Mesopotamian and Persian Costume and Decoration.* London: A & C Black Ltd., 1954.

Thompson, Georgina. "Iranian Dress in the Achaemenean Period." *Iran* 3 (1965).

CRIMINAL MIND

Boldt, Gerhard. *Hitler's Last Days, an Eye-Witness Account.* London: Weidenfeld and Nicolson Ltd., 1970.

Eysenck, H. J. *Crime and Personality.* London: William Heinemann Ltd., 1962.

Frischauer, Willi. *Goering.* Oldham Press Ltd., 1950.

Fromm, Erich. *The Anatomy of Human Destructiveness.* Jonathan Cape Ltd., 1975.

Trevor-Roper. *Last Days of Hitler: Analysis of the Nazi Mind.* London: Routledge and Kegan Paul Ltd.

GREEK WRITERS

Aeschylus. *The Persians.* Translated by Philip Vellacott. West Drayton, England: Penguin Publishing Co. Ltd., 1961.

Herodotus. *The Histories.* Translated by A. de Selincourt. West Drayton, England: Penguin Publishing Co. Ltd., 1972.

Plutarch. *Lives.* Vol. 3. Revised by Arthur Clough. Everyman, 1969.

Xenophon. *Cyropaedia.* Vols. 1, 2. Translated by Walter Miller. London: William Heinemann Ltd., 1968.

HISTORICITY

Bickerman, Elias. *Four Strange Books of the Bible.* Shocken, 1967.

Hoschander. *The Book of Esther in the Light of History.* Philadelphia: Dropsie College Press, 1923.

Wright, J. Stafford. "Historicity of Esther." *New Perspectives in Old Testament,* edited by J. Barton Payne. Waco, Texas: Word Books, 1970.

HISTORY (GENERAL)

Culican, W. *The Medes and Persians.* London: Thames and Hudson Ltd., 1965.

Ghershman. *Persia, the Immortal Kingdom.* London: Clifford House, 1971.

Herzfeld, E. *Iran in the Ancient East.* New York: Oxford University Press, 1941.

Hicks, Jim. *The Persians.* Emergence of Man Series. New York: Time-Life Books, 1975.

Olmstead, A. T. *History of the Persian Empire.* Chicago: University of Chicago Press, 1970.

Rogers, Robert W. *A History of Ancient Persia.* New York: Charles Scribner's Sons, 1929.

Stobart, J. C. *The Glory That Was Greece.* London: Sidgwick and Jackson Ltd., 1976.

Wilber, Donald. *Iran, Past and Present.* Princeton, N.J.: Princeton University Press.

INSCRIPTIONS

Cameron, George C. "An Inscription of Darius from Passargadae." *Iran* 5–6 (1967/8).

Kent, Roland. *Daiva Inscriptions of Xerxes.* Princeton, N.J.: Princeton University Press, 1934.

Pscheil. "Ancient Persian Inscription of the Achaemenid Found at Susa." *Memoirs de la Mission Archeologique de Perse* Book 21 (1929).

JEWISH HISTORY AND CULTURE

Baeck, Leo. *This People Israel.* London: W. H. Allen and Co. Ltd., 1965.

Biblical Books: *Ezra, Nehemiah, Esther, The Rest of the Chapters of the Book of Esther* (The Apocrypha).

Encyclopaedia Judaica. Vols. 2, 6, 7, 8, 12, 14. Jerusalem: Keter Publishing House Jerusalem Ltd., 1971.

Fraine, R. P. J. de, S.J. "La Communauté Juive au Temps des Perses." *Bible et Terre Saint.* 39 Series June 1961.

Jewish Encyclopedia. Vols. 1, 5, 6. New York: Funk and Wagnalls Co.

Rappoport, Angelo. *Myths and Legends of Ancient Israel.* Vol. 3. London: John Gresham, 1928.

Wiseman, Donald J., ed. *People of Old Testament Times.* Society of Old Testament Study. London: Oxford and Clarendon Press, 1973.

MISCELLANEOUS

Balcer, Jack Martin. "The Athenian Episkopos and the Achaemenid 'King's Eye'." *American Journal of Philology* (1977).
Bivar, ADH. "Document and Symbol in the Art of the Achaemenids." *ACTA IRANICA* (1975).
Bulsara, Sohrab J. *Laws of the Ancient Persians.* Bombay: Anklesavia, 1937.
Frye, Richard M. "Gestures of Deference to Royalty in Ancient Iran." *Iranica Antiqua* 9 (1972).
_____. "The Charisma of Kingship." *Iranica Antiqua* 4 (1964).
Gershevitch. *Avestan Hymn to Mithra from* Avesta. Cambridge: At the University Press, 1959.
Seibert, Ilse. *Women in the Ancient Near East.* Edition Leipzic (Prior).
Seitman. *Woman in Antiquity.* London: Thames and Hudson, 1956.

*The complete bibliography includes some 175 books and articles.